THE KING OVER THE WATER

SPONSORED BY

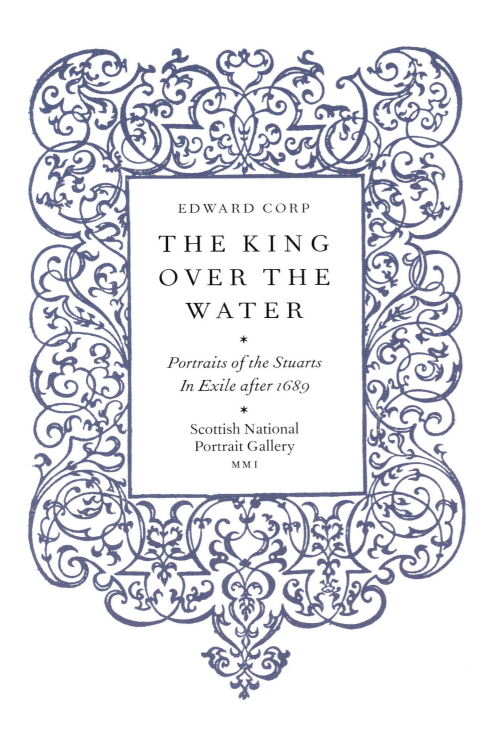

EDWARD CORP

THE KING OVER THE WATER

*

Portraits of the Stuarts
In Exile after 1689

*

Scottish National
Portrait Gallery
M M I

Published by the Trustees
of the National Galleries of Scotland
on the occasion of the exhibition
The King over the Water:
The Life of James Francis Edward Stuart (1688–1766)
held at the Scottish National Portrait Gallery,
Edinburgh from 27 April to
30 September 2001

© The Trustees of the National Galleries of Scotland 2001
ISBN 1 903278 19 8

Designed by Dalrymple
Typeset in Monotype Fournier by Brian Young
Printed by BAS Printers, Over Wallop

Jacket illustration: Unknown artist
James III and his Court in front of the Palazzo Muti
Scottish National Portrait Gallery, Edinburgh
(detail)

CONTENTS

SPONSOR'S PREFACE

Drambuie has a unique association with the Jacobite period. The recipe that forms the basis for our distinctive whisky-based liqueur was the gift of Prince Charles Edward Stuart – Bonnie Prince Charlie – to a MacKinnon of Skye as a thanks for his assistance while on the run in 1746. The Drambuie Liqueur Company, which remains in the hands of the MacKinnon family to this day, has always been aware of this direct link to a fascinating and turbulent period of history. We are delighted, therefore, to be able to support this exhibition and publication on the life of Charles's father, James Edward Stuart, the 'King over the Water' for whose cause so many rose and died in 1745–6.

Our rewarding association with the Scottish National Portrait Gallery began in 1996 with our sponsorship of *Look, Love & Follow: Prints and Medals of the Jacobite Cause* and, as on that occasion, it has been a particular pleasure to have the opportunity of lending works of art from our own collection of Jacobite art to the exhibition, allowing them to be seen by a wider audience and placed in context alongside the many generous loans from other collections worldwide.

The study of Jacobitism and the re-assessment of its place within British and European politics and culture have been notable phenomena of recent years and we continue to support such research through sponsorship and through the continuing development and study of our own collection. New discoveries are constantly being made and the most striking feature of this examination of the life of the *de jure* King James VIII and III is the revelation of just how rich the artistic life of the exiled Stuart court was. Regal in every sense, it frequently outshone its counterpart in St James's. It is fascinating to conjecture how life and culture in Britain might have differed had James ever reigned in the country of his birth.

ROBIN NICHOLSON
Company Curator

FOREWORD

'The King over the Water' was the toast of loyal Jacobites to their exiled monarch, Prince James Francis Edward Stuart. James spent all but a few months of his long life abroad while supporters, on both sides of the Channel, plotted his restoration. Had he succeeded his father King James VII and II on the latter's death in 1701, James Francis Edward Stuart, as King James VIII and III, would have ruled in England, Ireland and Scotland for over sixty-four years. His reign would have been the longest in British history.

The three centuries that have since passed have seen James and his supporters at first vilified, then glamorised and latterly marginalised. Recently, however, historians have begun a reassessment of James and Jacobitism, striving for a fairer assessment of their strengths and support. One of the new generation of scholars to specialise in the subject – and in the life of the courts at Saint-Germain-en-Laye near Paris and Palazzo Muti in Rome – is Professor Edward Corp of the University of Paris. This book, which accompanies his exhibition at the Scottish National Portrait Gallery, assesses the portraiture of the exiled Stuarts, hitherto a confusion of inaccurate dating and wrong attributions.

Portrait painters have always been employed to project the image and reinforce the recognition of monarchs. Their importance for a royal family in exile, anxious not to be forgotten, was even more crucial. The Jacobites were fortunate to be in a position to employ many of Europe's finest artists. Professor Corp has shown how portraits and the engravings derived from them often preceded military campaigns: portraiture serving as the first weapon of attack in a war fought on several fronts.

The exhibition and this book mark the acquisition by the Scottish National Portrait Gallery of a unique record of the Jacobite court in exile. *The View of Palazzo Muti* shows James Francis Edward Stuart stepping forward in front of his palace to welcome his younger son Henry, recently created Cardinal York. The busy street in front of the gaily decorated palace is thronged with activity and excitement as members of the Stuart court are jostled by the life of the Roman streets. In the final months of his life, Sir Walter Scott stood spellbound in front of this painting as he mused on the fate of Scotland's ancient royal house and the loyalty of its adherents. Thanks to generous donations from the Heritage Lottery Fund and the National Art Collections Fund this great painting will remain permanently on public display in the Gallery after the exhibition closes.

We would like to thank all those who have so generously lent their paintings to this exhibition. Baillie Gifford, for long benefactors of the Gallery, have once again offered their support. We also owe a particular debt to our sponsor, Drambuie, whose own connections with the Jacobites could hardly be stronger.

TIMOTHY CLIFFORD
Director-General of the
National Galleries of Scotland

JAMES HOLLOWAY
Director of the
Scottish National Portrait Gallery

ACKNOWLEDGEMENTS

In writing this book and preparing the exhibition which it accompanies, I have received very generous support and encouragement from James Holloway and the staff of the Scottish National Portrait Gallery. I should like to record my extreme gratitude to them. I should also like to thank Jan Newton, the exhibition designer, and Janis Adams and Christine Thompson of the Publications Department of the National Galleries of Scotland for their invaluable help.

Many people have kindly allowed me to see the Stuart portraits in their private collections, and I am very grateful to them all. Thanks also go to the keepers, curators and archivists at the National Portrait Gallery in London, the Royal Collection and the Royal Archives, and to Maurizio Ascari in Bologna, for all the help they have given me. Above all I should like to thank Alastair Laing of the National Trust, who for many years has generously shared his knowledge with me, helped me clarify many points and saved me from making several errors. For those which remain, I am, of course, solely responsible.

Finally I should like to thank the Institute for Advanced Studies in the Humanities of the University of Edinburgh for granting me a Visiting Fellowship and thus for providing me with an ideal base from which to prepare the exhibition.

EDWARD CORP

THE KING
OVER THE
WATER

After 1603 the separate kingdoms of Scotland, England and Ireland were ruled by the same monarchs, who called themselves Kings (or Queens) of Great Britain. James II of Great Britain was James VII of Scotland, James II of England and James II of Ireland. Thus his son was called James III or James VIII by the Jacobites.

To avoid confusion the King over the Water is referred to in this publication by his British title only, as James III. This was the title he used himself and by which he was recognised by half of Europe after 1701. He had been christened James Francis Edward, and created Prince of Wales in 1688.

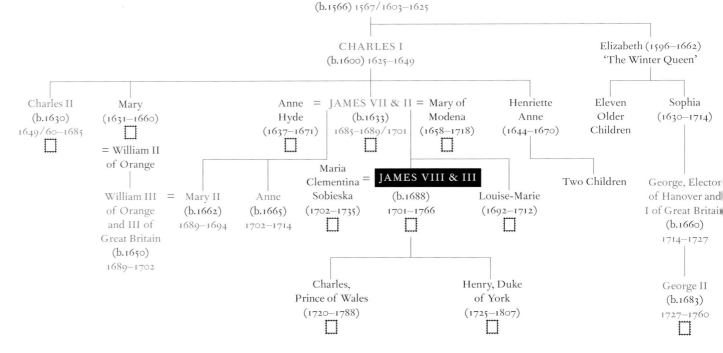

Henry Stuart, = Mary Stewart, Queen of Scots
Lord Darnley   and Dowager Queen of France

JAMES VI OF SCOTLAND AND I OF GREAT BRITAIN
(b.1566) 1567/1603–1625

CHARLES I
(b.1600) 1625–1649

Elizabeth (1596–1662)
'The Winter Queen'

Charles II
(b.1630)
1649/60–1685

Mary
(1631–1660)

= William II
of Orange

Anne
Hyde
(1637–1671)

= JAMES VII & II =
(b.1633)
1685–1689/1701

Mary of
Modena
(1658–1718)

Henriette
Anne
(1644–1670)

Eleven
Older
Children

Sophia
(1630–1714)

William III
of Orange
and III of
Great Britain
(b.1650)
1689–1702

= Mary II
(b.1662)
1689–1694

Anne
(b.1665)
1702–1714

Maria
Clementina
Sobieska
(1702–1735)

= **JAMES VIII & III**
(b.1688)
1701–1766

Louise-Marie
(1692–1712)

Two Children

George, Elector
of Hanover and
I of Great Britain
(b.1660)
1714–1727

Charles,
Prince of Wales
(1720–1788)

Henry, Duke
of York
(1725–1807)

George II
(b.1683)
1727–1760

Monarchs of Great Britain are shown in BLUE TYPE · A frame ☐ denotes those represented by portraits in the exhibition

PREFACE

HIS BOOK WAS WRITTEN TO ACCOMPANY THE EXHIBITION *The King over the Water* at the Scottish National Portrait Gallery in 2001. It marks the tercentenary of the death in exile of James VII and II, the last Stuart king to live and reign within the British Isles. If he had not been deposed in 1689 his son, also called James, might have had the longest reign in British history, from 1701 to 1766. The exhibition thus commemorates the accession of a king that we never had.

Those who wanted the restoration of King James and his family have always been known as the Jacobites. Their tragic and often dramatic story is well known. The same, however, is not true of the iconography of the Jacobite court in exile, and in particular that of the Stuart royal family. It is hoped that this book, like the exhibition, will clarify a subject which has for long been both confused and misunderstood.

From the revolution of 1688–9 to Bonnie Prince Charlie's invasion of England in 1745, or from the battles of Killiecrankie and the Boyne in 1689–90 to Culloden in 1746, the Jacobite saga has cast its spell over generations of people attracted by its romance, the heroism of its participants and the ultimate tragedy of Scotland's exiled royal family. Some events may be better known than others, but the general outline of the story is an accepted part of our common heritage. Forced into exile in 1688–9, the Jacobites attempted for over half a century to recover the thrones of Great Britain and Ireland for those whom they regarded as their rightful and lawful kings. After initial failures in 1689–90, they tried to organise invasions and uprisings, with French or Spanish help, from 1692 until the 1750s, of which the best known are the 'Fifteen' and the 'Forty-Five'. Eventually the disappointment of repeated failure and the passing of the generations allowed old wounds to be healed and a new loyalty and unity to be established.

Throughout this period the Jacobite court in exile commissioned various Continental painters to produce a steady flow of portraits. Their purpose was primarily political rather than aesthetic, to inspire loyalty at a particular moment and sometimes to coincide with another restoration attempt. Nevertheless, as works of art they maintained the great tradition of royal portraiture developed in England in the 1630s and after 1660. Today they compare favourably with the portraits commissioned by the major European courts of the late seventeenth and early eighteenth centuries. At the time, however, they were an essential ingredient in a long campaign of political propaganda which the exiled Jacobite court maintained without a break from 1689 until the late 1740s. No political history of Jacobitism should ignore them, yet the prevailing confusion has been so great that most historians have used them as little more than peripheral and non-essential illustrations.

It is not uncommon for the portraits of the exiled Stuarts to be misattributed and misdated. In some cases portraits are given no dates at all and attributed either to 'artist unknown' or else to 'after', or the 'school of', some painter who might (or might not!) have had a connection with the exiled Jacobites. Portraits painted in Rome may be attributed to a painter who worked in France, or vice-versa. Even the identity of the sitter is sometimes mistaken. Yet there is in fact a methodology and enough documentary evidence to allow us to give correct attributions, dates and identifications to all these portraits. That is the aim of this book.

What follows, therefore, is an examination of all the portraits of the exiled Stuart royal family, many of which are included in the exhibition *The King over the Water*, presented as a chronological narrative against the background of the familiar story of Jacobitism. Once every portrait has been identified and placed in its political context, others may then judge the impact that they had on the people who saw them at the time.

Note: the dimensions and locations of each portrait are given in the inventory of Stuart portraits at the end of the book. When several versions of a portrait exist, the information given is restricted to one or two examples only. The letter s with a number refers to the engraving of a portrait in the book by Richard Sharp, *The Engraved Record of the Jacobite Movement* (Scolar Press, 1996). Because court portraits were frequently supplied by painters in multiple copies of varying quality, with no prime versions, the best ones have not necessarily survived. Every attempt has been made to illustrate this book with high quality photographs, but they have not always been available.

INTRODUCTION

HE STUART ROYAL FAMILY (KNOWN BEFORE THE SEVENTEENTH century as the Stewarts) had already ruled Scotland for over two hundred years when James VI succeeded Queen Elizabeth as James I of England in 1603. For the next eighty-five years, until the end of 1688, the two independent kingdoms were ruled in a dynastic union by James himself, his son Charles I, and his two grandsons Charles II and James II. The latter was also James VII of Scotland, but in fact each ruler styled himself 'Magnae Britanniae Rex', King of Great Britain. Their British and English titles thus coincided.

This period of dynastic union was interrupted by the execution of Charles I in 1649 and the long period in exile of his legitimate heir Charles II. While the new Cromwellian government in England abolished the monarchy and established a republic, the majority of Scots declared their support for Charles II, who was crowned King of Scotland at Scone in 1650. In consequence, the British civil wars of the 1640s were succeeded by an Anglo-Scottish war of 1650–1, resulting in the defeat and occupation of Scotland by Oliver Cromwell and the republican New Model Army. It was not until 1660, after the death of Cromwell, that Charles II was restored to both his Scottish and English thrones and the Stuart dynastic union was re-established.

For many contemporaries the lessons of these years were clear. If any future Stuart king were to be deposed or even usurped in England, he might return to his ancient Kingdom of Scotland – though at the risk of an Anglo-Scottish war. If any future Stuart king was obliged to live abroad in exile, he might still be expected to return one day, however stable the new régime in Whitehall might appear. The memory of the years 1649–60 thus helped sustain the Jacobite cause in the sixty years following the revolution of 1688–9, when James VII and II and his son were indeed forced into exile and replaced on the thrones of both Scotland and England by William and Mary.

Seventeenth-century rulers were well aware that dynastic loyalty required visual stimulation, and that the images of the king and his family needed to be circulated as widely as possible. They therefore employed painters and engravers to produce their portraits, so that their appearance could become instantly recognisable to the great majority of their subjects. Large state portraits of the ruler triumphant, prominently displayed in the royal palaces and intended to impress, smaller portraits and miniatures reproduced in multiple copies for courtiers and other wealthy people, engravings, medals and coins distributed throughout the kingdoms – all created a cult of royalty which was then reflected in countless derivative images of a totally popular nature. The king himself was almost always shown with the insignia of the Order of the Garter, and frequently also with the symbols of royalty, most notably the closed crown which distinguished kings from other sovereign princes. To avoid any uncertainty, the engravings and medals were also inscribed with the names and titles of the people whose images they reproduced.

The revolution of 1688–9 had an important impact on the portraiture of the Stuart dynasty. Forced into exile at Saint-Germain-en-Laye in France, the king and his family were no longer present at Whitehall and could no longer be seen in London or the other places they had traditionally visited. Portraits of them previously displayed in public and in many private houses were now removed or hidden and replaced by those of the monarchs who had usurped them. Doubt was even cast on the legitimacy of the Prince of Wales, born to Queen Mary of Modena at St James's Palace on 10 June 1688, only a few months before the revolution. It became essential that a series of portraits, of all kinds, be produced at regular intervals to introduce the prince to the people of England and Scotland, and to make him familiar to them as he grew to manhood. The aim was that everyone should recognise him, even though virtually no one had ever seen him. The portraits had to be consistent, but they also had to show that the prince was unmistakably the son of both his parents. Each one had to contain an implied contradiction of the 'warming-pan myth', by which the Whigs pretended that a surrogate baby had been smuggled into the queen's bed during her labour. The portraits, moreover, had to be confidently produced, to suggest that the royal court was no longer at Whitehall but temporarily in exile, pending an inevitable restoration. They were to inspire Jacobites with loyalty, hope and even love, while anti-Jacobites might look on them with fear and perhaps admiration.

This continued when the son of James VII and II, who became the Jacobite King James III in September 1701, eventually married and had his own children. Dynastic policy demanded that the portraits of the exiled Stuarts should go on being produced at regular intervals. They had to maintain and even surpass the quality of portraiture established while the family was resident at Whitehall and able to employ Lely, Huysmans, Wissing, Kneller and the other successors of Van Dyck. It was essential that the new portraits should compare favourably with those of the rival dynasty in England.

Fortunately for the Stuarts this was not difficult. From 1689 to 1712 the Jacobite court was based at Saint-Germain-en-Laye, only a few miles from Versailles. Throughout that period the Stuarts were able to employ the same portrait painters who worked for the court of France, perhaps the best in Europe at that time and arguably more talented than the artists based in England. Of equal significance, Paris was the centre of the international print trade and contained some of the best engravers of the time. The French paintings and engravings of the Stuarts are notable for their consistently high quality.

When, after a period of instability, the Jacobite court settled in Rome in 1719 it was again able to command the services of some of the best portrait painters in Europe. This time, however, there were no local engravers capable of reproducing the Stuart portraits to the required standard. For many years this did not affect the high quality of engraved Stuart portraiture, because their Italian portraits were sent north to be reproduced in Paris, but as that was inconvenient the number of portraits suitable for engraving sharply declined. Eventually the Stuarts allowed some of their portraits to be reproduced in Rome, and then the decline in quality became very obvious.

The pivotal figure at the Stuart court in exile was always James III, referred to by his enemies as the 'Pretender' and eventually the 'Old Pretender', to distinguish him from his elder son. With the passing of the English Act of Settlement in 1701, the ratification of the Treaty of Union between England and Scotland in 1707 and the Hanoverian succession in 1714, he began to be frequently referred to in Scotland as James VIII. Whether as Prince of Wales until 1701 or 'King over the Water' thereafter, his image was constantly reproduced. There are approximately fifty original French and Italian oil portraits of him which are known to have been painted in the period 1689–1757, a figure which excludes copies, miniatures and, of course, engravings and medals.

The other Stuarts in exile were his parents, James VII and II and Mary of Modena; his sister, Princess Louise-Marie; his wife, Queen Maria Clementina Sobieska; and his two sons, Charles, Prince of Wales and Prince Henry, Duke of York. James lived with his parents and sister in France, and with his wife and children in Italy, mainly in Rome. The portraits of the exiled Stuarts thus fall into two clearly separate categories, the French ones, produced before 1715, and the Italian ones, produced after 1717.

Leaving aside the identification and ages of the Stuarts themselves, and the styles of the painters, the French and Italian portraits can be easily distinguished. In his French portraits, which were all painted before the death of his half-sister Queen Anne, James is never shown with a crown or any other royal regalia. To appease Tory opinion the legitimate king seems willing to await a peaceful restoration once the throne in London should become vacant. In his Italian portraits, all painted after the accession of the new Hanoverian dynasty, James is hardly ever shown without the closed crown of a king. The legitimate king had now to recover his thrones by force.

The other difference concerns the Orders of the Garter (St George) and the Thistle (St Andrew). In his French portraits James is always shown with the insignia of the Garter, normally the blue riband or sash falling from his left shoulder to his right hip, where the Lesser George would be pinned. He was given the honour by James VII and II at Saint-Germain, when he was three and a half years old, and at one time he briefly adopted the title 'Chevalier de Saint-Georges' as a convenient incognito.

James VII and II had previously revived the Order of the Thistle in 1687, but had stipulated that the order could not be worn with the Garter. In consequence, there are no Stuart portraits painted at Saint-Germain which show the Thistle. In 1716, however, James III changed the rules to allow the two orders to be worn together. The cross of St Andrew would be suspended from a ribbon worn around the neck, while the Lesser George would, as before, be pinned at the right hip to a blue sash worn over the left shoulder. In making this change James was consciously influenced by a precedent already established in 1700 by Louis XIV for the Spanish Toison d'Or and the French Saint-Esprit. The colour of the Thistle ribbon would be green, whereas that of the Toison d'Or was red, and the blue sash of the Garter would remain clearly identifiable, even in a monochrome engraving, because the *cordon bleu* of the Saint-Esprit fell in the diagonally opposite direction from the right shoulder to the left hip. The presence of both the Thistle and the Garter in a Stuart portrait is thus an indication that it was painted after 1717.

It is clear that the portraits of the exiled Stuarts were collected and highly prized by a large section of the population in both England and Scotland during the first half of the eighteenth century. Even the political opponents of the Stuarts were interested to see them, while making sustained efforts to stop them arriving from the Continent and to prevent their circulation. Most people in England and Scotland would not have seen the oil portraits themselves, nor perhaps even the better engravings made from them, but the recent study *The Engraved Record of the Jacobite Movement* by Richard Sharp has identified the very large number of popular prints derived for mass circulation from these original images. A similar study of the *Medallic Record of the Jacobite Movement* (Spink, London 1988) by Noel Woolf shows the large number of medals of the Stuarts produced by Norbert Roettiers in France and Ottone and Ermenegildo Hamerani in Italy. Other studies have examined the many popular portraits of the Stuarts, particularly those of Charles, Prince of Wales ('Bonnie Prince Charlie') produced in Scotland and England after the Jacobite rebellion of 1745–6. But there is considerable confusion surrounding the original paintings of the Stuarts produced at the Jacobite court itself. Which painters were employed, and when? What was the specific purpose of each portrait commissioned? How many of the portraits have survived and where are they today? Which portraits were copied and by whom? The largest and most comprehensive collection of these portraits is now in the Scottish National Portrait Gallery in Edinburgh, and this book is intended to place the gallery's permanent collection in its general context as well as to illustrate *The King over the Water*.

Fig.1 · *James VII and II*, 1685
Benedetto Gennari
Private Collection
[Gennari 1]

Fig.2 · *Mary of Modena*, 1687
Willem Wissing
Scottish National Portrait Gallery,
Edinburgh

HE EXILE OF THE STUART ROYAL FAMILY WAS THE RESULT OF the 'Glorious Revolution', an important turning point in the history of the British Isles. James VII and II had been on the throne for three and a half years when the revolution started on 5 November 1688 with the invasion of the south-west of England from Holland by William of Orange and a large mercenary army. William was married to James VII and II's elder daughter Mary, who had been heir to the throne until the birth of James, Prince of Wales, five months earlier.

William wanted England to pursue a pro-Dutch and anti-French foreign policy, and had been frustrated by James VII and II's policy of neutrality. He had, therefore, been waiting for his wife to succeed her father in order to achieve such a change. By 1688 a major war in Europe seemed imminent and William had become convinced that it was too dangerous to go on waiting. The birth of Prince James, destroying all his hopes, forced his hand and determined him to act. The enormous risks involved in invading England, particularly in the autumn, now seemed less significant than the danger of doing nothing. William felt that he could achieve his aim by assembling an overwhelmingly superior army with a large armada to carry it to England. If he could but safely land his army he felt that he could take control of the English government. He was helped by some extraordinary good luck. A 'Protestant wind' from the east enabled him to sail his fleet down the Channel and make his landing in Torbay. Shortly afterwards James VII and II suffered a nervous collapse and offered no military resistance. When James then escaped to France with Queen Mary of Modena and their infant son, a political vacuum was created which helped William and Mary get themselves proclaimed joint King and Queen of England in February 1689. These unexpected events seemed to have been brought about by the influence of divine providence, a political trump card in the hands of William and his supporters. James VII and II and the Prince of Wales were both deposed and all Catholics were excluded from the succession. The story of Jacobitism concerns the various attempts of James VII and II, his son, James III, and eventually his grandson (Prince Charles) to regain the throne which they had lost in that winter of 1688–9.

Apart from his military superiority, and his exceptional good luck, William was successful because he had convinced the political élite in the dominant Tory party that he had no designs on the throne itself. They believed that he had come to save them from James VII and II's unpopular religious policies. When they discovered his true intentions it was too late to stop him. The story of Jacobitism in England stems from the dilemma of a political party which knew it had been deceived, which never wanted James VII and II and his son to be deposed, but which feared that a Jacobite restoration would involve a return to the previous religious policies.

The story involves a series of invasions and rebellions, plots and negotiations, which lasted from 1689 until the 1750s. Before examining them, however, it is important to understand the context in which they took place. First and foremost James VII and II was King of Scotland and Ireland as well as England. Although the revolution started in England, it was not complete until William and Mary had successfully established themselves as king and queen in the two other kingdoms as well. In the case of Scotland, where James VII and II's government had also been unpopular, this meant a declaration by the Estates of the Kingdom in April that James had been replaced by William and Mary as joint monarchs. A civil war followed which the Jacobites had lost by May 1690, despite their early victory at Killiecrankie the previous July. The Jacobite restoration attempts were thus complicated by the fact that the Stuarts were trying to recover three thrones at the same time, while the interests of the English, the Scots and the Irish often differed.

Another important factor was the strong anti-Catholicism which was present in England and Scotland in the seventeenth and eighteenth centuries. Catholicism was associated in the minds of most people with tyranny and arbitrary government. The Whig party in England had even tried to exclude James VII and II from becoming king on the grounds that he was a Catholic. Now that he had been deposed they were determined to prevent his return. The Bill of Rights of December 1689 specified that no future monarch of England could be, or be married to, a Catholic. In

Scotland the Claim of Right of April 1689 had already used that principle to justify the transfer of the Crown. The Jacobites had the perpetual disadvantage of supporting a dynasty that was legally excluded from the succession on religious grounds.

A third factor concerned the way people interpreted the events of 1688–9, and the divided loyalties which resulted. Even today historians are unable to agree about the circumstances in England which led to the exile of James VII and II and his family. For many, and most notably the Whigs, James VII and II had tried to change the constitution by ruling arbitrarily without Parliament. A recent convert to Catholicism, James (according to this view) had tried to increase the powers of the Crown and to make himself more absolute, with a view to forcibly re-establishing Catholicism within his kingdoms. The revolution had therefore saved Great Britain from this menace, and any Jacobite restoration would inevitably pose a serious danger to Protestant liberties.

This view was challenged at the time, and has been rejected by many modern historians. Those who have disagreed with the Whigs have emphasised that James VII and II and his son wished to establish religious toleration. When James VII and II became king there were strong laws persecuting both the Catholics and the Protestant nonconformists, and other discriminatory laws (the English Test Acts) to prevent them from sitting in parliament or holding any public office. What James VII and II wished to do was repeal these laws to provide toleration and equality of opportunity for religious minorities. As the members of parliament refused to repeal the laws, the king had to use his prerogative powers to suspend the laws temporarily.

The opposing sides thus emphasised different points. The Whigs concentrated on James VII and II's methods, denouncing him as a tyrant. The Jacobites (and recent historians) concentrated on his aims. The Whigs replied that James was insincere and really wanted a Catholic absolutism: in their opinion he only pretended to want religious toleration and equality. The Jacobites insisted that he *was* sincere, and also denied that he acted unconstitutionally. Once in exile, James VII and II and particularly James III had to go out of their way to show their tolerance, by favouring Protestants at the exiled court. They also repeatedly declared that they would never again try to suspend the religious laws and that they would maintain the privileges of the established Protestant churches in their kingdoms.

The commitment to toleration had serious consequences, partly because it sometimes offended Louis XIV and the popes who gave them hospitality, but mainly because it encouraged James III in his refusal to convert from Catholicism to anglicanism. If he had been willing to do that he would probably have recovered his thrones, but he argued that if the king himself could not enjoy religious toleration, then there was no hope of anyone else obtaining it.

From the beginning, then, the dispute went far beyond the personalities of the rival monarchs. As the years went by other vested interests inevitably emerged to harden the opposing camps. Yet the conflict remained dynastic as well as religious and political. The hereditary succession in the legitimate royal line was in itself a point of great significance. It resulted in major divisions within the Tory party. It had been the Tories who had resisted James VII and II's religious policies in 1688, because they wished to maintain the full force of all the religious laws. They had thus helped William of Orange to conquer the country. But they had never wanted James VII and II to be deposed, and they now found themselves wanting two incompatible things: the Protestant succession and the legitimate succession. The refusal of James III to convert meant that they had to establish their priorities, and these would change several times in the seventy years after 1689. So, whereas committed Whigs and committed Jacobites had no need to make a choice, the Tories (and indeed most people) were constantly confronted by the problem of their divided loyalties. It is not surprising that many fell back on the prevailing religious belief, preached by the anglican and episcopalian churches, that legitimate authority should not be resisted. As it was so difficult to know which monarch should be regarded as the legitimate one, this often led to passive obedience, or merely doing nothing and waiting to see who would win. Then, as now, most people were not willing to risk themselves and their families for their political opinions. James VII and II and his son commissioned paintings and engravings of their portraits to remind or persuade people that they were the legitimate kings, but they knew that they had to rely on foreign support if they were to recover their thrones.

This passive obedience has made it very difficult for historians to assess the extent of support for the Stuarts in both England and Scotland. They have never been able to reach agreement. William III was personally unpopular, particularly after the death of his Stuart wife Mary II in 1694, but many people had disliked James VII and II as well. The succession of Mary's sister as Queen Anne in March 1702, shortly after the death of their father in September 1701, reconciled many waverers in the Tory party to the Protestant succession, but by then Anne's children had all died and there were no other Stuarts left except the family in exile. In consequence the problem of the succession had to be confronted. By the Act of Settlement of June 1701 it was laid down that all future English monarchs should be, and be married to, anglicans. The succession was settled on Sophia, Dowager Electress of Hanover and her son George, both Lutheran Protestants who were willing to become anglicans. Many, however, regarded this as merely a lever to force James to convert.

During the last years of Anne's reign, when for four years it had a majority in parliament, the Tory party was badly divided, one group being willing to repeal the Act of Settlement and restore James even if he remained a Catholic, the other insisting that there should be no restoration without a prior conversion. Nothing had been done when both Sophia and Anne died in the summer of 1714, so it was the Elector of Hanover who became King George I. In the years that followed, the Tory party was gradually reunited, as most people began to give priority to the legitimate hereditary succession, even if only as a way of opposing the new régime. Because the party commanded majority support in the country, that boded well for the popularity of a Jacobite restoration, but by then it was too late for this to happen peacefully. Parliament after the 1715 general election was dominated by the Whigs, to whom George I and then George II consistently gave their patronage and support. The opposition Tory party in parliament was generally pro-Jacobite, but the government was strong and few people in England could be relied on to show any active support for James until after he had been restored.

In Scotland, however, the situation was different, particularly after 1707. The Act of Settlement, establishing the principle of the Hanoverian succession, was only valid in England when it was passed in 1701, while the clause stating that all future monarchs had to be anglican was resented by the Presbyterians, who had only recently established their kirk as Scotland's established religion. The Scottish Parliament responded by passing the Security Act, which Queen Anne reluctantly signed in 1704. It opened the way for a Jacobite restoration in Scotland by stating that the succession must go to someone of 'the Royal Line of Scotland and of the true Protestant Religion', who should not be the 'successor to the Crown of England' unless the full sovereignty of Scotland were secured from English influence. It was to avert this that the Whigs in England and the anti-Jacobites in Scotland negotiated the Treaty of Union in 1706 and had it ratified by both parliaments in 1707. By uniting the two kingdoms, the Hanoverian and anglican succession was extended to all of Great Britain, while a special provision guaranteed the established status of Presbyterianism in Scotland. From this point onwards Jacobitism in Scotland attracted enormous support because the restoration of James, even as a Catholic, was seen as a way to break the unpopular union with England. While most Jacobites remained passive in England, there were many in Scotland who were prepared to come out in his support in order to encourage foreign countries to intervene.

The most powerful country in Europe, as well as the one geographically nearest to Great Britain, was France where Louis XIV had been the declared enemy of William III. As close ties already linked the Stuarts with the French royal family, Louis XIV had immediately offered James VII and II his support. He gave him the Château de Saint-Germain-en-Laye for as long as he needed it and committed himself to achieving a Stuart restoration. Thereafter, the Stuarts always looked to the French to help them regain their thrones.

For the next seventy years the French consistently sympathised with the Stuarts, but they had to consider their own interests as well. This meant that active French support could only be guaranteed when England and France were at war. During periods of peace the French might provide moral or even material support, but if ever the interests of the French government temporarily coincided with those of the government in London then the Stuarts found themselves politely but emphatically dropped. In the absence of active French support the chances of an immediate Jacobite restoration were very small indeed, unless another important power could be persuaded to intervene. The only one which actually prepared an invasion was Spain.

* * *

Shortly after William III's accession, England and France declared war. This conflict, known as the War of the League of Augsburg, lasted until 1697 and during it Louis XIV made three attempts to restore James VII and II. In 1689 he gave James an army and a fleet to transport him to Ireland. This resulted in James's defeat at the Boyne in 1690 and the Jacobite surrender at Limerick the following year. The second attempt was in 1692 when Louis assembled a large army near Cherbourg and attempted to win control of the Channel. This would have enabled James VII and II to invade the south of England, but the plan failed when the French fleet was defeated off Cap La Hogue. The third attempt was in 1696. Another army was assembled at Calais with orders to sail for England once news had been received that a planned Jacobite rebellion had broken out. When the Jacobites in England announced that they could not start their rebellion until the French army had already landed, the invasion had to be called off. In 1697, by the Treaty of Ryswick, Louis XIV recognised William III as the *de facto* King of England, Scotland and Ireland, while continuing to treat James VII and II as the *de jure* king and the Prince of Wales as his legitimate heir. When James VII and II died in September 1701, shortly after the Act of Settlement, Louis XIV similarly recognised his son as James III *de jure*.

William III, who like all kings of England described himself as king of France *de jure*, then used this recognition to persuade an angry Parliament to declare war on France, and to pass an Abjuration Act in 1702 declaring James, or rather the 'pretended Prince of Wales', guilty of high treason. The result was the War of the Spanish Succession, so called because a French prince had recently inherited the Spanish throne and because this was contested by the Austrian Habsburgs. The war was between the supporters of legitimism, in the persons of James III and Philip V of Spain, and those who favoured the Hanoverian succession in England and the Habsburg succession in Spain. Supported at first by the Tories as well as the Whigs, it was soon opposed by the Tories but pursued with vigour by the Whigs.

This war produced the crisis in relations between England and Scotland which led to the Union of 1707. The previous war had seriously damaged the Scottish economy, and the new one threatened to do the same. Moreover, many Scots resented having to wage war against France in the interests of England, and remembered with nostalgia the 'auld alliance' with France, which they wished to see revived. Once the Union had come into force Louis XIV decided to play the Scottish card by sending James with a small army to invade Scotland and provoke a nationwide Jacobite rebellion. The expedition sailed in 1708, but was prevented from landing in the Firth of Forth by the arrival of the English fleet. No rebellion took place, and perhaps the best chance of a Stuart restoration was thereby lost.

This lucky escape for the Whig government in London turned opinion against the long war, because the Protestant succession now seemed secure. In 1710 Queen Anne dismissed her Whig ministers and replaced them with Tories, enabling the latter to win a general election and dominate parliament. The next four years were of decisive importance. The Tories decided to make peace with France without consulting their allies, who included the Elector of Hanover. By the terms of the treaty, signed at Utrecht in 1713, Louis XIV had to recognise Anne as *de jure* Queen of Great Britain and to ask James to leave France. James went to Bar-le-Duc in Lorraine (at that time an independent duchy). The aim of the Tories was then to persuade James to convert to anglicanism so they could repeal the Act of Settlement and arrange for his restoration. His refusal to convert split the Tory party and prevented this plan from being carried through, so that it was George I who succeeded Queen Anne in 1714. The new king and his son (George II) never forgave the Tories for their support of James. The party was proscribed for the next forty years, during which period all ministerial offices and government patronage were reserved for the Whigs. It was this which reunited the Tory party and made its leaders hope for a Jacobite restoration.

Between 1715 and 1753 James and his supporters made many attempts to recover his thrones. The fact that they all failed has posed an historical problem. Should repeated failure be taken as evidence to support the Whig argument that the Jacobite movement had few supporters, and that it appealed only to a minority of reactionaries and malcontents, generally on the fringe of society? Or should each attempted invasion, rebellion and plot be examined separately to show how even a strong popular movement was unable to overthrow an unpopular government which had the support of a standing army and a large parliamentary majority? Two things are clear. Firstly, the Stuarts experienced extraordinary bad luck, so that divine providence really seemed to be against them. Secondly, Great Britain and France were at peace from 1713 to 1743, making it difficult to obtain foreign support. The circulation of portraits remained one of the few ways of keeping the Stuart cause alive.

In 1715 the Jacobites prepared an ambitious plan to overthrow George I. Irish troops serving in the French army and commanded by the Tory Duke of Ormonde would invade the south-west of England, where the Tories would rise in rebellion. Meanwhile diversionary rebellions would break out in Scotland and Lancashire, and the Hanoverian Whig government would be overthrown. The plan failed badly because it depended on the cooperation of Louis XIV. But the old French king died in the summer of 1715 and his successor, the Regent duc d'Orléans, cancelled the invasion and betrayed the rebels to the government in London. The diversionary rebellions in Scotland and Lancashire had to confront the forces of the Whig government without any assistance. Even then they might have succeeded, but for the chronically poor leadership of the Earl of Mar, who was defeated at Sherrifmuir in November. When James arrived in December, the rebellion had already been virtually put down, and he was obliged to return to Lorraine shortly afterwards. Once the crisis was safely over, these events enabled the Whigs to represent the Jacobite movement as marginal and easily defeated.

The new French government now turned against James, because the regent was on very bad terms with King Philip V of Spain and needed the diplomatic support of George I. The price that George demanded was the expulsion of James from both France and Lorraine. In 1716–17 James lived in Avignon, then an enclave of papal territory within the south of France, but George I soon obliged the regent and the Pope to expel him from Avignon as well. In 1717 James and his court, by then mainly Scottish and Protestant, crossed into Italy and settled in the Papal States, at first in the ducal palace of Urbino (1717–18) and then in Rome, where the Palazzo Muti was made permanently available.

Deprived of French help, James approached the enemies of George I and the regent in the hope that they would help him launch a fresh invasion of Great Britain. A Swedish expedition to Scotland seemed possible, but was cancelled when King Charles XII died in 1718. However, a project for a Spanish invasion of both England and Scotland went ahead. As before the plan involved a major invasion of England commanded by the Duke of Ormonde, while a minor diversionary force under the Earl Marischal and the Marquis of Tullibardine would provoke a Scottish rebellion in the Highlands. James travelled to Spain in 1719 hoping to join Ormonde, but bad luck struck again. The main Spanish fleet was seriously damaged by a terrible storm while sailing from Cadiz to meet James at Corunna. The invasion of England had to be cancelled. The expedition to Scotland did manage to sail but it could hardly succeed by itself. Partly as a result of divided leadership, the small Spanish force was defeated at Glenshiel in June.

James returned to Rome in the summer of 1719 to continue his negotiations for a restoration. It was then that he married the Polish Princess Maria Clementina Sobieska in September 1719. Their first child, the Prince of Wales, was born in December 1720 and named Charles. A second son, Henry, Duke of York was born in March 1725, ensuring the Jacobite succession into the next generation.

Although France remained at peace with Britain her relations with George I were no longer so close, and plans were now made for another invasion. These culminated in the so-called Atterbury Plot of 1722. Once again there was to be an invasion of England by the Irish troops serving in the French army, this time commanded by Lord Dillon. This would coincide with the general election of 1722, the first to take place since 1715 under a new Septennial Act (1716). While the election was on, and the gentry were dispersed on their estates, the Tories would raise a rebellion in London and the west country, and the troops would arrive from France. The invasion was betrayed by a leading member of the French government, so the regent had to cancel, while in England the Whig government identified and arrested the Jacobite leaders (including Bishop Atterbury of Rochester) by intercepting correspondence and seizing papers.

James's hopes were raised once again when he heard of the death of George I in June 1727. He travelled incognito to Lorraine, but discovered that George II had succeeded to the throne without difficulty. The new king maintained the stability of the Whig government by keeping on Sir Robert Walpole as prime minister. James therefore went back to Avignon, where he stayed for several months before returning to Italy.

These were very difficult years for the Jacobite movement. All the planned invasions and rebellions had failed and it was easy to be discouraged. James himself was becoming increasingly resigned to his fate, while his two sons were still too young to take up the challenge for him. It was particularly unfortunate that at this time James and his wife had a public disagreement which led to a two year separation. James left Rome and moved to Bologna, and it was from there that he travelled to Lorraine. By the time he returned in 1728 the quarrel had been made up and the queen was waiting for him at Bologna. They eventually returned to Rome in the following year.

After the accession of George II, James adopted new tactics. In the general election of 1727, made necessary by the change of monarch, the Whig party split into two factions, known as the 'ministerial' and the 'opposition' Whigs. This meant that there was now a group in Parliament with which the pro-Jacobite Tories might co-operate against the government. It also raised the possibility that one day there might be a hung parliament, with the Tories holding the balance. In 1733, when Walpole tried to increase the excise tax, he offended so many Whigs that in the general election of the next year his overall majority was considerably reduced. Jacobite hopes, therefore, were placed on the next general election, due to be held in 1741. By then the Stuart Prince of Wales would be twenty years old.

The Excise Crisis of 1733 also provoked another planned invasion. It was organised by Lord Cornbury with the French ambassador in London and the French foreign secretary in Versailles who, like many others at the French court, strongly disliked his government's unwillingness to support James. As in 1722 the French would invade the south of England, while the Jacobites in England would raise rebellions in London and the provinces. The plan came to nothing because the French foreign secretary was overruled by the elderly French chief minister, Cardinal Fleury, but it demonstrated that French support might still be forthcoming, particularly if the long period of peace between France and Hanoverian England could be brought to an end. The 1730s were a period of waiting, while the Prince of Wales and the Duke of York grew to manhood.

Walpole's achievement, helped by Cardinal Fleury, was to maintain the peace with France, thus largely negating the Jacobite threat for such a long time. By the end of the 1730s, however, this policy had become increasingly unpopular in parliament. In 1739 he was pushed into a war with Spain. Then, in 1740, a major war broke out on the continent, known as the War of the Austrian Succession. Great Britain and France were not at first involved, but as they supported opposing sides it seemed only a matter of time before they would go to war. French military support for a Jacobite restoration once again became possible.

It was in these circumstances that the general election took place in 1741. The ministerial Whigs lost their overall majority, thus giving the Tories the chance to combine with the opposition Whigs to bring Walpole and his government down.

When James gave them the order, Walpole was forced to resign in February 1742. Although the Whigs settled their differences and formed a new government (thus depriving the Tories of their influence in parliament), the way was now clear for a resumption of Anglo-French hostilities.

Cardinal Fleury, the other obstacle to war, died at the age of ninety in 1743. The leaders of the Tory party sent a message to Louis XV asking him to invade England on behalf of James. The French responded by assembling a large army at Dunkirk, intending to invade England in February 1744. The Prince of Wales secretly left Rome and travelled to France so he could accompany it. Once again, however, fate intervened. A terrible storm struck the Channel and destroyed the expeditionary force. The invasion was cancelled.

It was at this point, when no further French help was in prospect, that the Prince of Wales decided to sail for Scotland in 1745 to raise a rebellion. The dramatic events which followed, known as the 'Forty-Five', need not be repeated here in any detail. Lowlanders as well as Highlanders supported the prince in Scotland, and enabled him to take control of Edinburgh and invade England. But the predictably passive attitude of the Jacobites in England, coupled with bad communications and the very slow reaction of the French in sending help, undermined the confidence of the Scots and led to the fateful decision to retreat from Derby in December. A French invasion force had been assembled at Boulogne, but it was dispersed at the beginning of February 1746 and, as is well known, the prince's main Jacobite army was defeated at Culloden in April.

This was the moment when James realised that his family would never be restored. He was now fifty-eight years old, and the Hanoverian Kings had had over thirty years to establish their legitimacy in the eyes of a new generation of English people. Retribution in Scotland was so fierce that no further rebellion could be expected there. Even before Great Britain and France made peace in 1748, leaving the Stuarts without any prospect of military help, James agreed that the Duke of York should become a Cardinal and thus guarantee his status and security as a Prince of the Roman Catholic Church. This inevitably damaged the Jacobite cause in Great Britain. It also alienated the Prince of Wales, who refused to return to Rome and never saw his father again. All future Jacobite plans, such as the Elibank Plot of

1753, were conducted by the prince rather than James. New portraits of the Stuarts in Rome, to be sent to Jacobites in Great Britain, were no longer needed.

The Jacobite restoration attempts finally ended in 1759, by which time James was seriously ill in Rome. France and Great Britain were once again at war, in the Seven Years War of 1756–63, and the French briefly considered sending an invasion to restore the Stuarts. The idea was dropped after the decisive British naval victory at Quiberon Bay.

In England, Tory loyalty to the Stuarts had meanwhile collapsed during the 1750s. There were several reasons for this, including the behaviour of Prince Charles after his return from Scotland and the emergence of a new generation which accepted the status quo. So long as George II lived, there remained a lingering loyalty to the 'King over the Water', for George was a German and still regarded as a foreign ruler. His death in 1760 really marked the end of the Jacobite movement as a political force, because his grandson, the new King George III, had been born and brought up an Englishman.

When James died on 1 January, 1766 even the Jacobite succession in the direct Stuart line was insecure. Neither of James's sons had any legitimate children, so their claims seemed likely to pass one day to a distant cousin, a foreign prince unknown to the people of England and Scotland. Although James may only have visited Great Britain very briefly in the winter of 1715–16, and his son Charles for only one year in 1745–6, and although Prince Henry never once set foot on British soil, all three were known to the majority of the British people, thanks to the portraits painted and engraved in France and Italy over a period of approximately sixty years. The long series of Jacobite invasions, rebellions and plots was at least partly made possible because people knew for whom they were acting and could visualise the princes for whom they risked their lives.

Fig.3 · *The Prince of Wales*, 1691
Nicolas de Largillière
Scottish National Portrait Gallery, Edinburgh
[Largillière 1]

PART ONE · FRANCE · 1689–1715

THE EXILE OF THE STUARTS BEGAN IN THE WINTER OF 1688–9 when James VII and II, Mary of Modena and the Prince of Wales fled to France, following the successful invasion of England by William III of Orange. They were welcomed by Louis XIV, who lent them the Château-Vieux de Saint-Germain-en-Laye, to the west of Paris. Originally intended as only a temporary residence, pending a restoration, it became the home of the Jacobite court for about twenty-five years. James VII and II and Mary of Modena both died there, in 1701 and 1718 respectively. Their son James III remained there until 1712 when he moved to Bar-le-Duc in Lorraine, before eventually settling in Italy.

There are very few portraits which show James VII and II and Mary of Modena in exile, and none of them was engraved at the time. This is partly because the portraits which they commissioned were intended for the decoration of their apartments in the Château de Saint-Germain or for their private use. It was partly also because new portraits were not actually needed in England and Scotland.

During their short reign James and Mary (figs.1 and 2) had been painted by both Sir Godfrey Kneller (1646–1723) and Nicolas de Largillière (1656–1746). In addition, James had been painted by Benedetto Gennari (1633–1715) and Mary by Willem Wissing (1656–1687). The king and queen were unable to take any of these portraits to France with them, but the two pairs by Kneller and Largillière had already been engraved and were well known in England and Scotland. Produced before the revolution, these portraits showed the king and queen before they had been deposed. They thus represented continuity and legitimacy, and were deliberately not replaced by French portraits showing them in exile.

But James and Mary needed portraits for other reasons. In 1689 James VII and II went with a French army to Ireland to recover his British kingdoms, leaving his

Fig.4 · *The Prince of Wales*, 1689
[Gennari 2]

wife and son at Saint-Germain. By 1690 she wished to send him a double portrait. Later, in 1690, after the Battle of the Boyne, he returned to Saint-Germain and moved into the apartment previously used, and now decorated for him, by Louis XIV. He therefore wanted a large family portrait to be placed in a prominent position in his antichamber, to impress his visitors with the majesty of the British royal family. These circumstances lay behind the first portraits of the Stuarts in exile.

The choice of painters was also dictated by circumstances. Largillière, who had visited England three times and already painted the king and queen, was available in Paris and might have been commissioned by Mary of Modena to paint a double portrait. But Gennari, who had regularly worked for the British royal family since 1674, left England and joined the queen at Saint-Germain at the beginning of 1689. While James VII and II was in Ireland it was therefore Gennari, a fellow Italian, whom Mary of Modena employed. In 1689 he produced a large portrait of the Prince of Wales, wearing a silver dress and a lace stomacher, apron and bonnet (fig.4), which the queen placed in her bedchamber. The following year he painted the double portrait for James VII and II. It was not a very attractive work. Whereas the portrait of the prince by himself shows him seated on a cushion and holding a parrot on his right hand, the larger double portrait shows him in the same costume standing on a table beside his mother, who wears a blue dress and ermine-lined cloak (fig.5). The composition is stiff and the image of the queen not very flattering. As it happened, James VII and II returned to Saint-Germain before the painting could be despatched to Ireland, so it remained at the Jacobite court.

Gennari's list of works shows that he produced two more portraits of Mary of Modena, both now lost, one of which was for the convent of Visitation nuns where she regularly stayed at Chaillot. But the failure of his double portrait made the king and queen turn to Largillière for their family portrait in 1691. They might well have been influenced in their choice by the Earl of Melfort, a recognised connoisseur, who returned from an embassy to Rome at precisely this time and had never patronised Gennari. The painter left the court and returned to Italy in the spring of 1692, and was asked to take his double portrait with him as a present for the Duke of Modena.

Largillière, like Gennari, began with a portrait of the Prince of Wales, before proceeding to the larger canvas. The first picture is now in the Scottish National

Portrait Gallery and shows the prince sitting on a cushion with a spaniel (fig.3). The prince is naked, except for some material draped around his body. The family portrait has not survived. It was discovered in the château in the early nineteenth century in a terrible condition, and described as follows:

'The little prince is very beautiful, with dark eyes, bright complexion, and a profusion of clustering curls. He is dressed in a red and green tartan frock, with a long waist, and point-lace stomacher: and wears a sort of fanciful helmet cap of dark blue velvet, with a plume of black and blue feathers… He holds a robin red breast on his finger, on which he bestows a smiling regard. The elbow of that arm originally rested in the palm of his royal mother, while the King held him by the other hand; but the portrait of the prince was all that could be restored.'

Unfortunately not even the part showing the prince has survived.

In 1692 James VII and II and Louis XIV planned an invasion of England from the Cotentin peninsula. A large Franco-Jacobite army was assembled near Cherbourg, and the French navy was instructed to clear the Channel by defeating the Anglo-Dutch fleet. In anticipation of this, James VII and II left Mary of Modena, who was pregnant, and went to join the army. His hopes were dashed by the Anglo-Dutch naval victory at the Battle of Cap La Hogue, which inflicted severe damage on the French fleet under Tourville. The invasion had to be called off, and James VII and II returned to Saint-Germain. Shortly afterwards the queen gave birth to a daughter, named Louise-Marie.

The birth of the princess in 1692 meant that sooner or later the family portrait painted by Largillière the previous year would have to be replaced. The ideal choice of painter for a new family group was the elderly Pierre Mignard (1612–1695), the principal painter to Louis XIV, who had been spectacularly successful in portraying the family of the Dauphin in 1687. When Mignard was approached in 1694 he was eighty-two years old and reluctant to go to Saint-Germain to paint the Stuarts, alleging as his excuse that there was illness there. But he was persuaded to agree by Louis XIV, who allowed him to paint them in the king's *petit appartement* at Versailles. The result was the greatest of all the portraits of the Stuarts in exile, and the only one which has survived showing the family as a whole (Mignard 1). It occupied an entire wall in James VII and II's antichamber and was so positioned that it confronted any visitor to the court who was allowed beyond the king's guard chamber.

Fig.5 · *Mary of Modena and the Prince of Wales*, 1690
[Gennari 3]

Fig.6 · *The Family of James VII and II*, 1694
Pierre Mignard
The Royal Collection © 2001, HM Queen Elizabeth II
[Mignard 2]

It shows the king and queen seated at a table, upon which their little daughter sits on a cushion between them. The six-year-old prince stands on the other side of his mother, who thus dominates the centre of the picture. James VII and II wears the regalia of the Order of the Garter, including the collar with its Great George, whereas the prince has the Garter sash worn over an armour breast-plate. The crown has been placed with a sword on a large cushion at the feet of the queen, and the prince points to it with his left hand. In addition to the large painting, Mignard's preliminary sketches (Louvre) and finished *modello* (fig.6) have also survived.

The last portraits of James VII and II and Mary of Modena seem to have been commissioned in 1698. They were painted by François de Troy (1645–1730) and were probably exchanged as mutual presents, perhaps to celebrate their twenty-fifth wedding anniversary in November 1698. Although of similar dimensions, and composed as pendants, the portraits were not hung together. The elderly king is shown looking to the right and wearing the Garter over armour. He stands by a table, on which his left hand rests beside the crown (fig.7). The queen is shown looking to the left, in her blue coronation dress. She sits on a high backed chair beside what might be the same table, resting her right hand beside another crown. Both portraits survive, but the one showing the queen was later substantially reduced in size (fig.8) to make a false pair with a different portrait of the king.

By 1698 there were already several portraits of the Prince of Wales. The first had been painted by Kneller in 1688 when the Prince was still in England, and showed him as an infant lying on a cushion. Although the original painting has been lost, and we only have a miniature version (fig.9), it was engraved in mezzotint at the time by John Smith (s 71). Between 1691 and 1694 four more portraits were produced at Saint-Germain by Largillière, all of which were engraved and smuggled across the Channel. Largillière's portrait of 1691, already referred to, was engraved in reverse by Van Schuppen in 1692, though with the body fully clothed (s 91). A second portrait (Largillière 3), similar to the previous one but also fully clothed, was engraved in 1692 by Gantrel (missing from s). These two must have been finished by the spring of 1692 because neither shows the prince with the Garter which his father gave him in April of that year. Largillière's third portrait, which prominently displays the star and blue sash of the Garter, was based on the image of the prince in the original large family group. It shows the Prince with an elaborate feathered

Fig.7 · *James VII and II*, c.1698
[De Troy 1]

Fig.8 · *Mary of Modena*, c.1698
[De Troy 2]

Fig.9 · *The Prince of Wales*, 1689
Sir Godfrey Kneller
The Drambuie Collection, Edinburgh

Fig.10 · *The Prince of Wales*,1692
[Largillière 4]

helmet, and wearing a lace trimmed red costume (fig.10). It was immediately engraved by Edelinck (s 89). Largillière's fourth portrait was painted in 1694, when the prince was six years old. It was sent to Rome to be presented to Pope Innocent XII, but a copy was kept at Saint-Germain so that it could be engraved by Gantrel (s 116). It shows him wearing the Garter over an elaborately embroidered red coat (Largillière 5).

This last portrait made the prince look so handsome that in December 1694 the queen commissioned Largillière to produce a large double one showing both of her children. The image of the prince was to be exactly reproduced, and indeed the portion depicting his head has been stitched into the larger canvas (fig.11). The prince is shown in a plain scarlet coat, which contrasts with the blue of the Garter. He rests his right hand on the head of a large hound. His sister stands beside him wearing a white dress with lace stomacher and apron, and a newly fashionable high head-dress. She holds a sprig of orange blossom in her left hand and points up to her brother with her right. Behind her is a large stone vase, with an orange tree and a parrot, and an inscription which records that the prince and princess were then seven and three years old. They actually reached those ages shortly afterwards, in June 1695.

When this picture was finished the queen gave it to James VII and II, but she was so delighted with it that she immediately ordered at least three other full-size copies and several smaller busts. The latter show either the prince or the princess, and one of the prince was engraved by Drevet (s 115). In a half-length of the prince, Largillière presents him with his hand on the dog's head, but wearing his original elaborately embroidered coat (seen in Largillière 5).

Great Britain and France were at war from 1689 until the autumn of 1697. During those years engravings destined for England and Scotland were generally smuggled via the Spanish Netherlands or the United Provinces. The return of peace, however, enabled people once again to travel directly between England and France. In 1698 John Smith (*c.*1652–1742) travelled to Paris and secretly visited the Jacobite court at Saint-Germain-en-Laye. There he was given permission to make a large mezzotint of the double portrait of Largillière, which he published in Paris before returning to London (s 114).

No new images were produced at Saint-Germain between 1695 and 1698, but

Fig.11 · *The Prince of Wales and Princess Louise-Marie*, 1695
Nicolas de Largillière
National Portrait Gallery, London
[Largillière 6]

Fig.12 · *The Prince of Wales*, 1699
[De Troy 3]

Fig.13 · *The Prince of Wales*, 1700
[De Troy 5]

Fig.14 · *The Prince of Wales*, 1700
[De Troy 6]

the years which followed were the most prolific of all for the production of Stuart portraits. There were three reasons for this. In the first place the peace, which lasted until 1702, made it possible for Jacobites to go to France and visit the court. They were rewarded, depending on their status, with paintings, miniatures or engravings. Secondly, the Prince of Wales and his sister were growing up, so new pictures were needed. Thirdly, the question of the succession entered a new phase. The Act of Settlement of June 1701 specifically excluded the Prince of Wales and his sister, along with all other Catholics, from the succession to the English throne. After the death of Queen Anne, who succeeded William III in March 1702, the throne was to pass to the Electress Sophia of Hanover and then to her son George. In September 1701 James VII and II died, and the prince was recognised by France, Spain, Portugal, the Pope and most of the Italian states as King James III. The English Parliament responded in 1702 by passing the Act of Abjuration, by which all office holders were called upon to support the 'warming-pan myth' by taking an oath which repudiated James as 'the pretended Prince of Wales'.

For some reason Largillière was never again employed by the Stuarts after 1695. Instead, they turned in 1698 to François de Troy to produce a series of portraits of the Prince of Wales and his sister Princess Louise-Marie. It was a natural choice, because De Troy had become the leading portraitist to the French court at Versailles during the 1690s, while Largillière was increasingly employed by the wealthy merchants of Paris. In particular, De Troy had painted the three sons of the Dauphin, who were like older brothers to the Prince of Wales, in 1696. While the Stuarts commissioned their portraits from De Troy, the court of Versailles increasingly employed Hyacinthe Rigaud (1659–1743).

The choice of De Troy might have been influenced by the Earl of Perth, who had been appointed governor to the prince in 1696. De Troy lived only six doors away from the Scots College in Paris and had already painted several Jacobites, including Perth's son, Lord Drummond.

Between 1699 and 1701 De Troy produced seven separate portraits of the Prince of Wales. They are all private cabinet pieces, measuring a little less than 30 × 25 inches (76 × 63.5 cm). The first, painted shortly before the prince cut off his hair and began to wear a wig, was sent to Rome in 1699 as a present for Cardinal Caprara, the Cardinal Protector of England. It shows the young prince looking to his right,

Fig.15 · *The Prince of Wales*, 1701
François de Troy
Scottish National Portrait Gallery, Edinburgh
[De Troy 8]

Fig.16 · *The Prince of Wales*, 1700
[De Troy 7]

Fig.17 · *The Prince of Wales*, 1701
[De Troy 9]

wearing lace over the shoulder of his red coat and pointing with his left hand across the Channel to England. There are three versions in existence today (fig.12). In the second portrait the prince's face is virtually the same but his body is turned more to the right and both arms are by his side. Three versions of this one have also survived (De Troy 4). The third portrait was painted for the Electress Sophia of Hanover in 1700, before the Act of Settlement. The prince is shown looking to his left, wearing a breast-plate over his coat (fig.13). It is the first portrait, apart from the Mignard family group, in which the prince is shown wearing armour.

De Troy's fourth portrait is a variant of the the last one, in which the prince's right hand now rests on his hip. It is one of his best known portraits, and eight versions of it have survived (fig.14). It was engraved in reverse by Edelinck in the spring of 1700 (s 119), though care was taken to ensure that the sash of the Garter would still be shown over the prince's left shoulder. Later, the same year, De Troy and Edelinck collaborated on a fifth portrait. This time De Troy showed the prince in exactly the same costume, still with his right hand on his hip, but now looking to the right. The engraving was again reversed, with the sash of the Garter adjusted appropriately (s 118). There are three versions of the original picture (fig.16).

De Troy's sixth portrait is the one now in the Scottish National Portrait Gallery (fig.15), painted in 1701. It was probably commissioned by Mary of Modena at the time of the prince's thirteenth birthday in June. It is very similar to the portrait of the duc d'Anjou (by then King Philip V of Spain), painted in 1696 when he too had been thirteen. De Troy's seventh portrait is similar to this one, but shows the prince in a red rather than a grey coat. His body is placed at a slightly different angle, with his face looking further over his left shoulder. Three versions have survived (fig.17).

In addition to these seven portraits of the prince, De Troy also produced two of Princess Louise-Marie. The first was probably painted in 1699 and shows the princess when she was seven years old. There is a table on her right hand side where some orange blossom has been placed. She seems to be gathering up these flowers, because she holds some in her left hand and is in the process of picking up more with her right. Two versions of this picture have survived (De Troy 12). The next portrait, painted in 1700, seems to be a sequel. She now has some flowers in her hair, and holds others with a hyacinth in her left hand, which is extended to her right

Fig.18 · *Princess Louise-Marie*, 1700
François de Troy
The Drambuie Collection, Edinburgh
[De Troy 13]

Fig.26 · *Princess Louise-Marie*, 1704
Alexis-Simon Belle
Scottish National Portrait Gallery, Edinburgh

[Belle 14]

Fig.18 · *Princess Louise-Marie*, 1700
François de Troy
The Drambuie Collection, Edinburgh
[De Troy 13]

Fig.19 · *The Prince of Wales and Princess Louise-Marie*, 1699
[Belle 5]

Fig.20 · *The Prince of Wales*, 1700
[Belle 6]

shoulder. There are two known versions of this portrait as well (fig.18), one of them paired with De Troy's fourth portrait of her brother. This one of Louise-Marie was engraved in reverse by Duflos in 1700, but De Troy's name was omitted (s 171). An unauthorised copy of Duflos' print by Desrochers, in which the image is reversed back to its original state, incorrectly states that the original painting was by Largillière (s 170). This has resulted in confusion, encouraging people to think that the latter artist continued to work for the Stuarts after 1695.

With twenty-six known versions of nine original compositions, all painted between 1699 and 1701, De Troy must have employed assistants to help him in his work for the Stuarts. He seems to have received some assistance from Largillière's nephew, Jacob van Schuppen (1670–1751). There is an engraving by Desrochers which appears to be connected with De Troy's fifth portrait of the prince, but which is nevertheless attributed to Van Schuppen (s 148). It seems clear that De Troy also received some assistance from Alexis-Simon Belle (1674–1734). It is probably impossible, however, to determine which, if any, of the surviving versions were produced by De Troy's assistants.

Belle had begun to work independently for the Stuart court in 1699, but there is one portrait of 1698 which emphasises the problem surrounding correct attributions. This is a full-length portrait of the prince which shows him with his own hair, before he began to wear a wig in the spring of 1699 (Belle 4). Is it by De Troy or is it by Belle or perhaps by Van Schuppen? The dimensions are exactly the same as De Troy's portraits of James VII and II and Mary of Modena, also painted in 1698. The positioning of the arms and torso, and even the armour that the prince is wearing, are virtually the same as in the large family group by Mignard. The face recalls the earlier portraits by Largillière more than the seven (which had not yet been painted) by De Troy. An attribution to Belle, carrying out precise instructions, seems the safest conclusion.

Belle's earliest portraits tend to give the prince a narrower and more pointed face than those of De Troy. The first is large and must have been commissioned for a convent, perhaps even the one at Chaillot, because it shows the prince as a guardian angel, leading his younger sister by the hand under the protection of cherubims (fig.19). After this Belle produced two private cabinet pieces which make an interesting comparison. The first, of which there are two versions, dates from 1700 (fig.20). It is Belle's reinterpretation of De Troy's fourth portrait of the prince, which it closely resembles and which was painted during the same year. It suggests that Belle did not make many of the copies of that portrait by De Troy or that, if he did, he preferred on this occasion to stamp the composition with his own individuality. Before Belle had painted his second portrait, in 1702, James III had succeeded his father as the Jacobite king and Belle began to describe himself as 'peintre ordinaire du Roy d'Angleterre'. Great Britain and France declared war in 1702 and Belle's portrait of that year is the first one to show James in full armour (fig.21).

The accession of Queen Anne and the renewal of war in 1702 significantly reduced the contact between the Stuart court and England. It had the opposite effect, however, in Scotland where many resented the renewal of war against France, and where the Act of Settlement had no validity. The Scottish Parliament responded by passing a Security Bill in 1703, which eventually received the royal assent the following year. It declared that Scotland had the right to choose her own successor to Queen Anne. During these years contact with Scotland was significantly increased and the demand for portraits as essential weapons of political persuasion therefore continued.

The ideal gift for a Scottish emissary making a clandestine visit to Saint-Germain was a miniature rather than a cabinet portrait, and it was in the years following 1702 that three miniaturists are known to have worked for the court. The first was Jacques-Antoine Arlaud (1668–1746). The second was Anne Chéron (c.1663–1718), who married Belle in November 1701. The third was Jacqueline de La Boissière (fl.1690–1721). Arlaud and La Boissière produced original images, whereas Chéron copied the portraits done by her husband.

There are several miniatures traditionally attributed to Arlaud which date from the 1690s, all of them copied after the portraits by Largillière (Arlaud 1, 3), one of which shows the prince as a Knight of the Garter in 1692 (fig.22). But the first which can be definitely attributed to Arlaud was made in October 1702 (Arlaud 4). Another was made for Lord Lovat in May 1703 (Arlaud 6). They show James wearing armour and the blue sash of the Garter. The miniatures by Chéron are similar, but they can easily be distinguished because whereas Arlaud shows James facing right, Chéron (like Belle) shows James facing left. Various examples have survived, and the Scottish National Portrait Gallery's collection contains one by each artist. The

Fig.21 · *James III*, 1702
[Belle 7]

Fig.22 · *The Prince of Wales as a Knight of the Garter*, 1692
[Arlaud 2]

Fig.23 · *James III*, 1704
[Chéron 1]

Fig.24 · *James III*, 1702
[Arlaud 5]

one by Chéron is dated 1704 (fig.23). The one by Arlaud was produced in 1702 (fig.24) and later engraved by Simon in 1708, at the time of the planned Franco-Jacobite invasion of Scotland. There are two versions of Simon's engraving, one inscribed 'Jacobus III. Magnae Britanniae Rex', the other 'James VIII, King of Scotland and England' (s 124). La Boissière's miniatures, like Arlaud's, show James facing right, but they are half-lengths rather than busts (fig.25). Some include a red sash at the waist and one of them is dated 1710 (La Boissière 4).

Belle and his wife Anne Chéron began to live at Saint-Germain in 1702 and quickly became integrated into the British community there. In August 1703 he was elected to the Académie Royale de Peinture et Sculpture and commissioned to produce a large new portrait of James for the Scots College in Paris. James is shown full length in armour, in a composition which is reminiscent of Rigaud's portrait of 1702 of the duc de Bourgogne. James stands beside the Channel, in which several warships can be seen, pointing with his right hand to the cliffs and castle of Dover. He rests his left hand on his sword and is accompanied by a page in Polish costume (fig.27). It was this large picture which established Belle as the official painter to the Stuart court, and which brought him a regular flow of commissions from the Jacobites at Saint-Germain. He exhibited it at the Salon in 1704 (along with four other Jacobite portraits) and made various copies of the bust. Four of these have survived (Belle 8), one of which also includes both the warships and Dover Castle.

One of the other Jacobite portraits which Belle exhibited at the 1704 Salon was a charming new one of the twelve-year-old Princess Louise-Marie. There are three surviving versions (fig.26). The composition is deliberately similar to that of the De Troy portrait of 1700, and the princess wears peonies and orange blossom in her hair. Belle, however, has transferred the other flowers from her right shoulder and placed them on the right-hand side of her bodice. The flowers are now much larger.

Belle's next Stuart portraits were commissioned to commemorate the coming of age of both James and his sister Princess Louise-Marie, in June 1706 and June 1710 respectively. The portrait of James once again shows him wearing full armour, with the blue sash of the Garter. Two versions have survived (Belle 9), but we know that Belle made several others. One document records that four copies were sent to Scotland in September 1706, one of which was for Lord Strathmore. This portrait was engraved in reverse by Le Roi, and inscribed 'Jacobus III. Mag. Britan. etc Rex' (s 131). It is noteworthy because Le Roi, who was never employed again, omitted to keep the sash of the Garter on James's left shoulder, thus making it appear like the Saint-Esprit.

The portrait to celebrate the eighteenth birthday of the princess in 1710 was commissioned by Mary of Modena as a pendant to De Troy's portrait of James VII and II, with virtually identical dimensions (fig.28). In a pose which is similar to some of De Troy's portraits of Bourbon princesses, Belle shows Louise-Marie wearing a crimson cloak over her white satin dress and picking orange blossom from a tree in a large decorated gilt urn on her right hand side. The portrait was later engraved by Chéreau, in 1713, one year after the princess had died (s 175).

During these years Belle had a virtual monopoly on Stuart and Jacobite portraits, but De Troy still received commissions from time to time. In 1704 he produced two new portraits of James. One of them is a variant of Belle's full-length portrait for the Scots College in Paris (fig.29). In De Troy's version, which shows James three-quarter length without the page, the king still points with his right hand to warships in the Channel, but Dover Castle is not visible. His left hand is placed on a helmet. Curiously enough there is a copy of De Troy's portrait by Belle (De Troy 10), and even a later version of Belle's own portrait, painted three-quarter length without the page, in which a helmet has been placed in front of James as in the portrait by De Troy (Belle 8). The latter's other portrait of 1704 shows James wearing armour, holding a baton and looking over his right shoulder (De Troy 11).

De Troy's last commission was for a bust of Louise-Marie in 1711 (De Troy 14), not long before she died at the beginning of the following year. The princess was also painted, probably by Belle, in masquerade costume (Belle 16). When this portrait was eventually engraved in 1720, by someone who adopted the pseudonym 'Veraut', it was used to represent Queen Maria Clementina (s 178).

When Princess Louise-Marie died of smallpox in April 1712 James's long residence at Saint-Germain was drawing to a close. The attempted invasion of Scotland in 1708 had failed, and a new Tory government in London was negotiating peace with France. As an essential condition it was stipulated that James should leave Saint-Germain and transfer his court to Bar-le-Duc in the Duchy of Lorraine. No peaceful restoration, as in 1660, was felt to be possible so long as the 'King over the Water' remained associated with the French. James left Saint-Germain in the sum-

Fig.25 · *James III, c.*1710
[La Boissière 2]

Fig.26 · *Princess Louise-Marie*, 1704
Alexis-Simon Belle
Scottish National Portrait Gallery, Edinburgh
[Belle 14]

mer of 1712 and went to the frontier between France and Lorraine to await developments. Once the Treaty of Utrecht had been signed early in 1713 he crossed the border and moved into his new residence.

Before James's departure Mary of Modena commissioned Belle to produce yet another portrait. It had the same dimensions as De Troy's portrait of James VII and II and Belle's recent portrait of Princess Louise-Marie. These three were hung together in the queen's apartment at Saint-Germain to remind her of the family she had lost. The new one of James III was also intended to be copied and sent to England and Scotland. While the peace negotiations continued at Utrecht, and the life of Queen Anne was drawing to a close, it was essential to have a new portrait of James as part of the sustained Jacobite propaganda campaign. In addition to the original painting (fig.32), there are two full-size copies, and four copies in bust. The portrait was engraved by Chéreau in 1712 (s 128, 129) and immediately sent to Scotland and England, where it was copied many times by other engravers. There are several miniatures, some probably by Chéron, others painted after Chéreau's engraving. The image was received with so much approval that it remained James's official engraved portrait for the rest of his life.

Belle's portrait shows James's long face and jutting chin. He is standing three-quarter length in a tent, wearing a breast-plate over his coat and resting his outstretched left hand on a helmet. His right arm is placed on his hip, beside the blue sash and above the Lesser George of the Garter. By 1712 James had fought with distinction in three military campaigns, so the message conveyed by the picture is unmistakable. As usual, no crown or other indications of royalty are to be seen anywhere – and indeed the original plates of Chéreau's engraving did not name the person represented. James is therefore prepared to await the eventual death of Queen Anne. But a military solution will be necessary if no peaceful Jacobite restoration can be achieved thereafter.

When James moved to Lorraine he left Belle behind in Paris, but this did not interrupt the regular appearance of new Stuart portraits. Mary of Modena went to live with the Visitation nuns at Chaillot, where she could no longer see the portraits of her family, so James decided to send her a new portrait of himself from Lorraine. It was by Pierre Gobert (1662–1744), who was already there and who was instructed to take the work back to the queen at Chaillot, once it was finished.

Fig.27 · *James III with a Page*, 1703
[Belle 8]

Fig.28 · *Princess Louise-Marie*, 1710
[Belle 15]

Fig.29 · *James III*, 1704
[De Troy 10]

Fig.30 · *James VII and II, c.*1712
[Belle 2]

Fig.31 · *Mary of Modena, c.*1712
[Belle 3]

Although Mary of Modena rewarded Gobert with further commissions, she did not consider his portrait a good likeness of her son, and it has not survived (Gobert 1). James, therefore, summoned Belle to Bar-le-Duc to paint some more portraits.

During James's absence Belle had been working for various Jacobites. He had also produced posthumous portraits of James VII and II, wearing the same armour as in the 1712 portrait of his son, to emphasise the latter's legitimacy (fig.30). These he had sold as pairs with new reduced copies of De Troy's 1698 portrait of Mary of Modena (fig.31), thereby subsequently misleading people about the true attribution of the latter. Now in Bar-le-Duc he was ordered to make three new portraits of James III. They are among his best. Two of them are similar to the portrait of 1712, but one shows James's left side (Belle 11, see p.111) and the other his left profile (fig.33). The third, which unfortunately has not survived, showed James, for the first time, wearing the robes, collar and Great George of a Knight of the Garter (Belle 13, see p.111). Leaving aside all copies, it was Belle's tenth – and last – portrait of James.

In the summer of 1714 Queen Anne died sooner than had been expected and George I of Hanover succeeded unopposed to the throne of Great Britain. James was caught by surprise in Lorraine. He issued a protest from Plombières, insisting on his legitimate rights as King of England and Scotland, and annexed to it an elaborate genealogical tree which showed that George I was only fifty-eighth in the legitimate line of succession to the thrones. He also had the new Garter portrait engraved, this time by Marie-Nicolle Horthemels (who later became Belle's second wife), with two alternative inscriptions: 'Jacobus III. Magnae Britanniae Rex' for the English and Scots, and 'Jacques III. Roy d'Angleterre etc' for the French and other potential foreign supporters (s 145). In addition, the 1712 engraving by Chéreau was reissued and now identified as 'Jacques III. Roy de la Grande Bretagne' (s 128, 129).

The last original portraits of the Stuarts painted in France were made by Gobert for Mary of Modena. She sat for her own portrait, dressed as a widow and pointing sadly to the urn containing her husband's heart (Gobert 2). The picture was sent to James in Lorraine. She then commissioned two large allegorical paintings for the tribune of the chapel at Chaillot. One showed Mary of Modena herself as St Helen, holding the wooden cross of St Edward and presenting it to her son. The other was

Fig.32 · *James III*, 1712
Alexis-Simon Belle
UK Government Art Collection, London
[Belle 10]

Fig.33 · *James III*, 1714
[Belle 12]

Fig.34 · Detail of *Mary of Modena
Holding a Cross in her Hand and
Presenting it to James III*, 1713–15
[Gobert 3]

a posthumous double portrait, described as the apotheosis of James VII and II and Princess Louise-Marie (Gobert 4). All that survives of these two is the left side of the former, which shows the queen holding the cross in her left hand, while her right hand supports a crown (fig.34). The portrait of Mary of Modena as a widow disappeared during the nineteenth century.

If one considers the quarter of a century that the Stuarts were at Saint-Germain one cannot but be impressed by the large number of portraits that they commissioned. After the departure of Gennari, they employed five of the leading French portrait painters to produce more than forty original portraits (excluding all copies and miniatures) at an average of over three every two years. In addition to these, Van Schuppen exhibited *The Return of the King of England from Hunting* at the 1704 Salon, while Hyacinthe Rigaud's *Livre de Raison* records that he too painted James III in 1708, immediately before James departed for Scotland. The latter painting is lost and perhaps there were others by other portraitists of which we have no record.

Most of these pictures were sent away to England and Scotland, or to the other courts of Europe, but some were permanently displayed in the royal apartments at Saint-Germain. Paintings which were no longer needed were withdrawn to James's private cabinets, which became a family portrait gallery. In addition to the recent French paintings, there was also a copy of the second 1635 portrait of the *Three Eldest Children of Charles I* (fig.35), believed by the Stuarts to be by Van Dyck himself, and acquired by James VII and II during the 1690s. Much prized as a symbol of continuity, it remained with the family throughout their exile in France and Italy.

Fig.35 · *The Three Eldest Children of Charles I*
Sir Anthony van Dyck and his studio
Stanford Hall

FTER THE FAILURE OF THE JACOBITE REBELLION OF 1715 JAMES III and his court withdrew to Avignon, where they remained from April 1716 until February 1717. No new portraits were produced during this period, but it was in Avignon that James decided that wearing the Thistle should be made compatible with wearing the Garter. The Scots College in Paris was instructed to celebrate this decision by commissioning Belle to obtain a new engraving of his full-length portrait of 1703 (Belle 8). The basic composition was to remain the same, but Belle was to modify it in various respects. James was to appear taller by lowering the level of the sea in the background and slightly changing the pose of the page who accompanied him. His face and wig were to be altered to show them as they were in his most recent engraving (the Garter portrait of 1714, Belle 13). But the most important change concerned the Thistle and the Garter. The St Andrew medal was now to be shown on James's chest, suspended from the (green) ribbon of the Thistle around James's neck, and resting on the (blue) sash of the Garter. It was the first of the many Stuart portraits to show the orders together.

No painting has survived, and it is unlikely that Belle did more than supervise the new engraving. Unfortunately the prints were all seized by the French government before they could be distributed. The only copy which is known to have survived carries no inscription and does not identify the engraver (s 126).

Fig.36 · *Maria Clementina*, 1719
Francesco Trevisani
Scottish National Portrait Gallery, Edinburgh
[Trevisani 2]

AMES LIVED IN ITALY FOR NEARLY FIFTY YEARS AND commissioned approximately fifty more portraits. There are thus more Italian than French portraits of the Stuarts in exile. The annual average was less than it had been in France, but as the Italian portraits all date from the years 1717 to 1757 it was still well over one each year. Whereas in France the Stuarts had relied almost entirely on three painters, Belle (16), De Troy (14) and Largillière (6), in Italy they employed nearly twenty, of whom only three produced as many as six portraits.

The first portrait of James in Italy was actually commissioned by Pope Clement XI, to commemorate James's arrival in the Papal States in March 1717. Painted by Giuseppe Maria Crespi (1665–1747), who was present at the scene, it shows James being greeted by the Pope's nephew, Don Carlo Albani, beside the river Panaro on the road between Modena and Bologna (Crespi 1, see p.111). It also shows the leading Jacobite courtiers, among them James's private secretary, David Nairne. James stayed in Bologna and then travelled to Pesaro on the Adriatic coast. To get there he had to go via Imola, and there is a second large picture, this time by Antonio Gionima (1697–1732), which shows James and his courtiers being received at the archbishop's palace by Cardinal Gozzadini (Gionima 1, see p.110).

James resided at Pesaro for two months. He then visited Rome, from late May to early July, to meet the Pope and decide on a permanent residence. He was given the Palazzo Ducale at Urbino, but before leaving to go there he commissioned a new portrait from Antonio David (1684–1750), to be sent to Mary of Modena at Saint-Germain. James is shown standing three-quarter length beside a table, wearing both the Thistle and the Garter over armour. On the table has been placed, for the first time, the closed crown of a king, behind which can be seen a view of London (fig.37).

Fig.37 · *James III*, 1717
[David 1]

Fig.38 · *James III*, 1719
[Trevisani 1, copy of 1720]

David finished the portrait after James's departure, but before it was sent to France, James ordered him to supply eleven half-length copies and two miniatures. One of the copies was to be kept by James himself, the other ten to be given as presents to various cardinals and other supporters in Italy. For carrying out this large order, David was given a formal warrant appointing him to be 'one of our Painters'. All eleven copies, of which three still exist, were finished by April 1718, though the last ones had to be copied from a copy, so that the original could be sent to Saint-Germain. It reached Mary of Modena just before she died in May.

One of the copies was engraved without authorisation in Rome by Matthieu (s 156). The quality of this engraving, which is in reverse, with the Garter incorrectly falling to the left hip, was so bad that it helped convince James that future Stuart portraits would have to be engraved in Paris.

This particular one, however, never was engraved. The decision to employ the Italian-Swiss David had been taken on the advice of Cardinal Gualterio, previously Nuncio in France from 1700 to 1706 and now Cardinal Protector of England at the Papal court. Gualterio described David as 'the best [portrait] painter we have' in Rome. He was supported in his choice by James's private secretary, David Nairne, who felt that David would be a worthy successor to Belle and had helped him obtain his warrant. But the Jacobite Secretary of State, the Duke of Mar, disliked Nairne and was keen to turn James against his French background. He made no secret of his opinion that David's portrait was by no means a good picture and that too many copies had been made of it. A plan whereby the original picture would be copied by Belle and engraved in France was therefore cancelled.

This turned out to be an important decision. At some point James decided that he would no longer allow his own portraits to be engraved, either in Rome or Paris. Just as James VII and II had preferred to circulate the engravings of his English portraits, painted before he was forced into exile in France, so now James III preferred to rely on the engravings of his French portraits, painted before he was forced into exile in Italy. James's enemies eventually called him the 'Old Pretender', but in his engraved image he never did grow old.

Mar persuaded James that he should have his portrait painted by Francesco Trevisani (1656–1746) who, unlike David, had an international reputation. Nothing could be done so long as James remained at Urbino, but in November 1718 he moved temporarily to Rome, intending to travel on to Spain where an invasion of England and Scotland was being prepared. He only remained there until the beginning of February but during that time he was painted by Trevisani as a Knight of the Garter (Trevisani 1). The composition is similar to the earlier portrait by Belle, except that James is shown with a crown placed beside him. This portrait was intended as a present for James's new wife.

When James went to Spain in February 1719 he was still unmarried, but while at Urbino he had negotiated to marry Princess Maria Clementina Sobieska, the youngest daughter of Prince James Sobieski and thus a grand-daughter of the celebrated King of Poland, John III, who had saved Vienna from the Turks in 1683. For political reasons the Emperor Charles VI was opposed to this match, so when the princess travelled south through Austrian territory to meet James in Italy in the autumn of 1718 she was arrested and detained at Innsbruck. The marriage had to be postponed (and nearly cancelled), leaving James no choice but to go to Rome and thence to Spain without her.

Fig.39 · *Maria Clementina*, 1720
[Trevisani 3]

In the spring of 1719, however, Maria Clementina made a daring escape from Innsbruck and married James by proxy in Bologna. There she was presented with Trevisani's portrait of her new husband. A month later she arrived in Rome, where Trevisani (who had previously worked for her grandmother) made two identical copies of her own portrait as the new Queen of Great Britain, with a closed crown placed beside her. One of these was then immediately despatched to her husband in Spain. The other (fig.36) was kept by Maria Clementina, but copied in Rome by an unnamed painter (probably David!) for the Duke of Mar, who had left the court.

The portrait sent to James in Spain never reached him. Before it could arrive, the Spanish fleet preparing to take him to England was destroyed by a storm, leaving him no choice but to return to Rome. Only the small diversionary force intended for Scotland was able to sail, an expedition which culminated in defeat at Glenshiel. Trevisani's portrait of the new queen arrived after James's departure and was added to the Spanish royal collection.

Shortly after his return James and Maria Clementina were formally married at Montefiascone in September 1719. Many years later (in 1735) James ordered a large painting to illustrate the ceremony, but nothing was done at the time. The royal couple returned to Rome and took up permanent residence in the Palazzo Muti.

Fig.40 · *Maria Clementina*, 1719
[David 3]

Fig.41 · *James III with a Page*, 1721
[Pesci 1]

During 1720 James commissioned two more paintings from Trevisani. The first was a replica of his own portrait in the robes of a Garter Knight (fig.38), the second a new portrait of Maria Clementina wearing a gold bejewelled dress and a blue ermine-lined cloak, but without the crown or any other royal regalia (fig.39). The former was sent to the Duke of Mar, so that he and James both had a pair of portraits by Trevisani. The latter, of which two versions have survived, was to be engraved.

There is confusion concerning the early engraved portraits of Maria Clementina because the artists in Paris were not always aware which painters had produced the portraits they were asked to copy. The problem arose because Trevisani worked too slowly. An engraved portrait of Maria Clementina was urgently needed in 1719, to be sent to England, but there seemed no hope of getting a copy of Trevisani's painting to Paris in time. David was therefore commissioned to produce an alternative half-length portrait, including a crown, which was immediately despatched to Paris (fig.40). It was engraved by Drevet and correctly attributed to David (s 180). But two other versions were also produced, one by Dupuis (s 183), the other anonymous (s 187), both of which were busts without the crown and attributed to 'Trinisani'. It was not until 1720 that the authentic portrait by Trevisani reached Paris. It was then engraved in 1721 by Chéreau but also attributed to 'Trinisani' (s 181). As the portraits are fairly similar, and Chéreau did not exactly reproduce the painting which really was by Trevisani (he changed the costume), these engravings have caused the original paintings to be wrongly attributed.

It is anyway not always possible, and perhaps even unnecessary, to determine which paintings are 'originals' and which are copies. Once Mar had left the court, David could be employed again and in January 1720 he was paid for producing ten paintings. Some were modified copies of his 1717 portrait of James, two of which have survived (David 1), others were presumably copies of his 1719 portrait of Maria Clementina. He probably also made other copies of Trevisani's first portrait of her. This may be very confusing, but it emphasises that what actually matters in a study of court portraiture is the image itself, the number of times it was copied and the ways in which it was varied. David's copies of Trevisani's portrait of Maria Clementina were busts which deliberately omitted all royal regalia and other clues as to her identity. They could therefore be safely sent to England and Scotland.

During 1720, when Maria Clementina became pregnant, no new portraits were commissioned, but the birth of Charles, Prince of Wales in December prompted James to commission three new portraits. There was to be one of James himself, a second of Maria Clementina and a third, when the prince was old enough, of mother and son together. The painter selected was Girolamo Pesci (1679–1759). A former pupil of Trevisani, his reputation was more for his religious works and decorative ceilings than his portraits.

Pesci's portrait of James is not a good likeness. It is an updated version of the 1703 portrait by Belle which had been engraved in 1716. James is shown three-quarter length in armour, standing by the sea (fig.41). He is accompanied by a page and rests his left hand on a map of England. His right hand holds a baton which points across an invading army towards the sea. There is a heaviness to James's features which makes him almost ugly. It is certainly not a flattering image. The original picture was to be kept in the Palazzo Muti, but a smaller copy was sent to the Queen Dowager of Spain, who was one of Maria Clementina's aunts, at Bayonne. The Oxford antiquarian Richard Rawlinson visited Rome at this time and he was given a small copy of James's bust.

In 1721, once Maria Clementina had recovered from the birth, Pesci painted two identical portraits of her, one to be sent to Bayonne (fig.42), the other for the Duchess of Mar. (A small copy of the bust was also given to Richard Rawlinson.) These were in effect preliminary works, while the prince was still too young to be painted. At the end of 1721 Pesci finally produced a double portrait of Maria Clementina and the prince. The image of Maria Clementina herself is very similar, but the canvas is much larger, with exactly the same dimensions (fig.43) as Pesci's portrait of James. Both were to be kept in the Palazzo Muti and neither was engraved.

In the original composition Maria Clementina is shown standing three-quarter length. On her left side there is a table, where she rests her left hand near her crown. Her right hand holds some flowers across her bosom. The larger double portrait shows her sitting on a throne with the baby prince at her side in place of the table and crown. There is now a table on her right side, from which she is taking flowers and handing them to the prince. The queen is radiantly beautiful, with a poised and confident air which is not so evident in the earlier portraits by Trevisani and David.

With the Stuart succession now assured James redoubled his efforts to achieve a

Fig.42 · *Maria Clementina*, 1721
[Pesci 2]

Fig.43 · *Maria Clementina with Prince Charles*, 1721
[Pesci 3]

Fig.44 · *James III*, 1722
Antonio David
Private Collection
[David 2]

restoration. The result was the so-called Atterbury Plot of 1722, by which a Jacobite rising in England would take place during the general election of that year,
assisted by the Irish regiments of the French army. The plan failed because it was
betrayed at the last moment by the French government. James was therefore left in
Rome, with no immediate prospect of a restoration.

Shortly afterwards, in the autmn of 1722, he ordered new portraits from David.
The first was an impressive three-quarter length of himself (fig.44) wearing armour, with his left hand placed on the crown. In the background David included a
view of the Tower of London, closely based on an engraving published in *Britan-
nia Illustrata* (1707) by Knyff and Kip. James intended the original to remain in the
Palazzo Muti, but he ordered David in 1723–5 to supply several copies of the bust,
six of which have survived. To make a pair with these James also ordered David to
supply several copies of a new bust of Maria Clementina (fig.45). Some of them
were sent to the Duchess of Hamilton.

The following year, 1723, David received two more commissions. The first
demonstrated very clearly how he had now re-established himself as official painter
to the Stuart court. It was to make an improved copy of Pesci's portrait of James
with a page (fig.46). In David's version James now points with his baton to the map
rather than the sea. The face of the page remains the same, but the features of James
himself have been softened to make him much more handsome. David's second
commission was for a small portrait of Prince Charles (fig.47), who had been given
both the Garter and the Thistle on the previous Christmas Day. David continued to
supply copies and miniatures of this portrait for the next two years, but it was never
engraved (fig.48).

Maria Clementina's second child was born in March 1725 and named Prince
Henry, Duke of York. This was the occasion for the next portraits of the king and
queen, commissioned not from David but from Martin van Meytens (the Younger),
who was briefly in Rome at the time. The portraits were mutual presents between
Maria Clementina and James, each to be hung in the other's apartment in the
Palazzo Muti. They are busts and make an excellent pair. Each wears an ermine-
lined red cloak, James looking to his left, Maria Clementina to her right. James is
shown wearing the Garter and the Thistle as usual over armour, which has a
gorgoneion at the neck. His orders are then nicely balanced in the portrait of Maria

Fig.45 · *Maria Clementina*, 1722
[David 4]

Fig.46 · *James III with a Page*, 1721
[Pesci 1, copy by David, 1723]

Fig.47 · *Prince Charles*, 1723
[David 6]

Fig.48 · *Prince Charles*, 1723
[David 6, copy]

Fig.49 · *Prince Charles*, 1726
[David 7]

Clementina, who has a strip of blue material falling from her right shoulder to her left hip and a large jewelled brooch pinned to the front of her bodice. It was the most successful image of Maria Clementina and eventually became her official portrait (Meytens 1 and 2).

The fact that the pictures were commissioned from Meytens did not imply that the Stuarts had turned away from David. On the contrary, he was employed during 1726 to provide new portraits of the two princes. The first was a large full-length of the five-year-old Prince of Wales (fig.49). The second showed the one-year-old Duke of York, whole length, sitting on a cushion with ermine and flowers (David 11). The latter has been lost, but the former, of which several full-length and three-quarter length copies were made, was engraved in Paris by Edelinck in the winter of 1726–7 (s 202).

During the autumn of 1725 relations between James and his wife broke down because he insisted on giving the Prince of Wales a Protestant governor, James Murray, Earl of Dunbar. Maria Clementina retaliated by retiring to a convent in November. Unfortunately for James, Pope Benedict XIII sided with Maria Clementina and reduced his pension. Short of money, and keen to get away from Rome, James then went with his two sons to live in Bologna in October 1726.

The scandal of this separation had important consequences for the commissioning of Stuart portraits. James now wanted copies of the recent pictures of himself, Maria Clementina and the princes to be sent to him in Bologna. He also felt obliged to reassure his friends and supporters by commissioning and distributing a large number of portraits of himself and his wife. He quickly decided, however, that the painters in Bologna were not good enough, so he had to procure copies of the recent pair painted for him in Rome by Meytens. As the latter had left Rome for Vienna, where he was to be appointed court painter, they had to be made by someone else, and as cheaply as possible. Maria Clementina, meanwhile, who had no wish to economise, employed David to paint various pictures for her, including a new portrait of herself. The result was confusion, both then and for future historians, and the production of some relatively inferior copies. It is not even clear if the original paintings have survived.

The ones for James himself were painted in February 1727 by E. Gill (died 1749), an Englishman resident in Rome, about whom virtually nothing is known.

They were felt to be 'fuller in the face than their Majesties are', but nevertheless Gill was ordered to produce sixteen more copies (ten of Maria Clementina, five of James and one of Prince Charles) to be given away as presents. One copy of the queen's portrait was to be sent to Belle in Paris so that he could make further copies. (Belle had recently painted Maria Clementina's sister and signed the portrait 'Pictor Regis Britann.'.) Although Gill's work was not considered good enough, he was not told to stop until March 1728, by which time he had made ten of the sixteen planned, though not the one to be sent to Belle. Several examples of each of these copies of James and Maria Clementina have survived. The one of James in the Scottish National Portrait Gallery is notable because the colour has been changed: James's Thistle ribbon is maroon instead of green (figs.50, 51 and 52).

David's new portrait of Maria Clementina was painted while Gill was making these copies. It shows her modestly dressed and in mourning, holding a breviary beside her crown. She seems to have lost weight under the strain of the separation and her face, so full and beautiful in Meytens's portrait of 1725, is now pinched and thin. The original painting was sent to France as a present for the Dowager Duchess of Melfort, but David made various copies, and six versions of it have survived (fig.53).

Political developments continued to complicate the story of Stuart portraits. In the summer of 1727 George I died while travelling abroad to Hanover and James hastened to Lorraine in the hope of a restoration. A little later Maria Clementina agreed to leave her convent in Rome and join the court at Bologna. Before leaving, and despite his earlier opinion, James had commissioned new portraits of both his sons from the Bolognese painter, Lucia Casalini Torelli, probably because the Duke of York was given the Garter and the Thistle on his second birthday. When Maria Clementina arrived Casalini Torelli painted her portrait as well, but all three pictures are lost.

James remained in Lorraine for a short time only, and then spent several months in Avignon. It was not until January 1728 that he returned to Bologna and the Stuarts were finally reunited. James celebrated the fact by inviting the Florentine Giovanna Fratellini to paint the entire family. She worked in Bologna during the autumn of 1728 and produced five pictures (four originals and one copy). These portraits are also lost.

Fig.50 · *James III*, 1725
[Meytens 1, copy by Gill, 1727–8]

Fig.51 · *Maria Clementina*, 1725
[Meytens 2, copy by Gill, 1727–8]

Fig.52 · *James III*, 1725
Martin van Meytens
The Drambuie Collection, Edinburgh
[Meytens 1, copy by Gill, 1727–8]

In the spring of 1729 the Stuart court left Bologna and returned permanently to the Palazzo Muti in Rome. By this time the princes were eight and four respectively and James received letters from his friends in France and England asking for their portraits. The Duke of Bedford particularly asked for a double portrait, but James observed that 'I could not send them to you both in one, without spoiling the likeness, … since there are none here who could paint such a picture … well, that draws pictures like'. This is the reason why there are no Italian portraits of the Stuarts to be compared with the great family portrait by Mignard or the large double portrait of James and his sister by Largillière.

Bedford's request was the origin of the famous pair of portraits produced by David in the summer of 1729. The painter actually needed to be persuaded to carry out the commission, because a bill he had presented in 1727 for pictures ordered by Maria Clementina had been queried by James and reduced by a quarter before payment. This time he insisted on being paid in advance. When the portraits were finished in October 1729 James was delighted with them and commented that they were 'very like' (David 8 and 12). Three pairs were sent to Paris, one of which was copied twice by Belle. The pair for the Duke of Bedford was painted without the Garter or the Thistle, to make it safer to smuggle the pictures into England. Before being sent they were engraved anonymously and without inscriptions in Paris (s 204, 259), but because there was no Garter sash to be taken into account these engravings were simply reversed. The result was that the buttons appeared on the wrong sides of the princes' coats. An opportunity to rectify the mistake arose the following year when Simon made a copy of these engravings (s 208, 260), but he failed to use it. This was particularly annoying for the Stuarts because Simon reversed the engraving of the duke and actually took the trouble to transfer the buttons to the wrong side!

Despite this disappointment, James remained very pleased with the portraits themselves and asked David to continue making copies until 1732 (figs.54 and 55). This was possible because the original pictures made the princes look 'a little older than the life'. The composition of the portraits of the duke remained the same, though in some of the later ones he looks a little older. The image of the Prince of Wales did not change, but in two of the later ones he is shown wearing armour instead of his coat (fig.56).

Fig.53 · *Maria Clementina*, 1727
[David 5]

Fig.54 · *Prince Charles*, 1729
Antonio David
Scottish National Portrait Gallery, Edinburgh
[David 8, copy of 1732]

Fig.55 · *Prince Henry*, 1729
Antonio David
Scottish National Portrait Gallery, Edinburgh
[David 12, copy of 1732]

Fig.56 · *Prince Charles*, 1729
[David 9]

Fig.57 · *Prince Charles*, 1734–5
[David 10, miniature copy]

Fig.58 · *Prince Henry*, 1734–5
[David 13, miniature copy]

A few weeks after David had finished the original versions of these portraits, the princes were painted by Giovanni Paolo Pannini (c.1692–1765), walking with their father and Lord Dunbar through the Piazza Navona in Rome. The occasion was the lavish fête held there in November 1729 to celebrate the birth of the Dauphin (fig.59). The Stuarts can be seen with two other courtiers and seven of their liveried servants, while Swiss guards hold back the crowd.

No new Stuart portraits were painted until the end of 1734. During the intervening four and a half years, which coincided with the Cornbury Plot, the Excise Crisis and a general election in Great Britain, David was kept busy making many more copies of portraits of both James and Maria Clementina (probably those by Meytens), in addition to those of the princes already mentioned. It is impossible to keep an accurate count of how many were painted, and indeed how many still exist today, but the documents refer to four busts of James and six of Maria Clementina. One of the latter was sent to be copied by Belle. It has recently been suggested that by the late 1720s Belle might have delegated the task of copying Stuart portraits to his assistant, Jacques Aved (1702–1766).

The last portraits that David painted for the Stuarts date from the winter of 1734 to 1735, when the two princes sat for him again. Charles was now aged fourteen and Henry nine. The portrait of the duke is similar to the earlier one of 1729, though his left hand is now placed on his hip and he wears a breast-plate under his coat (fig.58). The Prince of Wales, by contrast, is shown looking over his right shoulder and wearing full armour, perhaps because he had been present earlier that year at the siege of Gaeta (fig.57, see p.110). Two other copies of the portrait of the duke and one of the prince have also survived.

While David was painting these portraits Maria Clementina died on 7 January 1735. She had lived a retired life since her return to Rome in 1729 and indeed had not sat for a new portrait since 1728. She lay in state in the Church of the Santi Apostoli to the left of the piazza beside the Palazzo Muti. Her body was then transferred to St Peter's, where a colossal monument was erected in her honour above the first doorway in the south aisle. A putto is shown holding a large bust of Maria Clementina in mosaic. It is the portrait originally made by Meytens in 1725, and subsequently copied by Gill and David, the last one to have been painted before her separation from James.

Fig.59 · *A Fête in the Piazza Navona to Celebrate the Birth of the Dauphin*, 1729
Giovanni Paolo Pannini
Musée du Louvre, Paris
[Pannini 1]

The death of his wife prompted James to commission a very large painting show-ing their marriage at Montefiascone in September 1719. It is by Agostino Masucci (*c.*1691–1758) and is now in the Scottish National Portrait Gallery (fig.60). James and Maria Clementina are shown kneeling before the bishop, Sebastiano Bonaventura, in the presence of courtiers and attendant clergy. A sceptre and the crowns of their three kingdoms are prominently displayed on a cushion beside James's right knee. An altar with large candlesticks can be seen behind the bishop. A smaller copy, which omits some of the spectators, still hangs in the sacristy of Montefiascone Cathedral, and there is also an engraving by Friz (s 697) based on the original painting but in-cluding some additional spectators. Unlike the original painting, it shows James putting the wedding ring on his wife's finger. It was the first posthumous portrait of Maria Clementina and was modelled on the early ones by Trevisani. James himself is shown in profile for the first time since he had been painted by Belle in 1714.

At about the same time, Masucci painted another posthumous portrait of Maria Clementina, which is only known from an engraving made by Sorello in 1737 (s 195). This time she kneels immediately in front of the altar, with a breviary in her right hand. The sceptre and one of the crowns are on her right side, beside a similar cushion. A large candlestick has been placed beside her.

James then asked Masucci for an even larger picture to illustrate the royal succes-sion that Maria Clementina had assured. It shows the baptism of the Prince of Wales by the Bishop of Montefiascone in the chapel of La Madonna dell'Archetto, behind the Palazzo Muti, at the end of December 1720, in the presence of various cardinals and courtiers. James is shown standing full length beside the bishop, wearing the Garter and the Thistle. The painting (fig.61) has been traditionally attributed to Pier Leone Ghezzi (1674–1755) in collaboration with Masucci. The faces of the leading participants are based on engravings published before 1722, while that of James him-self is based on his portrait by Trevisani.

After the death of Maria Clementina the story of Stuart portraiture becomes even more complicated. No new images were created at the court in Rome until 1737, when James gave commissions to two relatively young foreigners who were work-ing in the papal city, Jean-Etienne Liotard (1702–1789) who was Swiss, and Louis-Gabriel Blanchet (1705–1772) who was French. The work of these two painters has often been confused.

Fig.60
*The Solemnisation of the
Marriage of James III and Maria
Clementina Sobieska at
Montefiascone, 1 September, 1719,*
1735
Agostino Masucci
Scottish National Portrait Gallery,
Edinburgh
[Masucci 1]

Fig.61
*The Baptism of Charles, Prince of
Wales, 31 December 1720,* 1735
Agostino Masucci and
Pier Leone Ghezzi
Scottish National Portrait Gallery,
Edinburgh
[Masucci 3]

Fig.62 · *Prince Charles*, 1737
[Carriera 1]

Fig.63 · *Prince Henry*, 1737
[Liotard 2, miniature copy]

In June 1737 the Prince of Wales visited Venice and sat for two identical pastel portraits by Rosalba Carriera (1675–1757). The original was sent to James in Rome; the second version was sent to Owen O'Rourke, the Jacobite diplomatic representative in Vienna (fig.62). Prompted by this, James agreed during that summer to let Liotard make two further pastels, of himself and the Duke of York (Liotard 1 and 2). As James thought highly of these new portraits he agreed to let Liotard make a third pastel portrait of the Prince of Wales when he returned to Rome (Liotard 3). It was finished in December 1737, and when James compared it with the one done by Carriera he felt that Liotard's was the better likeness of the two. In 1738 he therefore ordered Liotard to have miniatures made from each of his pastels (which have not themselves survived). A set of three was sent to Vienna so that they could be shown to the empress (the wife of Charles VI), who was known to be sympathetic to the Jacobite cause. A miniature of Prince Charles was sent to Dorotea, the Dowager Duchess of Parma and mother of the Queen of Spain, who had met him the previous year, and various other miniatures were sent to England and France. One of Prince Henry is now in the Scottish National Portrait Gallery (fig.63). Meanwhile some copies of the original pastels of the princes were made in oils, probably by Liotard himself, and these are now also in the Scottish National Portrait Gallery (figs.64 and 65). In these various pictures, none of which was engraved, the princes are shown with the Garter only and not the Thistle. (A double miniature of the two princes, however, includes a touch of green to suggest that they might be wearing the Thistle under their coats.) The portrait of James has only survived in a miniature, which shows him facing right and wearing a brown coat with gold buttons (Liotard 1, see p.111).

Although the Duchess of Parma received the miniature of Prince Charles by Liotard, she let James know that what she really wanted were large full-length portraits of both the princes. In November 1737, therefore, while Liotard was working on his pastels, James commissioned Blanchet to produce two large portraits based on them, with the faces copied exactly from the pictures by Liotard. They were both finished by June 1738, when the princes were seventeen and thirteen respectively, and immediately sent to Parma (figs.66 and 67). Blanchet's images of the princes are so similar to Liotard's that it is difficult to distinguish between them, particularly as the duke is shown wearing the same embroidered brown coat. The only obvious

Fig.64 · *Prince Henry*, 1737
Jean-Etienne Liotard
Scottish National Portrait Gallery, Edinburgh
[Liotard 2, copy]

Fig.65 · *Prince Charles*, 1737
Jean-Etienne Liotard
Scottish National Portrait Gallery, Edinburgh
[Liotard 3, copy]

Fig.66 · *Prince Henry*, 1738
Louis-Gabriel Blanchet
National Portrait Gallery, London
[Blanchet 4]

Fig.67 · *Prince Charles*, 1737–8
Louis-Gabriel Blanchet
National Portrait Gallery, London
[Blanchet 2]

Fig.68 · *Prince Charles*, 1739
[Blanchet 3]

Fig.69 · *Prince Henry*, 1739
[Blanchet 5]

difference is in the costume of the Prince of Wales. Because the duchess already had the miniature, Blanchet had to make the full-length portrait seem different. He did this by giving the prince an armour breast-plate over the embroidered red coat which he wears in the portrait by Liotard. The prince stands confidently, with his right hand placed on a helmet, his left hand on his hip. The duke, by comparison, seems delicate and even timid, accompanied by a hound with its two front feet raised on a chair. Both princes wear the Garter, but neither has the Thistle.

In the following year, 1739, Blanchet was commissioned by a Jacobite courtier in Rome named William Hay to paint another pair of portraits. They are similar to the previous ones, but the princes, who have matured in the intervening year, are now shown to below the waist only (figs.68 and 69). Whereas the Prince of Wales wears both the Garter and the Thistle over his armour (indeed the star is actually welded on to his breast-plate), the duke has his red coat open to show that he is wearing both orders beneath it. Once again these portraits were not engraved.

In December 1738 the Prince of Wales had achieved his majority and the attention of Jacobites in Great Britain was now increasingly focused on the two princes rather than James himself. Political events also increased their potential importance. In 1739 Great Britain went to war against Spain, where Philip V was still James's main supporter. Walpole was steadily losing his parliamentary majority by defections within the Whig party, particularly since 1737, and the forthcoming general election of 1741 threatened to produce a hung Parliament with the pro-Jacobite Tories holding the balance. The War of the Austrian Succession broke out in 1740, and there was at last a possibility that France and Great Britain might go to war again, for the first time since 1713. Under these circumstances it became imperative that new images of the handsome young princes should be available, to inspire the loyalty of the dissatisfied in Great Britain and the support of the pro-Jacobites in France and Spain. But no engravings had been circulated since 1730.

The painter selected to produce new portraits of the princes, to be engraved in Paris, was not David but Domenico Dupra (1689–1770), who had previously been employed by the Sabaudian court at Turin. He seems to have been chosen for this politically important commission because he had recently (1739) painted William Hay and a group of his friends at the exiled court. He painted two portraits of each of the princes, and all four were strikingly successful. In the first pair both princes

Clockwise from top left

Fig.70 · *Prince Charles*, 1740
[Dupra 2, copy]

Fig.71 · *Prince Henry*, 1740
[Dupra 5]

Fig.73 · *Prince Henry*, 1740
[Dupra 6]

Fig.72 · *Prince Charles*, 1740
[Dupra 3]

Fig.74 · *Maria Clementina*, 1725
[Meytens 2, copy by Blanchet, 1741]

Fig.75 · *James III*, 1741
[Ponzone 1, copy]

are shown in armour, with an ermine-lined red cloak. The picture of the prince has been lost and is only known from a slightly reduced copy (fig.70). The one of the duke shows him holding a baton in his left hand and resting it on a table (fig.71). In the second pair they are both holding batons in their right hands. The duke's armour extends to above his elbow (fig.73), whereas the prince is wearing a breast-plate (fig.72). In all four the Garter and the Thistle are both clearly visible on their chests. James preferred the second pair, and ordered at least four copies to be made, one of them for the Tory leader Sir John Hynde Cotton, as well as several pairs of miniatures. The engravings were done by Daullé and Wille (s 209, 262) and are of outstanding quality. These portraits quickly established themselves as the official images of the princes, were copied by other engravers and very widely circulated in the years which followed, which coincided with the 'Forty-Five'.

An important aspect of Stuart portraiture at this time was the creation and circulation of sets of four pictures showing all the members of the royal family in Italy. The portraits themselves were intended to invite comparison with those of the Hanoverians in London. The sets implied the unity of the Stuart family, whereas George II, who had also lost his wife, was known to have very bad relations with his eldest son.

During the summer of 1740 the Duke of York had asked Blanchet to paint a portrait of his mother. He wanted a copy of the one by Meytens (1725), painted shortly after his own birth, which was then being reproduced in mosaic for her tomb (unveiled in December 1742). William Hay then asked Blanchet for another copy, of the same approximate dimensions as his 1739 portraits of the princes. To match those, Blanchet extended the original composition to show Maria Clementina to below the waist, with her left hand resting on a crown (fig.74). Although only a copy, Blanchet's is in fact the best-known of the various versions of Meytens's portrait that have survived, and has consequently misled people into thinking that his was actually the original.

Then, unexpectedly, Hay was obliged to leave the court in April 1741. He had quarrelled with a friend, drawn his sword, apologised, and then done the same to another friend shortly afterwards. He settled at Sens in France, where there was a Jacobite community, but before leaving he gave enough money to his friend James Edgar, James III's private secretary, to pay Blanchet to paint a new portrait of James.

Fig.76 · *James III*, 1741
Louis-Gabriel Blanchet
National Portrait Gallery, London
[Blanchet 1]

Fig.77 · *James III*, 1742
[Dupra 1]

This was intended to complete his set and console him for his enforced departure. James was not willing to sit for a new portrait, but Edgar had in his possession a pen and ink drawing of James's head in profile, which he felt was a very good likeness. It had been drawn in January 1741 by Francesco Ponzone (see p.111). Edgar lent this drawing to Blanchet, who then used it (in reverse) to paint the new portrait (fig.76). James wears a cloak over most of his chest, so the Thistle is obscured, but the Garter is the same as in Blanchet's 1739 portrait of the Prince of Wales. The picture is smaller than the other three in Hay's possession, because Blanchet had not been left enough money for a larger picture, but in all other respects it was intended to be part of a set. Most notably, James is shown wearing a fashionable pointed glove on one of his hands only, as are the princes.

Once Blanchet had finished with Ponzone's drawing, Edgar sent it to Paris to be given to the Duchess of Buckingham, an illegitimate daughter of James VII and II. A copy had already been made in Rome showing the bust as well as the head (fig.75), and this was subsequently engraved in reverse in 1747, with a false inscription claiming that it was 'publish'd according to act of Parliament' (s 158). The engraving is interesting because it has subsidiary images of the two princes which are based on some other pen and ink drawings. These latter are by Giles Hussey (1710–1788), who had been in Rome in the mid-1730s.

During the winter of 1741–2 the political crisis at Westminster came to a head and James instructed the Tories to cooperate with the 'opposition' Whigs to bring down Walpole's government. This was achieved in February and, at a time of renewed hope, James decided to commission Dupra to paint a second set of four portraits. The ones of the princes were reduced copies of those he had already made in 1740 (Dupra 3 and 6). James now agreed to sit for his own portrait (fig.77) and Dupra, like Blanchet, made a copy of Meytens's portrait of Maria Clementina. The dimensions were virtually the same as the oil copies of Liotard's 1738 portraits of the princes, and it may be that they were intended to be interchangeable. Dupra made several other copies of these portraits, and a smaller one of the new portrait of James himself was sent to Lord John Drummond. In 1742 Dupra also painted two new portraits of the princes which James kept for himself. Both are half length and show an ermine-lined cloak over armour. Prince Charles looks over his right shoulder (Dupra 4), and Prince Henry looks over his left (Dupra 7, see p.111).

Great Britain and France finally declared war in 1744. At the very end of the previous year the Prince of Wales left Rome and travelled to Paris, where he hoped to persuade Louis XV to prepare an invasion of England. In May 1744, while he was in Paris, he asked to be sent miniature portraits of his father, mother and brother. He specified that he wished these miniatures to be done by Pompeo Batoni (1708–1787), 'coppid from the likest pictures', but for some reason James gave the commission to Veronica Telli (1717–1807) instead. Not wishing to disappoint his brother, the duke then ordered Dupra in July to paint a new portrait of himself, holding a miniature of the Prince of Wales (Dupra 8), which was then copied in miniature by Batoni. At first the duke disliked Batoni's copy, so he employed Telli to produce an alternative, intending to send to Paris the one he preferred. In the end none of the four miniatures by Telli was considered to be a good copy, and only the one by Batoni met with general approval! So the duke sent his brother the miniature by Batoni of himself and the ones by Telli of his parents.

In the following year, when the prince had sailed to Scotland, the duke also went to Paris to request a French invasion of England. Like his brother he too omitted to take any miniatures with him, so Telli was again employed by James. This time it was to make a set of four, including all the members of the family. In the years that followed Telli continued to make these sets. Her portrait of the king was based on the one by Dupra of 1742; that of the queen was after the Meytens of 1725, recently copied by both Blanchet and Dupra; while for the princes she used either the 1740 or the 1742 portraits by Dupra.

The defeat at Culloden in 1746 inevitably had important consequences for the commissioning of Stuart portraits by the court in Rome. In the first place the Prince of Wales never returned there until after his father's death. Secondly, the Duke of York decided to become a cardinal to ensure the continued status and financial security of the family in Rome. His appointment to the rank of cardinal deacon on 3 July 1747 was a catastrophe for his elder brother and for the Jacobite cause in Great Britain, because it associated the exiled Stuarts even more closely with the papacy, but for James, who now realised that he and Henry would never leave Rome, it was an important achievement. He celebrated the event by decorating the Palazzo Muti and the adjacent buildings in the Piazza Pilotta. There is a large commemorative painting (fig.78) in which the palace is shown with large shields placed on the top of

Fig.78 · *James III and his Court in Front of the Palazzo Muti During the Celebrations of
the Appointment of Prince Henry as a Cardinal, July 1747* and detail
Unknown Artist
Scottish National Portrait Gallery, Edinburgh

the centre of the building. The arms of Pope Benedict XIV are flanked by those of James himself on the left and those of Rome on the right. Above the arms are the papal tiara, the crown of Great Britain and a coronet intended to be that of an English duke. James can be seen greeting the new cardinal in the centre foreground, supported by his guards. He pays his son the honour of coming forward to receive him, not just at the entrance to his guard chamber nor even at the foot of the grand staircase, but beyond the gates of the palace in the piazza outside. The Duke of York is shown in the customary black coat, scarlet stockings and black shoes worn by cardinals in the mid-eighteenth century, rather than in his full scarlet robes of state. The Prince of Wales was in France at the time, so he is not shown, but James's household (probably headed by the Earl of Lismore and James Edgar) can be seen lined up behind him. From the windows of the palace on the left, and the convent on the right, people can be seen looking out and admiring the façade of the Stuart residence. Recent restoration work suggests that two or more artists probably collaborated on this picture, but the identities of the painters are at present unknown.

Nine days after the Duke of York's appointment as cardinal deacon he and his father attended a performance of a *componimento dramatico* by Niccolò Jommelli at the Teatro Argentina, to celebrate the second marriage of the Dauphin to a daughter of the King of Poland. The occasion was recorded in a well-known painting by Pannini, which shows the interior of the crowded opera house while the cantata is being performed (fig.79). As one looks at the stage, James and his son can be seen on the right-hand side, accompanied by another cardinal and various guests and courtiers. The Stuarts have a triple box (all the others are single), at the centre of which James sits on a large high backed chair. The columns in front of him are specially decorated, to be easily distinguished from all the others in the house, and the audience on the other side of the theatre are looking up at him rather than at the stage.

The new Cardinal of York, as he was styled, was ordained a priest in September 1748 and given the parish of Santi Apostoli as a benefice. He and James immediately commissioned some new portraits, both for themselves and for their supporters. Two were painted before the cardinal was ordained and two immediately after. The artists were Domenico Corvi (1721–1803), Blanchet and Anton Raphael Mengs (1728–1779).

Fig.79 · *A Concert in the Teatro Argentina*
to Celebrate the Marriage of the Dauphin, 1747
Giovanni Paolo Pannini
Musée du Louvre, Paris
[Pannini 2]

Corvi was the first to produce a portrait of the cardinal. In a large three-quarter length picture Prince Henry is shown seated at a table, holding a letter in his left hand and a quill pen in his right. Beyond the letter a bell can be seen, placed on some closed books (fig.84). This portrait was painted in 1747 and engraved in Rome by Campana the following year (s 270).

In 1748, before he was ordained, the cardinal was painted by Blanchet. This time he is shown standing full length, with his right arm outstretched before a draped curtain. He is beside a large and richly gilded chair and holds a biretta in his left hand (fig.80).

Once he had been ordained the cardinal commissioned a second portrait from Corvi. Like the previous one he is shown seated at a table, though this time full length, holding a paper. The book is now open, with the bell placed beside it. The cardinal wears a richly jewelled cross on his chest, suspended from a string of pearls around his neck where once he had worn the Thistle. At his feet there is a coronet like the one placed on the top of the Palazzo Muti. The original portrait was given to Ottavio Angeletti, the Bishop of Gubbio (fig.81), but many copies were also made, see p.111. There are two half-lengths and five busts (fig.83).

In 1748 Cardinal York was painted by Mengs. The original painting has been lost, but a most sensitive study in oils of his head and shoulders has survived (fig.82). It is similar to the busts by Corvi, except that the cardinal is shown looking to the right instead of to the left. It was engraved the same year in Rome by Pazzi, though not attributed to Mengs, as an illustration for *Effigies Cardinalium* (s 272). The engraving shows a jewelled cross around the cardinal's neck, though none is shown in the sketch. Like the one by Campana, it shows how relatively inferior the Roman engravers were, compared with the French.

It is possible that Mengs also painted a new portrait of James, presumably to make a pair with his portrait of the cardinal, and perhaps to mark the king's sixtieth birthday in June 1748. Three versions have survived. One is a bust and shows James looking to his left, with a crown above his raised right hand. He wears the Garter over a mole-coloured coat, trimmed with gold lace, and the Thistle under it, though the St Andrew medal can be seen on his chest (fig.85). The other two are the same, but both show James three-quarter length and wearing armour. The king now holds a baton in his right hand, and the Thistle ribbon is shown around his neck below the

Fig.84 · *Cardinal York*, 1747
Domenico Corvi
Wadsworth Atheneum, Hartford
[Corvi 1]

sash of the Garter (fig.86). In each case the king's image is clearly a development of the earlier portrait by Dupra. In 1748 Mengs was only twenty-years-old and at the very beginning of his career, so he might well have accepted a commission of this type. The dimensions of the bust are virtually the same as two of Corvi's busts of the cardinal, so it might perhaps be by the latter rather than by Mengs. In any event, the 1748 portraits are interesting because they present to us the image of the 'King over the Water' as he would have appeared to the people of Great Britain had the Jacobite rising and invasion of 1745 succeeded.

Copies of these pictures were perhaps made from time to time in the years which followed. There is, for example, a document which records that Blanchet painted portraits of both James and the cardinal in 1752, to be sent to Paris. But the last portraits of James during his lifetime were painted a few years later, at the beginning of 1757. The Earl Marischal's younger brother, James Keith, who was a field marshal in the Prussian army, informed Edgar that Frederick the Great would like a portrait of the elderly king. The timing was unexpected, because Frederick had dropped his earlier support for the Jacobites and was about to enter the Seven Years War as an ally of George II. James agreed to be painted by both Placido Costanzi (1701–1759) and Pompeo Batoni, and both portraits were sent to Berlin. The one by Batoni is lost, but it is probable that the one by Costanzi has survived. There is a portrait which shows James in a formal pose, standing full length with a cloak opened up to show armour beneath (fig.87). He wears both the Garter and the Thistle, while his right hand holds a baton resting beside the crown on a table. It recalls the pictures by Mengs (or Corvi), but the king is now a very much older man.

James's health began to fail at the end of the 1750s. He grew weaker until at last he became bed-ridden and almost speechless. He died on 1 January 1766 and lay in state in the Church of the Santi Apostoli. The scene was recorded in a large engraving by Vasi (fig.88), in which James's body can be seen placed in front of the high altar, illuminated by many large candles. While it lay there someone made a pencil sketch of his face and torso. He wears a crown and has an orb placed on his left side. It was his last portrait.

By the 1760s the Palazzo Muti must have contained a very large collection of Stuart portraits, including several which had been brought to Rome from France. It seems that, contrary to the practice at Saint-Germain-en-Laye, the portraits in Italy

Fig.85 · *James III*, 1748
Anton Raphael Mengs
National Portrait Gallery, London

[Mengs 1]

Fig.86 · *James III*, 1748
[Mengs 2]

Fig.87 · *James III*, 1757
[Costanzi 1]

were not used to decorate the royal apartments as a whole, but were rather grouped together in three rooms. Two of these were in James's apartment, situated on the first floor; the other was in Maria Clementina's apartment on the floor above. In James's apartment the portraits were kept in the private cabinets immediately beyond his bedchamber, while in the queen's apartment they were in the bedchamber which they shared. In 1726, for example, there were twenty-eight pictures in the two rooms below, and eleven 'great pictures' in the bedchamber above. These figures must have steadily increased year by year, though not all the pictures would have been portraits of the Stuarts themselves. As the princes grew up and acquired their own collections, they also kept family portraits in their bedchambers. When the queen died in 1735 her apartment was left empty and the large pictures by Masucci were probably placed there. Finally, when Charles succeeded his father in 1766 he created a family portrait gallery in one of the largest rooms of the king's apartment.

This alternative royal collection must have made an impressive display because the Stuarts, in Rome as at Saint-Germain, had employed many of the very best portrait painters of the period from 1689 to 1748. Some, like Meytens, Corvi and Mengs, were still relatively unknown when they were given their commissions, but others, notably Trevisani and Dupra, were already established masters. Some important painters in Rome were never employed by the Stuarts, such as Pierre Subleyras (1699–1749), while Batoni's connections with his British patrons were mainly developed after the Stuarts had stopped commissioning portraits. Nevertheless, James did patronise most of the leading portraitists of his time, a significant achievement when it is remembered that his annual pension from the Pope (£3000) was only a small fraction of the £50,000 he had received each year from Louis XIV. Works by Gennari, Largillière, De Troy and Belle would have been displayed alongside those of David, Pesci and Blanchet. The family collection also contained the painting after Van Dyck brought from France, and a portrait of Charles II believed to be by Lely. This was the one that had been painted in 1660 to celebrate the successful restoration of James's uncle. The previous Stuart restoration was a source of hope and consolation throughout the long period of the Jacobite exile. It was exactly one hundred years later that the accession of George III confirmed that no second Stuart restoration would ever take place.

Fig.88 · *James III Lying in State*, January 1766
Giuseppe Vasi, after Giovanni Baptista Marchetti and Paolo Posi, 1766
Scottish National Portrait Gallery, Edinburgh

Fig.89 · *Maria Clementina*, 1725
Rosalba Carriera
Private Collection, London
[Meytens 2, copy by Carriera]

PART THREE · MISCELLANEOUS PORTRAITS FROM ITALY AND FRANCE · 1717–1752

HE DEMAND FOR IMAGES OF JAMES III AND HIS FAMILY continued throughout his life-time and beyond. The portraits commissioned and kept at the exiled court were copied and no doubt re-copied in Great Britain, and some very primitive pictures have survived which testify to this practice. Engravings were also copied, often very badly, being reversed and re-reversed in the process, with little regard for the positioning of the sash of the Garter. These poor quality by-products of Stuart court portraiture made the images of the 'King over the Water' and his children familar to most people in Great Britain, so that even a false inscription on an engraving could not hide the true identity of the person represented. 'Cognoscunt mei me,' as one inscription read: 'My own know me.'

There was also a market for semi-official images of good quality, alongside the official portraits already described. For example, the Swiss engraver Jacob Frey (1681–1752), who lived permanently in Rome, made a large portrait of Maria Clementina when she first arrived from Innsbruck, perhaps in an unsuccessful attempt to attract Stuart patronage (s 188). The Scottish painter John Smibert (1688–1751) visited Rome in 1719–22 and was allowed to copy portraits of James and Maria Clementina on to a single canvas, which was then taken back to London and re-copied several times. Numerous miniatures were painted by unknown artists, with or without the involvement of David, Pesci or Meytens (fig.89). When the Duke of Beaufort visited Rome in 1726 he obtained two miniature portraits of James, set into rings (Wolfgang 1). They were by Georg Andreas Wolfgang (1703–1745). Domenico Muratori (c.1661–1744) painted a portrait of Maria Clementina in about 1734, according to an engraving by Rossi (s 194), as did Bernard Luttrell, according to an engraving of 1737 by Miller (s 157). In the mid-

Fig.90 · *James III*, 1748
[Telli 2]

Fig.91 · *James III*, 1749
[Alexander 1]

1730s Giles Hussey made some drawings of the princes which were taken back and later engraved in England. He then continued to draw and paint portraits of Prince Charles until at least 1765. Another minor portraitist who did this was Matthew Saunders (dates unknown). His copy of Meytens's portrait of Maria Clementina is dated 1756.

Not all of these miscellaneous Stuart portraits were intended to be sold. Between 1717 and 1729 the Senate of Bologna commissioned a remarkable series of nine pictures on vellum (39 × 53 each), showing various episodes in the lives of the Stuarts (Bologna State Archives, *Insignia degli Anziani* XIII). Five are by Leonardo Sconzani (1695–1735), two by Angelo Michele Tosi (dates unknown) and two are anonymous. They show the arrival of James at the River Panaro in March 1717, his departure from Nettuno for Spain in February 1719, his proxy marriage with Maria Clementina in May 1719, the baptism of Prince Charles in December 1720, the visit of James and Maria Clementina to the church of San Petronio in Bologna in October 1722, the baptism of Prince Henry in March 1725, the arrival of James and his sons in Bologna in October 1726, the ball to celebrate the sixth birthday of Prince Charles in December 1726, and the departure of Maria Clementina and Prince Henry from Bologna for Rome in May 1729. Meanwhile, the monastery of Santa Scolastica at Subiaco commissioned a full-length fresco of James as a Roman emperor. He is shown wearing the Thistle but not the Garter, and with an open, not closed, crown at his feet!

As already stated, it was during the 1740s that artists began to produce sets showing James, the deceased Maria Clementina, and the two princes. Telli's earliest miniatures of the princes are dated 1743 and based on the portraits by Liotard (Telli 4 and 6). Having been employed by James to make the set of three miniatures for Prince Charles in 1744, and the set of four for Prince Henry in 1745, she continued this lucrative practice. Her portraits of James (fig.90) and Maria Clementina were still copied from the ones by Dupra and Meytens respectively, but she eventually stopped reproducing the ones by Dupra of the two princes. In a set dated 1748 she seems to have copied Blanchet's new portrait of Prince Henry as a cardinal deacon (Telli 9) and a French engraving of the Prince of Wales, who had been absent for over four years (Telli 5).

The most important set of four was made in Rome by Cosmo Alexander in

Fig.92 · *Prince Charles*, 1748
Maurice Quentin de la Tour
Scottish National Portrait Gallery, Edinburgh

Fig.93 · *Maria Clementina*, 1749
[Alexander 2]

Fig.94 · *Prince Charles*, 1752
[Alexander 4]

1749. The portrait of James (fig.91) was after the recent one by Mengs (or Corvi). That of Maria Clementina was based on her early portraits by both Trevisani and David (fig.93). For the Prince of Wales he used a recent French engraving of one of Dupra's portraits of 1740 (Alexander 3, see p.111), and for Cardinal York he used the first (1747) portrait by Corvi (Alexander 5). All four compositions were altered just enough to give an appearance of originality. In 1752, when Alexander was in Paris, he was commissioned to paint portraits of the two princes. Once again he achieved the appearance of originality while really basing his pictures on other portraits. He made a modified copy of his earlier portrait of the cardinal after Corvi (Alexander 5) and paired it with a new portrait of Prince Charles (fig.94) based on an engraving of a recent pastel (fig.92) by Maurice Quentin de La Tour (1704–1788). When painters were not able to get the Stuarts to sit for them, they had to resort to such practices to meet the constant demand for new portraits. Their choice of originals was probably more influenced by availability than taste.

After the dramatic events of 1745–6 this demand was chiefly for new images of the Prince of Wales. These, of course, could not be provided by the court in Rome, which therefore lost all control over his iconography. A new engraving of 1745 by Robert Strange (1721–1792), itself really copied from a 1743 miniature by Telli, and the engraved portraits after (1747) Louis Tocqué (1696–1772) and Maurice Quentin de La Tour (1748) were among the many images of the hero prince which helped to create the cult of 'Bonnie Prince Charlie'. Among these are the so-called Harlequin portraits, which show the prince standing full-length with a red tartan or check coat and breeches. Rather surprisingly he is shown in all these portraits with the Garter but not the Thistle. It is curious to note that the best, which shows the prince landing at Loch nan Uamh with the 'Seven Men of Moidart', is by Gill, the English painter who was employed in Rome making copies for James in 1727–8.

EPILOGUE
THE FINAL PORTRAITS · 1770–1802

FTER 1760, WHEN THE ENGLISH-BORN GEORGE III BECAME king in London, it was clear that the Jacobite cause had totally failed. Neither James nor Cardinal York saw the need to commission any more portraits, and when the king died in 1766 not even the papacy recognised the Prince of Wales as King Charles III. There is only one portrait which shows Charles as the Stuart king-in-exile. It was painted in Rome by Laurent Pecheux (1729–1821) in 1770, when Charles was still unmarried. It shows him three-quarter length in armour, pointing with his right hand across his chest to a coastline where a battle is being fought on the beach, with warships out at sea. Beside him are placed the crowns of England and Scotland (Pecheux 1).

The only other portraits from this period of Charles's life are a pen and ink drawing by Ozias Humphry, dated Florence 1776, and an oil of *c.*1785 by Hugh Douglas Hamilton (*c.*1738–1808). Charles wears the Garter (though not the Thistle) but otherwise there is nothing to indicate that he might be the Jacobite claimant to the throne (National Portrait Gallery, London).

Charles, who had no legitimate children, was succeeded in 1788 by his brother as 'Henry IX', 'non desideriis hominum sed voluntate Dei' (Not by the desire of man but by the will of God). There is a pen and ink drawing by David Allan (1744–1796) which shows the cardinal at morning prayer in St Peter's in 1773 (National Gallery of Scotland). There is also a portrait of the cardinal aged about sixty-one (*c.*1786) by Hamilton in which he is shown looking to the right and wearing a decorated red cape (National Portrait Gallery, London). He is an older man, but otherwise the portrait is little different from the busts by Corvi of nearly forty years earlier. The only portrait to show the cardinal as the Jacobite claimant to the throne is a copy of Hamilton's portrait, apparently commissioned by the Scots College in Rome, in which the corner of a table supporting a closed crown has been added.

The last of all the paintings of the Stuarts in exile shows the Villa Muti at Frascati in 1802 (fig.95), and has been tentatively attributed to Louis Ducros (1748–1810). Cardinal York had been appointed Bishop of Frascati in 1761, and the Villa Muti there became his favourite country residence. The town and surrounding area were sacked by the French in 1799 and for a time the cardinal was obliged to take refuge in Venice. When he returned, helped by a pension from the British government, he was seventy-seven years old and it was clear that the legitimate Stuart descendants of James VII and II would soon be no more. The cardinal's heir was King Charles Emmanuel IV of Sardinia, directly descended from James VII and II's youngest sister. Charles Emmanuel reigned from 1796 to 1802 when, having been deposed by the French, he abdicated the Sardinian throne in favour of a younger brother. In the autumn of 1802 shortly before his abdication, he and Pope Pius VII both visited Cardinal York at Frascati, and spent the afternoon at the restored Villa Muti. The cardinal and the Pope arrived first, followed shortly afterwards by Charles Emmanuel. In a large painting, which shows the town of Frascati in the distance, the Villa Muti can be seen on the left. At the top of a staircase leading to the entrance the elderly cardinal and the Pope are greeting the cavalcade of the king. It is thus with the apparent blessing of the Roman Catholic Church that the last of the exiled Stuarts seems to hand on the Jacobite claim to his cousin, who succeeded him in 1807.

Fig.95 · *The Visit of Pope Pius VII and King Charles Emmanuel IV of Sardinia to Cardinal York at the Villa Muti, Frascati in 1802*
Attributed to Louis Ducros
Private Collection

opposite
Detail of fig.95

A NOTE ON PORTRAITS OF THE JACOBITES IN EXILE

Many of the Jacobites who joined the Stuart court in exile at Saint-Germain-en-Laye commissioned their own portraits, generally to be sent back to the members of their families who had remained in Great Britain and Ireland. Most of these Jacobite as opposed to Stuart portraits have probably not survived, and of those which have there are several which cannot be identified. There are, however, sufficient to give us a general idea of the extent of Jacobite patronage in France, particularly when supplemented by documentary evidence. The significant point is that nearly all the painters who worked for the Stuarts in France were also employed by their courtiers.

By contrast, few of the Jacobites at the Stuart court in Italy seem to have commissioned good quality portraits. As a result, only three of the artists who worked for the Stuarts in Rome are known to have painted their courtiers. This note provides some details of both these French and Italian Jacobite portraits.

BENEDETTO GENNARI 1633–1715

Between 1689 and 1692 Gennari painted nine of the Jacobites at Saint-Germain: Francesco Riva (Master of the Queen's Robes), Robert Strickland (Vice-Chamberlain to the Queen), Bishop Philip Ellis, Captain Randall Macdonnell (Groom of the Bedchamber), James Porter (Vice-Chamberlain to the King), Giuseppe Ronchi (Gentleman Usher of the Presence Chamber), the Countess of Almond (Lady of the Bedchamber), the Duke of Berwick and his brother Lord Henry FitzJames (later Duke of Albemarle).

Only the portrait of Riva has survived. It shows him with his English wife, Mary (née Newcombe), and their two sons (Pinacoteca Nazionale, Bologna). The portrait of Berwick was engraved by Drevet in 1693 (S 316).

FRANÇOIS DE TROY 1645–1730

De Troy did not work for the Stuarts until 1698, but his earliest Jacobite portrait dates from several years earlier. It shows the Duke of Tyrconnell, who visited France between September 1690 and January 1691. He wears the blue sash and the star of the Garter, which he was given by James VII and II during November (National Portrait Gallery; National Gallery of Ireland). The portrait is noteworthy because the star is shown upside down.

The next surviving portraits by De Troy probably date from 1692 and were commissioned by the Duke of Powis (Lord Chamberlain). There are two different portraits of the latter's daughter Mary, Viscountess Montague (Coughton Court; Powis Castle), and one of her sister, Lady Lucy Herbert (Powis Castle). Powis himself is shown in his robes as a Knight of the Garter, an honour he received from James VII and II in 1692 (Powis Castle).

Other surviving portraits by De Troy include those of Lord Drummond, later 2nd Duke of Perth (1694, Drummond Castle), the Duke of Berwick (c.1695–1700, Althorp), the first Duchess of Berwick (c.1695–7, Palacio da Liria, Madrid; Kilkenny Castle), Anthony Hamilton (c.1700, National Portrait Gallery), and the Viscountess Clare (Château de Breteuil).

Much later, in about 1722, De Troy painted Maréchal de Camp Charles Skelton (Barrett-Lennard Collection), and his wife Lady Barbara, a daughter of the Earl of Sussex (Barrett-Lennard Collection).

JACOB VAN SCHUPPEN 1670–1751

Sir William Waldegrave, the private physician to James VII and II, owned a portrait of the Prince of Wales by Van Schuppen. In addition to pursuing his medical practice, Waldegrave devoted himself to playing the lute and guitar, for which he had long been celebrated in English society. There is a family portrait by Van Schuppen which might tentatively be identified as showing Waldegrave with his Italian wife, Isabella (née Ronchi), whose brother was painted by Gennari. While Waldegrave plays a guitar, a little girl dances beside what seems to be the balcony of the Château de Saint-Germain (Walker Art Gallery, Liverpool).

HYACINTHE RIGAUD 1659–1743

Rigaud painted the Duke of Berwick in 1708 to commemorate his having become a Chevalier du Saint-Esprit. The portrait has only recently been identified, partly because it is one of the very few which are missing from Rigaud's *Livre de Raison*. The painter shows Berwick in exactly the same composition he had already used for other portraits, most notably that of the Dauphin, merely altering some of the background details. Several copies have survived (Versailles; Château de Breteuil).

NICOLAS DE LARGILLIÈRE 1656–1746

Despite his work for the Stuarts between 1690 and 1695, it seems that it was not until much later that Largillière was commissioned to paint any of the Jacobites. Only three portraits have so far been identified. There is one of the Duke of Perth (Gentleman of the Bedchamber) wearing the blue sash and the star of the Garter, which he received in 1706 (Drummond Castle; Neûchatel, Musée Historique). The two others date from the 1720s and show Lieutenant-General Michael Rothe, the son-in-law of the 2nd Earl of Middleton (Potsdam), and the Duke of Berwick. The latter is an oil sketch (Musée de Nîmes).

ALEXIS-SIMON BELLE 1674–1734

When Belle replaced De Troy as the official painter of the Jacobite court, he and his wife, Anne Chéron, settled at Saint-Germain. The Jacobite courtiers whom he painted there included Roger Strickland (Page of Honour) in c.1703–4, (Sizergh Castle), John (later 2nd Lord) Caryll (Gentleman Usher of the Privy Chamber) in 1704 (lost), Sir John Gifford (Groom of the Bedchamber) in 1704 (lost), Bernard Howard of Glossop (Equerry) in c.1705 (Arundel Castle), the Duke of Berwick in c.1705 (Palacio da Liria; Château de Breteuil), and the duke's sister-in-law Henrietta Bulkeley (daughter of

a Lady of the Bedchamber) in 1705 (lost). He also painted several English Jacobites who were not attached to the court, such as Thomas Strickland in 1703 (Sizergh Castle).

Belle remained at Saint-Germain after the departure of James, but was invited to join the court at Bar-le-Duc in 1714. There he produced several copies of a portrait of David Nairne, the king's private secretary (private collection), one of Charles Leslie, his anglican chaplain (s 484), and another of Sir Carnaby Haggerston, who was studying in Lorraine (National Gallery of Ireland). When he returned to Paris later the same year he painted the Duke of Perth (copy on loan to the Scottish National Portrait Gallery) and the Duc de Lauzun (Musée d'Arts décoratifs, Saumur), both of them wearing their robes as Knights of the Garter. At around the same time he painted Count Anthony Hamilton, the poet and novelist (Lennoxlove).

Belle received several commissions from Scottish Jacobites in exile after the 'Fifteen'. These included Maurice Murray of Abercairny in c.1716–17 (private collection), Arthur Elphinstone (later 6th Baron Balmerino) in January 1717 (private collection), the 4th Lord Forbes of Pitsligo in 1717 (private collection), and the Duchess of Mar in November 1718 (lost), followed during the 1720s by Lord Erskine (son of the Duke of Mar) (lost) and James Keith (Marischal College, Aberdeen).

ANTONIO DAVID 1684–1750
AND FRANCESCO TREVISANI 1656–1746

In the autumn of 1717, after finishing his first portrait of James and before starting the eleven copies already referred to, David was commissioned to paint Robert Freebairn, one of the many Scottish Jacobites who had followed the king into exile (lost). Thereafter he was too busy working for James to accept other Jacobite commissions. By the time David finished making the copies in 1718, the Duke of Mar and his relations had decided that it was not a good picture.

It was therefore Trevisani who was commissioned to paint the Duchess of Mar and her daughter in 1719. They are shown beside a harpsichord, on which can be seen an aria from Bononcini's opera *Erminia*, first performed in January of that year (private collection). A portrait of the Duke of Mar, which shows him with the Garter (given him by James in 1717) as well as the Thistle (given him by Queen Anne in

1706) might also have been painted by Trevisani at the beginning of 1719 (private collection). Later the same year, or perhaps in 1720, Trevisani painted both James Murray (Scone Palace) and his sister Marjory, Countess of Inverness (Scone Palace), whose husband was a Groom of the Bedchamber. At the time Murray (later Earl of Dunbar) was acting Secretary of State, but he left the court in January 1721 and did not return until 1725, when he was appointed Governor of the Prince of Wales.

By 1720 David was again working for James, but there are only two other Jacobite portraits by him which have survived. They are similar and both show the Countess of Inverness, whose husband had replaced Murray as acting Secretary of State. They were painted in 1723. One was destined for her husband and shows her holding some flowers (Perth Art Gallery and Museum), while the other, for Lord Dunbar, shows her with a bow and arrow (Scone Palace). After finishing these pictures David began work on two copies of a companion portrait of her husband John, Earl (after 1727 Duke) of Inverness, but before they could be finished he was sent by James on a mission to Paris. Deprived of his sitter, David's likeness was then judged by a group of courtiers to be unrecognisable, so that he was totally discouraged from continuing. When Inverness returned to Rome in 1724 the commission to paint his portrait was consequently given to Trevisani (on loan to the Scottish National Portrait Gallery).

These are the only known Jacobite portraits painted in Rome before the end of the 1730s. Although Trevisani painted several other British people on the Grand Tour, most notably the Jacobite Duke of Beaufort in 1726–7, he does not seem to have been employed again by the members of James's court. David continued to work for James himself until 1734, and painted Lady Inverness again in 1727 (lost), but no evidence has survived of any commissions from other courtiers.

DOMENICO DUPRA 1689–1770

Dupra was first brought to the attention of James when he painted the portraits of William Hay and a group of his friends.

The presence of many Scots at the Stuart court in exile encouraged their fellow countrymen to visit Rome when making a Grand Tour. Even those of limited Jacobite sympathies were pleased to take advantage of their hospitality and to satisfy their curiosity.

In 1739 some Scottish visitors, all of whom would later be involved in the 'Forty-Five', formed a 'Society of young Gentleman Travellers in Rome' and commemorated their friendship by having their portraits painted by Dupra. They included Lord John Drummond, later 4th Duke of Perth (Scottish National Portrait Gallery; Drummond Castle); David, Lord Elcho, the eldest son of the 4th Earl of Wemyss (private collection); and two others named Carnegie of Boysack and Bellingham Boyle (both lost). These visitors were entertained by two members of the court, whose portraits were also painted, thus making a group of six. The courtiers were Dr James Irvin, who was Physician to James (Scottish National Portrait Gallery) and William Hay of Edington, not a salaried member of the royal household but someone who then lived at the court permanently on a pension from the king (Scottish National Portrait Gallery).

A NOTE ON THE SOURCES

The primary source material for any study of the portraits of the Stuarts in exile is necessarily the pictures themselves. Most of them may be studied in the rich photographic archives of the Scottish National Portrait Gallery in Edinburgh and the National Portrait Gallery in London. Others may be found in the *service de documentation* at the Louvre in Paris.

Many of the portraits are referred to in the Stuart Papers, now part of the Royal Archives at Windsor Castle. These contain correspondence explaining why, when and for whom portraits were commissioned, as well as details of some of the payments to the painters.

The Stuart Papers, however, are disappointing and difficult to use. They refer only to the portraits painted in Italy after 1719 and contain nothing at all about any painted at Saint-Germain-en-Laye. Moreover, the relevant information is overwhelmed by a mass of irrelevant material in well over five hundred large bound volumes of documents, in three different languages, and often in poor condition and barely legible handwriting! This is an obstacle which seems to have deterred most people from making the effort.

There is another reason. Shortly after the Second World War a serious attempt to study the Italian portraits was made by the Hon. Clare Stuart Wortley. When she died in 1948, her researches were still very far from complete and many of the important documents had not yet emerged. Nevertheless, her notes were assembled into narrative form by the eminent Jacobite historian Henrietta Tayler and deposited in the Royal Archives. They were edited so well and contained so many details that further research in the Stuart Papers seemed unnecessary. As a result, little progress was made in the half century after Clare Stuart Wortley stopped her pioneering research. It was during these same fifty years that the enormous expansion of the photographic archives made it possible to carry out a comprehensive study of the many portraits still in existence.

My own researches have revealed a mass of additional material in the Stuart Papers, much of which refers to pictures of which Clare Stuart Wortley was unaware. They also show that several of her conclusions, which she had made only tentatively but others accepted as fact, were wrong.

For the various Stuart portraits painted in France and Lorraine, and in Italy before 1719, the Stuart Papers tell us nothing. Instead we need to turn to the various papers of Sir David Nairne, an under-secretary at the Jacobite court who became James's principal private secretary. His private diary of 1691–1708 in the National Library of Scotland (MS 14266), his letter books of 1710–12 and diary of 1717 in the Bodleian Library (Carte MSS 208, 212), and his letters to Cardinal Gualterio of 1717–18 in the British Library (Add MSS 20298, 20312–13, 31260–61) provide much of the information which is missing from the Stuart Papers and thus enable a correct chronology to be established.

Contemporary quotations in the text have been kept to a minimum and, with one exception, are all from the Stuart Papers, arranged chronologically and thus easy to locate (p.65, SP 104/57; p.67, SP 130/85; p.67, SP 131/181; and p.83, SP 257/57). Cardinal Gualterio's opinion of Antonio David (p.58) is a translation from the Italian in the British Library (Add MSS 20306, f.445). The nineteenth-century description of the lost family portrait by Largillière (p.35) is taken from Agnes Strickland, *Lives of the Queens of England*, ix (1846), p.313.

Of the published sources used, by far the most important has been *The Engraved Record of the Jacobite Movement* by Richard Sharp. This has enabled me to check the attributions and the dates of many of the paintings, and to identify which ones were made publicly available. The importance of his work will be evident to anyone who looks at the present book.

INVENTORY NOTE

The inventory is organised in chronological sequence. The dates after each artist refer to the periods when the artist was working for the Stuart court. Miniature copies have not been included. All measurements are in centimetres, height preceding width. All works marked with an asterisk* were included in the exhibition *The King over the Water: The Life of James Francis Edward Stuart (1688–1766)* held at the Scottish National Portrait Gallery, Edinburgh from 27 April to 30 September 2001.

I · FRANCE

BENEDETTO GENNARI (1689–91)

1 James VII and II, 1685, copied in 1689, 200 × 127 (private collection)
2 *Prince of Wales, 1689, 129.5 × 96.5 (Stonyhurst College)
3 Mary of Modena and the Prince of Wales, 1690, 216 × 157 (private collection)
4 Mary of Modena, 1690 (lost)
5 Mary of Modena, 1691 (lost)

NICOLAS DE LARGILLIERE (1691–2; 1694–5)

1 *Prince of Wales, 1691, 102.2 × 81.3 (Scottish National Portrait Gallery 2191)
2 James VII and II, Mary of Modena and the Prince of Wales, 1691 (lost)
3 Prince of Wales, 1692 (lost)
4 Prince of Wales, 1692, 76.2 × 63.5 (private collection)
5 Prince of Wales, 1694, 70 × 56.5 (private collection)
6 *Prince of Wales and Princess Louise-Marie, 1695, 190.5 × 143.5 (National Portrait Gallery 976)

PIERRE MIGNARD (1694)

1 *The Family of James VII and II, 1694, 247 × 293 (private collection)
2 The Family of James VII and II, 1694, 46 × 80 (Royal Collection)

FRANCOIS DE TROY (1698–1701; 1704; c.1711)

1 James VII and II, c.1698, 137 × 106 (Barrett-Lennard Collection)
2 Mary of Modena, c.1698, 137 × 106? later reduced to 99 × 79 (Sizergh Castle)

3 Prince of Wales, 1699, 76 × 62.9 (Holyroodhouse)
4 Prince of Wales, 1699, 73.5 × 62 (private collection)
5 Prince of Wales, 1700, 71 × 58 (Niedersächsische Landesgalerie)
6 Prince of Wales, 1700, 76.5 × 64.3 (Holyroodhouse); 71 × 55.9 *(Drambuie Collection)
7 Prince of Wales, 1700, 70 × 53 (Palazzo Corsini, Rome)
8 *Prince of Wales, 1701, 76.8 × 64.2 (Scottish National Portrait Gallery 909)
9 Prince of Wales, 1701, 75.2 × 64 (private collection)
10 James III, 1704, 127 × 94 (Parham Park) copy by Belle, 112 × 76 (private collection)
11 James III, 1704, 92.1 × 74 (private collection)
12 Princess Louise-Marie, 1699, 73.5 × 61 (private collection)
13 *Princess Louise-Marie, 1700, 71.8 × 59.7 (Drambuie Collection)
14 Princess Louise-Marie, c.1711, 73.6 × 62.2 (private collection)

JACOB VAN SCHUPPEN (c.1700, 1704)

1 Prince of Wales, c.1700 (probably based on De Troy 7) (lost)
2 The Return of James III from Hunting, 1704, 98 × 131 (Sanssouci, Potsdam)

HYACINTHE RIGAUD (1708)

1 James III, 1708 (lost)

ALEXIS-SIMON BELLE (c.1698–1714)

1 James VII and II, after Kneller, c.1700, 99.5 × 80 (Sizergh Castle)
2 James VII and II, after Kneller, c.1712, 71.2 × 58.4 (private collection)
3 Mary of Modena, after De Troy, c.1712, 71.2 × 58.4 (private collection)
4 Prince of Wales, after Largillière, c.1698, 137 × 106 (possibly by Van Schuppen) (Sizergh Castle)
5 Prince of Wales and Princess Louise-Marie, 1699, 188.5 × 131.9 (Holyroodhouse)
6 *Prince of Wales, 1700, 75.3 × 65.2 (Scottish National Portrait Gallery 1215)
7 James III, 1702, 72 × 57.6 (Palazzo Doria Pamphilij, Rome)
8 James III with a page, 1703, 170 × 114 (Collège des Ecossais, Paris) copy without a page, 125 × 105 (Museo de San Carlos, Mexico City)

9 James III, 1706, 76.2 × 63.5 (Chiddingstone Castle)
10 *James III, 1712, 136 × 107 (Government Art Collection)
11 James III, 1714, 74 × 59.5 (private collection)
12 James III, 1714, 80 × 65 (Government Art Collection)
13 James III as a Knight of the Garter, 1714 (lost)
14 *Princess Louise-Marie, 1704, 73 × 59 (Scottish National Portrait Gallery 1216); 75.3 × 62.5 (National Portrait Gallery 1658)
15 Princess Louise-Marie, 1710, 135 × 103 (Sizergh Castle)
16 Princess Louise-Marie in Masquerade Costume, c.1711 (lost)

JACQUES-ANTOINE ARLAUD

1 Prince of Wales (attributed to Arlaud, copied after Largillière 4), 4.9 × 4 (Royal Collection)
2 *Prince of Wales as as a Knight of the Garter, 1692 (attributed to Arlaud, copied after Largillière 4), c.7 × 5.5 (private collection)
3 Prince of Wales (attributed to Arlaud, copied after Largillière 6) (Arundel Castle)
4 James III, October 1702 (private collection)
5 *James III, 1702 (Scottish National Portrait Gallery L 297)
6 James III, May 1703, 8.7 oval (private collection)
7 James III (Public Record Office, Atterbury Papers)
8 James III, 1710 (private collection)
9 Princess Louise-Marie, c.1710, 8.9 oval (Drummond Castle)

ANNE CHERON

1 *James III, 1704, 6 × 4.8 (Scottish National Portrait Gallery 1210)
2 James III, 1704, 5.4 × 4.3 (Royal Collection)

JACQUELINE DE LA BOISSIERE

1 James III, 8.6 × 6.4 (Royal Collection)
2 James III (private collection)
3 James III, 8.2 × 6.1 (Wallace Collection)
4 James III, 1710, 8.9 × 6.3 (private collection)
5 Princess Louise-Marie, 1710, 8.9 × 6.3 (private collection)

PIERRE GOBERT (1713–15)

1 James III, 1713 (lost)
2 Mary of Modena, 1713 (lost)
3 Mary of Modena holding a Cross in her Hand and Presenting it to James III, 1713–15, 84 × 108 later reduced to 80 × 65 (private collection)
4 The Apotheosis of James VII and II and Princess Louise-Marie, 1713–15, 84 × 108 (lost)

II · ITALY

GIUSEPPE MARIA CRESPI (1717)

1 The Meeting of Prince Albani and James III on the Banks of the River Panaro outside Bologna, 17 March, 1717, 149 × 225 (Narodni Gallery, Prague)

ANTONIO GIONIMA (1717)

1 Cardinal Gozzadini Receiving James III in the Archbishop's Palace in Imola, March 1717 (Castel Sant'Angelo, Rome)

ANTONIO DAVID (1717–35)

1 James III, 1717 (Palacio da Liria, Madrid) copy of 1719, 72.4 × 55.9 (Holyroodhouse)
2 James III, 1722, 134 × 96 (private collection)
3 Maria Clementina, 1719, 97.5 × 76 (Lambeth Palace)
4 Maria Clementina, 1722, 97 × 74 (private collection)
5 Maria Clementina, 1727, 73.7 × 61 (private collection)
6 Prince Charles, 1723, 68.6 × 59.7 (private collection)
7 *Prince Charles, 1726, 147.3 × 111.8 (Stonyhurst College)
8 Prince Charles, 1729, 73.5 × 61 (private collection); 63.5 × 48.3 (National Portrait Gallery 434) *copy of 1732: 73.4 × 60.3 (Scottish National Portrait Gallery 887)
9 Prince Charles, 1729, 65 × 48.5 (private collection)
10 Prince Charles, 1734–5, 83 × 65 (private collection)
11 Prince Henry, 1726 (lost)
12 Prince Henry, 1729, 73.5 × 61 (private collection); 65.4 × 49.2 (National Portrait Gallery 435) *copy of 1732: 73.4 × 60.6 (Scottish National Portrait Gallery 888)
13 Prince Henry, 1734–5, 83.2 × 64.8 (private collection)

FRANCESCO TREVISANI (1719–20)

1 James III, 1719, 97.8 × 74.6 (Holyroodhouse)
   *copy of 1720, 96.8 × 73.8
   (Scottish National Portrait Gallery 159)
2 *Maria Clementina, 1719, 98 × 73
   (Scottish National Portrait Gallery 886)
3 Maria Clementina, 1720, 76 × 63.5 (private collection)

GIROLAMO PESCI (1721)

1 *James III with a page, 1721, 167.6 × 116.8 (Stanford Hall)
   copy by David, 1723: 170.2 × 121.9
   (Blairs College, Aberdeen)
2 Maria Clementina, 1721, 102? × 80? (Prado, Madrid)
3 *Maria Clementina with Prince Charles, 1721, 167.6 × 116.8
    (Stanford Hall)

MARTIN VAN MEYTENS (1725)

1 James III, 1725, c.76 × 63 (lost ?)
   *copies by Gill, 1727–8: 76.4 × 63.5
   (Scottish National Portrait Gallery 1836)
   76 × 63.5 (Drambuie collection)
2 Maria Clementina, 1725, c.76 × 63 (lost ?)
   *copies by Gill, 1727–8: 76.5 × 63.7
   (Scottish National Portrait Gallery 1837)
   copies by David?, 1730 (private collection)
   copy by Blanchet, 1740 (Royal Castle, Warsaw)
   copy by Blanchet, 1741: 99.1 × 71.1 (private collection)
   copy by Dupra, 1742: 63.5 × 48.3 (private collection)

GUSTAV ANDREAS WOLFGANG (1726–7)

1 James III, 1726: miniatures in rings
   (Victoria and Albert Museum)
2 James III, 1726–27: miniatures (lost ?)

LUCIA CASALINI TORELLI (1726–7)

1 Maria Clementina, c.1727 (lost)
2 Prince Charles, c.1726–7 (lost)
3 Prince Henry, c.1726–7 (lost)

GIOVANNA FRATELLINI (1728)

1 James III, 1728 (lost)
2 Maria Clementina, 1728 (lost)
3 Prince Charles, 1728 (lost)
4 Prince Henry, 1728 (lost)

GIOVANNI PAOLO PANNINI (1729, 1747)

1 A Fête in the Piazza Navona (November 1729), 1729,
   110 × 252 (Louvre, Paris)
2 A Performance in the Teatro Argentina, (July 1747), 1747,
   204 × 247 (Louvre, Paris)

DOMENICO MURATORI (1734)

1 Maria Clementina, 1734 (lost)

AGOSTINO MASUCCI (1735)

1 *The Solemnisation of the Marriage of James III and
   Maria Clementina Sobieska at Montefiascone,
   1 September, 1719, 1735, 243.5 × 342
   (Scottish National Portrait Gallery 2415)
2 Maria Clementina, 1735 (lost)
3 *The Baptism of Charles, Prince of Wales,
   31 December, 1720, 1735, 243.9 × 350.3
   (Scottish National Portrait Gallery 2511)

ROSALBA CARRIERA (1737)

1 Prince Charles, 1737, pastel, 54.3 × 41.5 (private collection)

JEAN-ETIENNE LIOTARD (1737–8)

1 James III, 1737, pastel (lost)
2 Prince Henry, 1737, pastel (lost)
   *copy in oil: 63.5 × 47.3
   (Scottish National Portrait Gallery 1518)
3 Prince Charles, 1737, pastel (lost)
   *copy in oil: 63.5 × 48.5
   (Scottish National Portrait Gallery 1519)

LOUIS-GABRIEL BLANCHET
(1737–9; 1741; 1748)

1 *James III, 1741, 63.5 × 48.3
   (National Portrait Gallery 5573)
2 Prince Charles, 1737–38, 190.5 × 141
   (National Portrait Gallery 5517)
3 Prince Charles, 1739, 96.5 × 72.4 (Holyroodhouse)
4 Prince Henry, 1738, 186 × 140.3
   (National Portrait Gallery 5518)
5 Prince Henry, 1739, 96.5 × 72.4 (Holyroodhouse)
6 Cardinal York, 1748, 248.5 × 177.3 (private collection)

FRANCESCO PONZONE (1741)

1 James III, drawing, 1741, 23 × 15.3 (Royal Collection)
copy: 20.3 × 16.5 (National Portrait Gallery 4535)

DOMENICO DUPRA (1740; 1742; 1744)

1 James III, 1742, 64.1 × 48.3 (private collection)
2 Prince Charles, 1740 (lost)
3 Prince Charles, 1740, 71.8 × 59.1 (private collection)
copy of 1742: 64.8 × 48.3 (private collection)
4 Prince Charles, 1742 (Palacio da Liria, Madrid)
5 Prince Henry, 1740, 72 × 62 (Drambuie Collection)
6 Prince Henry, 1740, 71.8 × 59 (private collection)
copy of 1742: 64.8 × 48.3 (private collection)
7 Prince Henry, 1742 (Palacio da Liria, Madrid)
8 Prince Henry, 1744 (lost)

VERONICA TELLI (NÉE STERN)
(1743–5; 1748)

1 James III, 1744, after Dupra 1 (lost ?)
2 James III, 1748, after Dupra 1 (private collection)
3 Maria Clementina, 1744, after Meytens 2 (lost ?)
copy, 1748 (private collection)
4 Prince Charles, 1743, after Liotard 3 (Drummond Castle)
5 Prince Charles, 1748 (private collection)
6 Prince Henry, 1743, after Liotard 2 (Drummond Castle)
7 Prince Henry, 1744, after Dupra 6 (lost ?)
8 Prince Henry, 1744, after Dupra 8 (lost ?)
9 Cardinal York, 1748, after Blanchet 6 (private collection)

POMPEO BATONI (1744; 1757)

1 Prince Henry, 1744, miniature after Dupra 8 (lost ?)
2 James III, 1757 (lost)

DOMENICO CORVI (1747–8)

1 *Cardinal York, 1747, 130.5 × 96.8
(Wadsworth Atheneum, Hartford)
2 Cardinal York, 1748, 172.1 × 127.3 (Holyroodhouse)

ANTON RAPHAEL MENGS (1748)

1 *James III, 1748, 74.9 × 61 (National Portrait Gallery 433)
2 James III, 1748, 119.4 × 111.8 (Stonyhurst College)
3 Cardinal York, 1748 (lost)
study in oils, 44 × 35 (Musée Fabre, Montpellier)

COSMO ALEXANDER (1749, 1752)

1 James III (after Mengs 1), 1749, 99.2 × 76.2
(private collection)
2 Maria Clementina (after Trevisani and David), 1749,
99.2 × 76.2 (private collection)
3 Prince Charles (after Dupra 2), 1749, 99 × 74 ?? (lost)
28.5 × 25.5 (Sizergh Castle)
4 Prince Charles (after La Tour), 1752, 77.5 × 74.9
(Drambuie Collection)
5 Cardinal York (after Corvi 1), 1749, 99 × 74
(Château de Versailles)
copy of 1752: 77.5 × 74.9 (private collection)

UNIDENTIFIED (1747)

1 *James III and his Court in Front of the Palazzo Muti
during the Celebrations of the Appointment of Prince
Henry as a Cardinal, July 1747, 195.5 × 297
(Scottish National Portrait Gallery)

PLACIDO COSTANZI (1757)

1 *James III, 1757, 76 × 44 (private collection)

UNIDENTIFIED (1766)

1 *James III lying in state, drawing, 1766 (private collection)

LAURENT PECHEUX (1770)

1 Prince Charles, 1770, 140 × 96.5 (Stanford Hall)

PUBLIC COLLECTIONS

The portraits of the exiled Stuarts are very widely dispersed and may be seen in many museums abroad, in the Czech Republic (Prague), France (Azay-le-Rideau, Montpellier, Versailles), Germany (Hanover), Italy (Rome), Mexico (Mexico City), Poland (Warsaw), Spain (Madrid) and the United States of America (Hartford). In addition there are many which are in private collections throughout Great Britain, Europe and America.

Within Great Britain itself the largest collections are at the Scottish National Portrait Gallery, Holyroodhouse and the National Portrait Gallery, but whereas the two former collections are both in Edinburgh, the latter collection is no longer all in London. The richest collections open to the public are at the following places:

SCOTTISH NATIONAL PORTRAIT GALLERY, EDINBURGH

Largillière 1; De Troy 8; Belle 6; Belle 14; David 8; David 12; Trevisani 1; Trevisani 2; Meytens 1; Meytens 2; Masucci 1; Masucci 3; Liotard 1; Liotard 3; Corvi 2; unidentified (1747) 1.

PALACE OF HOLYROODHOUSE, EDINBURGH

De Troy 3; De Troy 6; Belle 5; David 1; Trevisani 1; Blanchet 3; Blanchet 5; Corvi 2.

SIZERGH CASTLE, CUMBRIA (THE NATIONAL TRUST)

De Troy 2; Belle 1; Belle 4; Belle 15; Alexander 3; Alexander 5.

CHIDDINGSTONE CASTLE, KENT

Largillière 6; Belle 9; David 3.

NATIONAL PORTRAIT GALLERY, LONDON
London except where shown

Largillière 6; Belle 10 (Lyme Park, Cheshire, National Trust); Belle 14 (Beningbrough Hall, Yorkshire); David 8 (Beningbrough Hall, Yorkshire); David 12 (Beningbrough Hall, Yorkshire); Meytens 2 (British Embassy, Warsaw); Ponzone 1; Blanchet 1; Blanchet 2; Blanchet 4; Mengs 1.

ADDITIONAL ILLUSTRATIONS

The Family of James VII and II, 1694
[Mignard 1]

The Prince of Wales, 1700
[De Troy 7]

Prince of Wales, *c.*1698
[Belle 4]

James III, 1706
[Belle 9]

Cardinal Gozzadini Receiving James III, 1717
[Gionima 1]

Prince Charles, 1734-5
[David 10]

The Prince of Wales, 1699
[De Troy 4]

James III, 1704
[De Troy 11]

Princess Louise-Marie, 1699
[De Troy 12]

Princess Louise-Marie, *c.*1711
[De Troy 14]

James VII and II, *c.*1700
[Belle 1]

James III, 1714
[Belle 11]

James III, 1714
[Belle 13, copy]

The Meeting of Prince Albani and James III, 1717
[Crespi 1]

James III, 1737
[Liotard 1, copy]

James III, 1741
[Ponzone 1]

Prince Henry, 1742
[Dupra 7]

Cardinal York, 1748
[Corvi 2, copy]

Prince Charles, 1749
[Alexander 3, copy]

INDEX

PHOTOGRAPHIC CREDITS

medieval realms

for common entrance and key stage 3

Colin Shephard **Martin Collier** **Rosemary Rees**

Hodder Murray

A MEMBER OF THE HODDER HEADLINE GROUP

Also available: *The Making of the UK for Common Entrance* ISBN-10: 0 340 89983 2
ISBN-13: 978 0 340 89983 0

The authors and publisher would like to thank Bob Pace of Belmont School, Mill Hill, and Niall Murphy of Radley College, Abingdon, for their valuable feedback.

Note: The wording and structure of some written sources have been adapted and simplified to make them accessible to all pupils, while faithfully preserving the sense of the original.

Words printed in SMALL CAPITALS (first mention only) are defined in the glossary on page 187.

Although every effort has been made to ensure that website addresses are correct at time of going to press, Hodder Murray cannot be held responsible for the content of any website mentioned in this book.

Hodder Headline's policy is to use papers that are natural, renewable and recyclable products and made from wood grown in sustainable forests. The logging and manufacturing processes are expected to conform to the environmental regulations of the country of origin.

Orders: please contact Bookpoint Ltd, 130 Milton Park, Abingdon, Oxon OX14 4SB.
Telephone: +44 (0)1235 827720. Fax: +44 (0)1235 400454. Lines are open from 9.00a.m. to 5.00p.m., Monday to Saturday, with a 24-hour message answering service. Visit our website at www.hoddereducation.co.uk.

Artwork by Tony Jones/Art Construction, Janek Matysiak, Edward Ripley, Steve Smith
Typeset in 12pt ITC Officina Book
Layouts by Fiona Webb
Printed in Italy

A catalogue record for this title is available from the British Library

ISBN-13: 978 0 340 89984 7

CONTENTS

The Middle Ages: an overview

This book has three sections. The first is in roughly chronological order. But Sections 2 and 3 overlap with Section 1.

SECTION 1   GOOD AND BAD MONARCHS

SECTION 2   RELIGION IN THE MIDDLE AGES

SECTION 3   HOW DID ORDINARY PEOPLE LIVE?

The chart opposite will help you to get an overview and piece the three sections together. You can also make your own copy of the chart (you can download a free Word version from www.hoddersamplepages.co.uk). Then you can add your own notes and information to it to help you revise.

We also have a couple more tips to help you to sort out who is who. When there are so many kings with such similar names (all those Edwards, all those Henrys), it is easy to mix them up. Here are some ideas that may help you:

1 Nicknames: some of the kings have nicknames. These names help us to remember them and tell them apart. No one mixes up William the Conqueror and William Rufus. Other kings don't have nicknames. So give these kings your own nicknames and add them to your chart. Make sure your name sums up something memorable about each king. For example, you could call Richard II 'the boy-king' or 'the peasant-basher'. Remember not to use your made-up nicknames in the exam!

2 Drawings: it will be even better if you also draw your own stick-man portrait of the king holding or doing something that reminds you of his nickname.

Monarch	Nickname	Notable events	Dates	Age at death	Cause of death	Pages
Norman						
William I	the Conqueror	Conquered England/Battle of Hastings	1066–87	59	Riding accident	6–27
William II	Rufus	First Crusade	1087–1100	40	Hunting accident (or was it?)	28
Henry I		Brought peace and stability to England	1100–35	67	Natural causes	28
Stephen		Civil War, chaos. Cousin Matilda took over 1141–42 while he was in prison	1135–54	58	Natural causes	29–32
Angevin						
Henry II	Curtmantle	Murder of Thomas Becket	1154–89	56	Hounded to death by son	33
Richard I	the Lionheart	The Third Crusade	1189–99	42	Shot by an arrow	33
John	Lackland or Softsword	Magna Carta	1199–1216	49	Dysentery (bolt-wound went septic)	34–39
Plantagenet						
Henry III		First 'Parliament'	1216–72	65	Natural causes	40–42
Edward I	Longshanks	Conquered Wales. Castle builder	1272–1307	68	Died in battle	44–53
Edward II			1307–27	43	Probably murdered	56
Edward III		Started Hundred Years War with France	1327–77	65	Natural causes	56–57
Richard II		The Peasants' Revolt	1377–99	32	Probably murdered or may have starved himself to death while in prison	58–65
Lancaster						
Henry IV	Bolingbroke		1399–1413	47	Got leprosy. Son took over before he died of natural causes	66–73
Henry V		Battle of Agincourt	1413–22	35	Dysentery	66–73
Henry VI			1422–61	50	Went mad. Murdered	74–75
York						
Edward IV			1461–83	40	Died suddenly of natural causes	75
Edward V	One of 'The Princes in the Tower'		April–June 1483	12	Possibly murdered by his uncle	89–92
Richard III		Battle of Bosworth	1483–85	32	Killed in battle by Henry Tudor's army	76–93

SECTION 1

Good and bad monarchs

Source

A medieval king pictured in the Westminster Psalter.

What made a good medieval monarch?

The first part of this book investigates a number of medieval monarchs to see how well they did their job. When you have finished studying them you will be asked to make some decisions about how good these monarchs were.

In the Middle Ages the MONARCH was the most important person in the country. He (and it was usually a 'he' in those days) had an enormous amount of power. He was helped by the fact that people believed that he was chosen by God to rule the country. However, being a monarch could also be a dangerous occupation. Monarchs had to keep on good terms with the NOBLES and with the Church. They also had to try to avoid uprisings by the peasants. As you will see, there are several examples of monarchs being killed, murdered or deposed (thrown off the throne)!

Task

1 On the facing page is a summary of the duties of a medieval king. Now look at the list of characteristics below. Choose the three most important ones for a medieval monarch. Add more qualities if you wish.

handsome cruel brave musical honest

feared healthy lazy fair educated

trustworthy strong greedy male

respected hated clever popular

ruthless

2 Choose one duty and explain how your chosen characteristics would help the king perform that duty.

4

Did you know?

Of the eighteen kings who reigned between 1066 and 1485, only four died of old age. Four were murdered (one with a red hot poker), two died of dysentery and two died in battle!

A medieval king had to ...

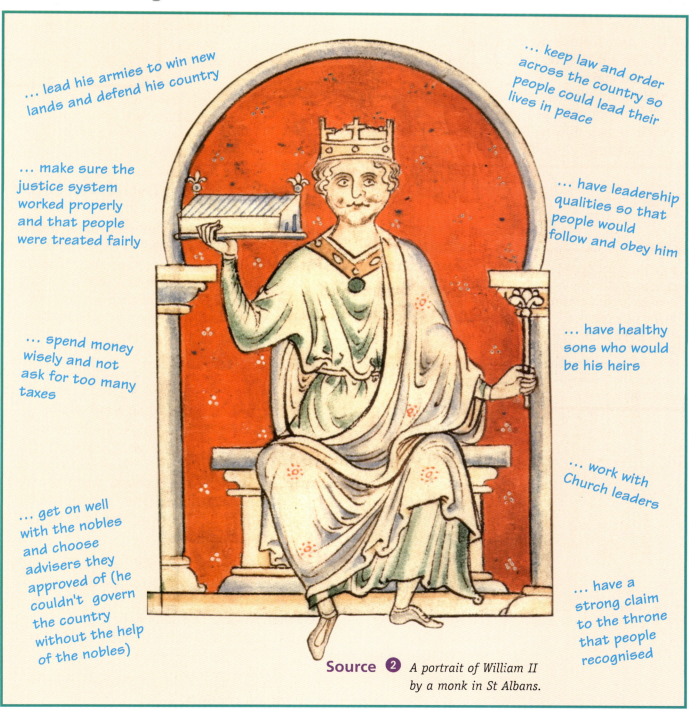

... lead his armies to win new lands and defend his country

... make sure the justice system worked properly and that people were treated fairly

... spend money wisely and not ask for too many taxes

... get on well with the nobles and choose advisers they approved of (he couldn't govern the country without the help of the nobles)

... keep law and order across the country so people could lead their lives in peace

... have leadership qualities so that people would follow and obey him

... have healthy sons who would be his heirs

... work with Church leaders

... have a strong claim to the throne that people recognised

Source ❷ *A portrait of William II by a monk in St Albans.*

5

UNIT 1 How did William and the Normans conquer England?

Who... ?

EDWARD THE CONFESSOR
Edward was called the Confessor because he was very religious. He spent a lot of time praying. He also built the first Westminster Abbey.

What is this all about?

In 1066, a huge fleet set sail from Normandy, bound for England. The ships carried the soldiers, horses and armour of William, Duke of Normandy. He was on his way to England to press his claim to be the rightful King of England.

This unit focuses on three issues:

- Why did William think he should be the King of England? Was his a good claim?
- How did William win the Battle of Hastings? Was it William's skills, his opponents' bad luck, or something else?
- There is a difference between winning a battle and gaining control of a country. So how did the Normans gain control of England?

1.1 Did William have a good claim to the throne?

Who ... ?

THE ANGLO-SAXONS
Originally came to England from Germany in the fifth century. They cleared the Celts out of England and then defended England against the Viking invasions.

In January 1066 the King of England, Edward the Confessor, died. He and his wife Edith had failed to produce a child to succeed to the throne. Anglo-Saxon customs were not clear about how a successor should be chosen in this situation. The problem was made worse because, over the years, Edward had promised the throne to a number of people. Now the struggle to succeed Edward as King of England had come to a head. The two strongest claims for the English throne in 1066 were:

- Harold Godwinson, who was the most powerful man in England
- William, Duke of Normandy.

There was also a third contender, the Viking king Harald Hardrada of Norway. You will find out more about him later.

Flashback: William visits Edward

By the winter of 1051–52 it was clear to many that Edward was probably not going to have a son. His wife Edith was childless and, in 1052, she had been sent to a convent because her father, Godwin, was in disgrace. The question was, who was going to succeed Edward?

- In 1052, the *Anglo-Saxon Chronicle* tells that 'Earl William' of Normandy visited the court of his cousin King Edward. The *Chronicle* does not mention that William was promised the throne.
- The Normans later suggested that Edward had sent Robert of Jumièges, Archbishop of Canterbury, to Normandy sometime in 1051 or 1052 to offer William the throne.

Whatever the truth, the Normans claimed that from this moment onwards William was the rightful heir to Edward's throne.

The rise of Harold Godwinson, 1052–66

The 27-year-old Harold Godwinson was made Earl of Wessex on the death of his father in 1053. For the next twelve years he was to be the most powerful nobleman in England.

- His sister, Edith, was married to Edward the Confessor.
- His brothers were also in powerful positions, for example Tostig was made Earl of Northumbria in 1055.
- The Godwins controlled much of England and had strong armies.

In 1063, when the Welsh decided to invade England, the Godwin family led an army that crushed them.

Did Harold swear an oath of loyalty in Bayeux?

In 1064 or 1065, Harold travelled to France. Why he did so is not known and what happened when he got there has caused considerable debate. It has been suggested that Harold was visiting William as Edward's ambassador. One account suggests that he was captured on his way to see William by the Count of Ponthieu. William then came to Harold's rescue. What happened next is the important part of the story. The Bayeux Tapestry clearly shows Harold swearing an OATH to William. He is touching the relics of a saint. What the oath was about, we are not too sure.

Who... ?

HAROLD GODWINSON
Harold's father Godwin, Earl of Wessex, had been the most important Anglo-Saxon in England apart from the king. When Godwin died in 1053 his son took over his job as Earl of Wessex. You can see how he got his surname!

Source check

THE BAYEUX TAPESTRY
Stitched together in the 1070s on the orders of William's half-brother, Odo of Bayeux, the Tapestry is the Normans' side of the story. Therefore you can't necessarily believe all of it. As you can see from Source 1, there are three basic parts to the tapestry:
- In the middle are the main events.
- Above the pictures is a description in Latin of story told. You may be able to work out what it says.
- In the top and bottom margins there are symbolic decorations of animals and objects.

Source ❶

Scene from the Bayeux Tapestry. ❓ *Can you find: Harold; William; an altar; the box containing saint's relics?*

Source check

The *Anglo-Saxon Chronicle* said that on Edward's death in 1066:
Yet did the wise king entrust his kingdom To a man of high rank, to Harold himself.

- The Norman writer William of Poitiers (writing in the 1070s) insisted that Harold swore to support William's claim to the English throne when Edward died. He also said that Harold swore fealty (loyalty) to William as his lord. But a Norman in 1070 would say that, wouldn't he? There are other possibilities.
- Perhaps Harold swore an oath out of gratitude for being rescued.
- Maybe he was forced to do so as condition of his release.
- Harold might have sworn an oath of friendship (on Edward's behalf) between England and Normandy, not an oath of fealty.

Whatever the truth, the claim that Harold had broken a sacred oath was used by the Normans as the reason for war. To break such a promise was seen at the time as a terrible crime against the Church and God. William portrayed his invasion of England as a religious CRUSADE to punish Harold. He received the support of Pope Alexander II, which was thought to be very important.

Edward's deathbed wishes

As King Edward lay dying in December 1065, the leading nobles of England gathered to discover who he would nominate as the next king. It is interesting that William did not travel to England despite the Norman claim that he had been promised the throne by Edward in 1052 and by Harold in 1064 or 1065. However, all of the sources, whether English or Norman, are clear about what happened next. On his deathbed Edward nominated Harold to be his successor.

On 6 January 1066 Edward was buried in his magnificent new Westminster Abbey and Harold was crowned the same day.

Source 2

King Edward's funeral shown in the Bayeux Tapestry. ? *What do you think is happening at each of the numbered points?*

Harold was in a strong position:

- Harold had been chosen by his brother-in-law, King Edward, to be his successor.
- He had the support of the English nobles, including Earl Morcar and Earl Edwin.
- He had been accepted as king by the *witan*, the gathering of nobility and clergy.
- Harold had a strong reputation as a military leader. This put him in a good position to resist any invasion attempts.

In the eyes of most English people, this was enough to make him the rightful King of England.

Source exercise

The sources below give evidence about the events of 1064 when Harold supposedly visited France.

Throughout the book, you will find source exercises and investigations, which will help you to practise analysing sources. Exam-style questions on sources can be found on pages 179–184.

Source Ⓐ

[In 1051] Edward, King of the English, having no heir, sent Robert, Archbishop of Canterbury, to William of Normandy to appoint him as the next King of England. But he also, at a later date [in 1064], sent to him Harold so that he should swear loyalty to William.

Adapted from The Deeds of the Norman Dukes *written by William of Jumièges, a Norman monk. He wrote the book after a request from King William in 1070 that he write an account of the conquest.*

Source Ⓑ

When they met … Harold swore loyalty to William using the sacred ritual recognised among Christian men. In front of other people, he swore without anyone making him do so that he would represent William at the court of his lord, King Edward; secondly that he would make sure that, after the death of King Edward, William would be confirmed as King of England.

Adapted from The Deeds of William, Duke of the Normans and King of England *by William of Poitiers (1071). He was one of King William's priests.*

Questions

Study Sources A and B carefully.

1 Look at **Source A**.
   How had Edward promised William the throne of England before 1064?
2 Look at **Sources A** and **B**.
   To what extent do these sources tell similar stories? Explain why as part of your answer.
3 Look at **Source 1** on page 7.
   How does Source 1 support the accounts of Sources A and B? Give reasons for your answer.
4 Look at **all** the sources.
   Why do they tell similar versions about the oath of 1064?

Summary task

'William had a strong claim to the English throne'.

Using **all** of the sources and the information you have studied in the last four pages, explain how much you agree with this statement.

1.2 1066: The year of three battles

A third claimant: Harald Hardrada

It might seem complicated enough to have two claimants to the English throne. There was a third! He was Harald Hardrada, King of Norway. Why did he think he should be king of England? For 36 years, from 1016 to 1042, England had been ruled by Norwegians. The last one, who was called HarthCnut, had promised that when he died, Magnus, King of Norway, could have England too. But that never happened. When HarthCnut died, his half-brother Edward (the Confessor) seized the English throne.

Now Magnus' son, Harald Hardrada, decided to resurrect his claim.

It was a complicated time. Hardrada's claim to the throne was not strong but his armies most certainly were. He was one of the most feared Viking warriors in Europe. And to add to King Harold's problem, Hardrada was supported by Tostig, Harold's estranged brother.

So although Harold was now king, he knew his position was not secure. He knew he might have to fight to stay in power. So Harold raised his armies and waited for nine months. His army in the south watched the English Channel for signs of a Norman invasion. His army in the north waited for an attack from Scandinavia.

As September came, Harold was forced to send his armies home. The harvest needed to be brought in and he no longer had the food to keep his army fed. Just as his soldiers started on their way home, his rivals struck.

Hardrada sailed a fleet of 300 ships up the River Humber. He landed at Riccall on the Ouse and marched towards York. While on his way back to London, Harold heard the news that Hardrada had landed in Northumbria and burnt to the ground Scarborough, Cleveland and Holderness.

The Battles of Fulford Gate and Stamford Bridge

Hardrada found his way to York barred by Harold's loyal allies, his brothers-in-law: Edwin, Earl of Mercia, and Morcar, Earl of Northumbria. But at the Battle of Fulford Gate, Hardrada and Tostig defeated this northern Anglo-Saxon army and massacred thousands of experienced troops. They then carried on to York, which surrendered.

In response to this defeat, Harold marched north with his southern army, covering 190 miles in four days.

On 20 September Harold surprised and defeated the Viking army at the Battle of Stamford Bridge (see Source 3). Hardrada and Tostig were killed. However, despite Harold winning a famous victory, the impact on his army was severe. This is very important when trying to understand what happened next. Again, thousands of his best troops including many housecarls and archers died in battle. Harold returned south with a much weakened and very tired army.

Source 3

1

One third of the Viking army was miles away at Riccall guarding the Viking ships. The rest of Hardrada's army were relaxing in the fields by the river at Stamford Bridge. They had just won a great victory. They were waiting for hostages to be delivered from the city of York. Most had discarded their mail shirts and helmets in the hot sun. A few were guarding the bridge over the River Derwent.

2

Harold's arrival caught them completely off guard. Viking guards on the bridge kept Harold's army back for long enough for the rest of Hardrada's army to put on their armour and take up position away from the river. They formed a shield wall.

3

Harold's army battered at the wall in hand-to-hand combat for hours. Reinforcements arrived from Riccall led by Eystein. But when Harald Hardrada was killed the Norwegian army crumbled. The Vikings ran away and were pursued all the way back to their fleet at Riccall. Many were killed including Tostig. Only 24 out of the 300 Norwegian ships sailed back to Norway.

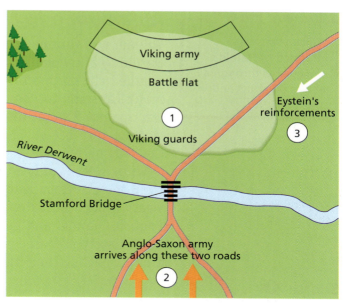

Plan of the Battle of Stamford Bridge.

Source 4

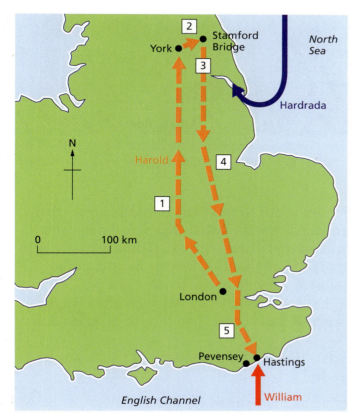

Battles in England, 1066.

What ... ?

HOUSECARL
A member of the king's bodyguard.

Did you know?

Why did Tostig fight against his brother Harold?
Tostig was Earl of Northumbria. In 1065 the Northumbrians accused Tostig of murder and misrule and staged a rebellion. Instead of siding with Tostig, Harold supported the rebels, threw Tostig out of England and made Morcar Earl of Northumbria.

Task

Make your own rough copy of this map (left) and add labels at the points numbered 1–3 to explain:

- the movement of Harold's troops
- what happened in each battle.

You can add labels 4 and 5 using the next two pages.

Meanwhile in Normandy

William was furious at the news that Harold had been crowned king: was Harold's oath worthless? The Normans believed that Harold should have guarded the throne for William. In a clever move, William sent the Norman monk Lanfranc to Rome to get the support of Pope Alexander II for a holy war against Harold. Alexander gave his blessing and sent William a banner to carry into battle. This was a boost to William's campaign. He could claim God was on his side.

William was ready with his ships. All he needed now was a favourable wind to take them across the Channel. And on 28 September, with Harold's weary army still marching south, the wind came. William crossed the English Channel and landed without opposition at Pevensey. His army immediately prepared for the hoped-for battle with Harold. They wanted a quick battle. They had little food for a long wait in enemy territory.

Source ❺

William's preparations for invasion as recorded in the Bayeux Tapestry. ❓ *Do the preparations look careful or rushed to you? Give reasons.*

Harold arrives

Harold's army marched 260 miles south to meet the Norman threat. Many of his best soldiers had been killed or wounded at Stamford Bridge and Edwin and Morcar could not offer immediate support. Harold was forced to recruit new soldiers as he made his way south. Many of his army came from Kent and Essex. They started arriving at the south coast on 13 October. The men were tired but their confidence was high after Harold's victory against Hardrada's army. It had shown Harold to be a skilled and brave leader.

On arrival at the south coast, Harold decided where the battle was to take place. He chose Caldbec Hill.

- It was quite heavily forested and not suited for open battle.
- The hill was steep and difficult to attack.

Task

Study the first five bullet points here. Do you think Harold chose a good site? Why? Give reasons.

- The hill gave Harold a clear view of the countryside around.
- To the south of Caldbec Hill was open ground known as Senlac Ridge. The ground sloped down to the position held by the Normans.
- The low land surrounding Caldbec Hill and Senlac Ridge was marshy while Harold's army was on the high, dry land.

When should he fight? This was a hard decision. There were three good reasons to wait.

- Not all of Harold's army had arrived, some were still marching south. On the night of 13 October he only had an army of around 7,500 men. This was the same as the Normans but if he waited, he would have a much larger army.
- William had already been in England for two weeks. His army was rested and well fed – they had taken as much as they could from the surrounding area. However their food might soon run out.
- William's army consisted of three groups: Bretons led by Alan Fergant; Flemish troops led by Eustace of Boulogne; and Normans. If they were forced to wait for action, divisions might appear.

But Harold did not wait; he ordered that his troops be ready for battle the next day. Why did he do this?

- Maybe he thought the Normans would not wait so he wanted to be ready.
- It might be that Harold knew William's troops were spreading terror amongst the local people with their looting and that he wanted to do something about it straight away.
- It is possible that Harold thought, if he waited, some of his own troops might lose heart or desert.
- Harold might have been very confident that, after defeating Hardrada's army, he could defeat William's forces with some ease.

> **Did you know?**
>
> William liked a good battle. He was just 19 when he took part in his first battle at Val-es-Dunes in 1047. According to one chronicler of the time he 'hurled himself at his enemies and terrified them with slaughter'.

Night fell. The Normans were camped 16 miles away near Hastings, with Harold's army camped on Caldbec Hill. The meeting point for Harold's troops was the Old Hoare Apple Tree. Few soldiers slept much. Instead they spent their time preparing themselves for the battle ahead. Prayers were said and weapons sharpened.

Before dawn, William's troops began marching towards the battlefield.

William's army was well disciplined. The march from Hastings to the battlefield would not have taken more than a few hours. However, the approach to Caldbec Hill was quite tricky: there were two streams and plenty of marshy ground to cross. For soldiers weighed down by armour and weapons, these were not easy obstacles to overcome. However, they managed it with little fuss and approached the battlefield in good order.

Source 6

The battle line-up

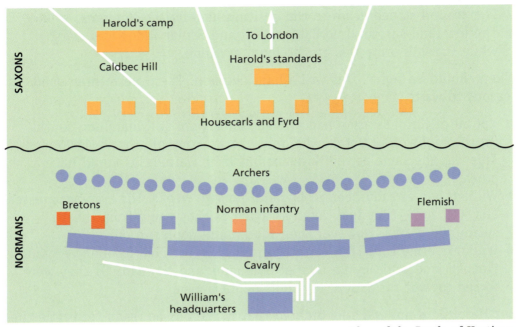

Plan of the Battle of Hastings.

As the sun rose on the battlefield, the armies moved into position (see Source 6).

William placed his Norman foot soldiers in the middle of his army. There were archers at the front and CAVALRY to the rear.

As the Normans came into view, Harold moved his troops down Caldbec Hill and settled about 250 yards away from William's army. Harold put his best troops, the housecarls, in the front row of the Saxon army. They were responsible for forming a shield wall to give protection against the Norman arrows. Behind them were the foot soldiers known as the fyrd. Harold took up his position to the rear. The Saxons did not use archers.

The troops stared at each other across the battlefield. They shouted rude things at each other and chanted like a crowd at a football match. The Saxons shouted 'ut, ut, ut' which meant 'out, out, out'. The battle was about to begin.

The Normans attack

Suddenly a young man called Taillefer broke from the French ranks. He charged up the hill to the Saxon lines. The Saxon housecarls chopped him down. The battle had begun. The Normans fired their arrows into the Saxon ranks but the housecarls used their shields effectively and few were killed. Soon the Normans ran out of arrows and their archers were not equipped to fight hand to hand with the Saxon housecarls. First advantage was with Harold.

The Saxons have the upper hand

The Saxons now attacked. Harold's soldiers threw anything that they could find including rocks and stones on the soldiers below. William ordered his cavalry to counter-attack. The Norman cavalry charged up the hill towards the shield wall. As they neared the Saxon lines they threw their spears then turned and returned to their lines. However, they too failed to make much of an impression:

Did you know?

Taillefer was a minstel. He led the Norman troops in songs such as the popular *Song Of Roland*.

Did you know?

William is known to history as William the Conqueror because he conquered England. Because his mother wasn't married to his father when he was born he was known at the time by the less appealing name of William the Bastard.

- Many housecarls used heavy axes with which they cut down the Norman horses and their riders.
- The Norman cavalry had to ride up the steep hill which slowed them down.

There was no doubt about it; the Saxons really did have the upper hand. By midday, the Bretons on the right of William's line were in retreat and some of his soldiers began to panic. As the Saxons chased the Bretons down the hill the rumour spread that William had been killed. William had to do something – quickly.

William is alive!

William took off his helmet and rode along the Norman lines to prove that he was still alive. This calmed the nerves of many of his troops. At around that time, some of the Norman cavalry led by Odo went to the aid of the Bretons. The Saxon troops who had chased the Bretons down the hill were now stranded. It was too muddy for them to return to their ranks and they were cut down by the Normans on horseback. Harold could have ordered a full attack but he did not do so. At this point in the battle, Harold's brothers Gyrth and Leofwine were killed, possibly by Odo's cavalry.

'Half time'

The Norman attacks had not succeeded but nor had the Saxons pressed home their advantage. Around 2 p.m. the battle paused. Both sides reviewed their situation.

- To win a battle like this you had to kill the enemy's leader. This was a battle about who should be king. If you got rid of the other claimant you had won.
- Some Saxons from Harold's right flank had been lost but otherwise his troops were in good shape. They had a strong position. They could hold out until the end of the day.
- William's archers had run out of arrows, the hill had proved too steep for his cavalry. He needed the Saxons to come and fight in his ground.

What should William or Harold do next?

A cunning plan

William came up with a cunning plan. He thought about what had happened in the morning when the Bretons ran away. The Saxons had lost their discipline and had chased the Bretons down the hill. Stranded, they became an easy target for the Norman cavalry. William's plan was to trick the Saxons into thinking that the Normans were running away, thereby drawing them into battle at the bottom of the hill. He issued a new set of orders to the cavalry telling them of the plan.

Did you know?

William had a terrible temper. During the siege of the French town of Alençon, the defenders were very rude about the fact that William's mother had been born a peasant. He was not happy. When he took the town he ordered 32 of the leading citizens to have their hands chopped off.

The Norman foot soldiers and cavalry were ordered forward. The cavalry charged up the hill, fought with the Saxons and then turned, pretending that they were running away. The Saxon army fell for the trick; housecarls and fyrd breaking ranks to chase the Normans down the hill. A number of reports from the battle suggested that this happened twice. It is not certain whether Harold gave an order for his soldiers to chase the French or if they acted against his orders. Whether he ordered it or not, Harold now had good reason to be very worried.

Source 7

The Bayeux Tapestry shows Harold's death. The Latin inscription says 'King Harold is killed'. ❓ *Which of the two soldiers do you think is supposed to be Harold? The one on the left or the one on the right or both?*

Harold dies

The battle was now opening up. The Norman archers were able to pick up a number of their used arrows and began firing them into the Saxon lines. With the housecarls engaged in hand-to-hand fighting, the shield wall had gone. The arrows now caused many more casualties. This was the crucial turning point of the battle. Harold had remained at the top of the hill, surrounded by his housecarl bodyguard. However, even they were unable to prevent a stray arrow hitting the king. The Bayeux Tapestry appears to show Harold being hit in the eye but that is not definitely what happened. What is sure is that news of Harold's death spread quickly amongst the ranks of the Saxon army.

Source 8

From the Bayeux Tapestry. ❓ *From what you know about the battle, write a caption to explain what you think it shows here. If you can read Latin, try to translate the inscription.*

William wins

Sensing victory, William ordered his foot soldiers forward. Many Saxons soldiers bravely fought on but some began to flee into the forests that surrounded the battlefield. A number of the Norman cavalry chased the Saxons into the forest although this was a dangerous thing to do. Some were ambushed by the Saxons and were killed. But this would not change the course of the battle. The housecarls fought to the end but were killed to the last man. A Norman knight rode up to Harold's body and drove his sword into his heart. Harold had been killed. His banner showing a red dragon was in William's possession. The Normans had won.

Source exercise

Questions

1 Look at **Source A**. Why did William have an advantage in the battle?
2 Look at **Source B**. What words show that the writer did not think much of the Anglo-Saxons?
3 Why do you think that the two sources give different accounts of the battle?

Source Ⓐ

King Harold assembled a large army but he was taken by surprise by William and the Normans before he was fully ready. But the King nevertheless fought hard against William, with the men who were willing to support him, and there were heavy casualties on both sides. There King Harold was killed and Earl Leofwine his brother, and Earl Gyrth his brother, and many good men, and the French were masters of the battlefield.

Adapted from the Anglo-Saxon Chronicle *of 1066.*

Source Ⓑ

Harold's large army were ready and lined up in close formation. Realising that they could not attack such an army without taking big losses, the Normans and their allies pretended to run away. The barbarians … thinking that they were winning, shouted with triumph … and chased the Normans who they thought were running away. But the Normans suddenly turned their horses round, surrounded Harold's men and cut them all down so that not one was left alive. The Normans played this trick twice with great success.

Adapted from Gesta Willelmi *by William of Poitiers. He was one of King William's priests.*

Summary task

1 Using all the information in the last four pages, copy and complete a diagram like this. Add at least one point to each arm.

William's army was well prepared — **WHY DID WILLIAM WIN?** — William was a skilful leader

William was lucky — Harold made mistakes

2 Once you have completed your diagram, highlight what you think is the most important reason that William won and write some sentences to explain why this was so important.

1.3 How did William gain control of England, 1066–87?

William was crowned King of England on Christmas Day 1066 in Westminster Abbey. London and the south east of England had surrendered to the new king but much of the rest of England lay out of his control. William's main problems were how to **keep** control of what he had and how to **gain** control of the rest of England.

1 Castles

Castles were William's main weapon in seizing control of England. They had an obvious function – to house Norman soldiers and knights – but castles were also meant to frighten the local population. They became a symbol of Norman military power and control. They reminded people that the Normans were in England to stay.

William ordered that castles be built in London, Hereford and Winchester to remind the 'rich, untrustworthy and bold' Saxon citizens that the Normans were now in charge.

The Normans usually built their castles in important places, for example on high ground dominating a town, at the mouth or crossing point of a river, or at an important road junction. Although the first castles were made out of wood and earth, they towered over other buildings around them.

Source ❾

The White Tower at the Tower of London.

Source check

The Norman writer William of Poitiers wrote that castles in London were built 'against the fickleness of the vast and fierce populace'.

- The motte of the castle was a hill on which was placed a fort known as a keep. The keep also served as living quarters. Initially the Normans built the keep out of wood but soon changed to using stone, which was easier to defend. The most famous Norman stone keep is the White Tower at the Tower of London (Source 9).
- Below the motte was a compound called a bailey, with living quarters, animals and even a church. The bailey was often surrounded by a moat or ditch and was also difficult to attack.
- All around both motte and bailey was a strong wall with lookout towers. Again, stone quickly replaced wood.
- Within the motte and bailey could be found all that was needed to survive a siege including a water supply and food reserves.

Source ⑩

What ... ?

MOTTE
A mound or hill.
BAILEY
A compound.
KEEP
A strong and central tower of a castle.

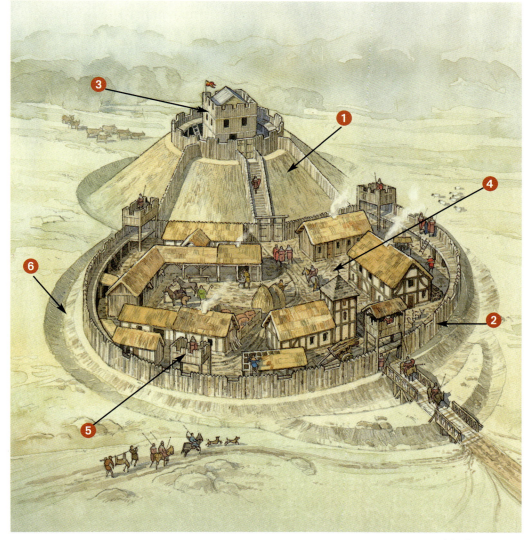

A motte and bailey castle.

Task
Use the text on this page to name correctly the features numbered on Source 10.

2 Land

William knew that Norman rule would be fully more secure when the vast majority of land was in Norman hands. Many Normans had supported William's campaign in 1066 and expected to be rewarded with land.

William immediately gave to his closest friends and followers the land taken from the families of the Saxon leaders who had died at Hastings.

- In 1067 William handed Harold's land to one of his closest and most loyal friends, William fitz Osbern.
- The lands of Harold's brothers Gyrth and Leofwine were given to Ralph the Staller and William's own brother Bishop Odo.

However, at this stage at least, William did not want to upset the remaining living Saxon earls and he did not take the lands of Edwin, Morcar and Waltheof. William was aware that rebellion might break out at any point.

There was an uprising against the Normans in Devon and Cornwall but this was crushed by a Norman army in early 1068. In response William took more land from the Saxons and gave it to Norman families.

This set a pattern that was to continue throughout William's reign.

3 Violent suppression

In the summer of 1068, William and a large army went north. Saxon lords Edwin, Earl of Mercia and Morcar, Earl of Northumbria were resisting the Normans. William ordered castles to be built at Warwick, Nottingham and then at York. As he returned to London for the winter, William ordered more castles to be built in Lincoln, Huntington and Cambridge. The arrival of William at York and the construction of castles was a clear sign to the Saxon nobles in the north that Norman rule was permanent. They had a choice, to fight against it or accept it; many chose to fight.

William had left a small army, led by Robert Comin, in the north. In January 1069 this Norman army was attacked in Durham and massacred. The Saxons were becoming more confident. Very soon after, one of the recently built Norman castles at York was destroyed. Although York was soon brought back under Norman control, a far greater danger than a few rebellious Saxons loomed into view. A large army led by King Swein of Denmark had set sail, aiming to conquer England.

Rebellions

Once the Danish army had landed in the north of England in September 1069, the last great Saxon earls rallied to Swein's cause: Waltheof of the East Midlands, Edwin of Mercia and Morcar of Northumbria. They were not enthusiastic about Swein's claim to the throne but felt that their power was under threat from Norman rule and saw Swein as their chance to drive back the Normans. York was again attacked and this time burned to the ground. The Norman garrison was butchered. Rebellion then broke out in the west. A Saxon army invaded from the English/Welsh border area known as the Marches. William's rule was seriously threatened. His response was rapid and ruthless.

● William fitz Osbern led a Norman army down to the West Country where it crushed the Saxon rebels outside Exeter.
● Another Saxon force from the west was defeated at Stafford by an army led by William himself.
● The King then successfully bribed Swein's brother to withdraw from York, and recaptured the burned city. Straight away, in December 1069, William repaired York's two castles and sent his soldiers out into the countryside to ensure that all resistance was crushed.

The Harrying of the North, 1069

William was determined that he would not have to face such an uprising again. It was time to teach the Saxons a lesson. What followed, the so-called 'HARRYING of the North', was to prove to be a turning point in the Norman conquest of England. Across the north of England, property and land was burned or destroyed and all food seized. As a result, thousands of Saxons died of starvation. The cruel plan worked: Saxon resistance was all but crushed; opponents such as Waltheof surrendered and begged for mercy.

Source ⑪

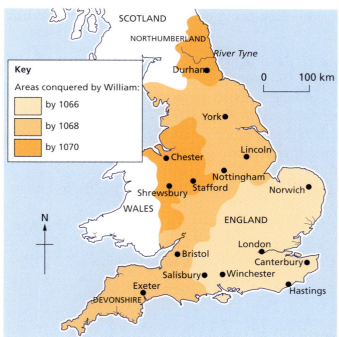

A map showing the Norman conquest of England. ❓ *Find where you live, or where your school is, on this map. When, if ever, was your area conquered by William?*

Task

Below is an account from the *Anglo-Saxon Chronicle* of the 'Harrying of the North'. Read it carefully, then answer the questions.

And there came to meet them Prince Edgar and Earl Waltheof and Maerleswegen and Gospatric with the Northumbrians and all the people riding and marching with an immense army rejoicing exceedingly and so they all went resolutely to York and stormed and razed the castle and captured an incalculable treasure in it and killed many hundreds of Frenchmen and took many with them to the ships ... When the King found out about this he went northwards with all his army ... and utterly ravaged and laid waste that shire.

a) What impression does the author give about the mood of the Saxons and the Danes?
b) What was the response of King William to the uprising?
c) Which side do you think that the writer favours? Explain your answer fully.

The Saxons' last stand

At the end of 1069, William appointed the warrior priest Thurold of Fecamp to be Abbot of Peterborough. The locals, led by the Saxon Hereward the Wake, invited the Danes led by King Swein to protect them. They asked the wrong people for help! The Danes stripped Peterborough of its wealth before returning home to Denmark much the richer.

Hereward led his followers into the fens and set up a fortified camp on the Isle of Ely. There he was joined by Morcar. This was to be the Saxons' last stand. The only way to get to Ely was using secret paths through the fens that were only known to the Saxons. Whilst the people of Ely supported Hereward, the monks in the cathedral did not and they told the Normans how to cross the fens. In 1071 the Saxons were forced to surrender to the Normans although Hereward managed to escape, never to be heard of again.

4 The Feudal System

William was now very much in control. The final stage in the destruction of the power of the Saxon nobility began. With Edwin dead and Morcar in exile in Normandy, William set about handing out all of the rest of the Saxon lands. He completed this exercise as part of the creation of the FEUDAL System.

The aim behind the Feudal System was that every group in society owed military service. In that way the King could quickly raise an army to crush any revolts.

- **The King** In theory, all of England belonged to the King. In practice, William kept about a sixth of the land.
- **Barons** The great Saxon earldoms such as Wessex, Mercia and Northumbria were broken up, because the holders of these positions had proved to be too powerful. Instead, much of England was divided among around 170 Norman barons who gave an oath of military service and paid HOMAGE to the King.
- **Knights** The barons gave smaller amounts of lands to knights in return for a promise of military service.
- **Villeins** The knights' lands were farmed by peasants called villeins who could also be called up for military service if need be.
- **Serfs** At the bottom of the pile were the serfs who were owned by the knights.

More castles

A network of more castles was built to support the Feudal System. As William appointed new regional rulers, so castles such as Durham Castle were built. Such castles acted as places to rule from as well as serving a military purpose. Castles were also built to protect the borders of William's lands in places such as Chester, to prevent attacks from Wales, and Newcastle-upon-Tyne, to prevent attacks from Scotland.

What … ?

FENS
Wet marshlands in the east of England. They have now been drained but in the eleventh century you needed a boat and local knowledge to get around.

Source ⑫

THE KING

THE BARONS
(NOBLES)

THE KNIGHTS

THE VILLEINS

THE SERFS

The Feudal System. There were many more people on the bottom rung than this picture can show. The vast majority of people in England were villeins or serfs.

5 The Church

For a couple of years after 1066, William allowed the Saxon leaders of the English Church to continue their work. Stigand, who had been a friend of the Godwin family, was allowed to remain as Archbishop of Canterbury. But after the events of 1069 William mistrusted all Saxon leaders. William realised that his control of the Church was crucial if he was to maintain control of the country.

- In 1070 he sacked Stigand, replacing him with the Norman bishop Lanfranc.
- The leading Saxon monks and abbots were thrown out of their jobs and the monasteries were looted of their Saxon treasure.
- Norman bishops were appointed to York, Rochester and Winchester.

With Lanfranc in charge, the Church in England was brought under closer control of the King. During the reigns of Edward and Harold, it had been very much under the control of the Pope. Under Lanfranc:

- New monasteries and church schools were set up.
- The King's courts developed independently of Church control.

William and Pope Gregory

In 1066 William had fought under the banner of Pope Alexander II but he was not prepared to allow any Pope great influence in the running of England. In particular he did not want the Pope to appoint bishops. In 1073 a new Pope, Gregory VII, was chosen. Gregory was a great reformer who hated the way important jobs in the Church were given out by political leaders to people who did not have the best interests of the Church at heart.

In 1075 Gregory demanded that William swear him an oath of fealty (loyalty) as King of England but William refused.

Instead William insisted that he, not the Pope, appointed bishops and abbots. He also insisted that no letters from the Pope could be read out in English churches without his permission.

> **Did you know?**
>
> A letter from the Pope was called a Papal Bull.

Source 🔵

Pope Gregory VII in 1073. He was probably the single most powerful person in Europe. ❓ *Explain how the engraver has made him look important.*

6 Local administration

Some of William's measures to control England were new ones. Castles were new. The Feudal System was new. Some of his measures were not new. He simply took over control of the structures that already existed. How he dealt with the Church is one example; another is local administration. William kept the main features of Anglo-Saxon government and administration but used them to his own advantage.

> **Did you know?**
>
> The Normans also built many new churches and cathedrals. You will find out more about these in Section 2.

What ... ?

DANEGELD

A tax originally raised by Alfred the Great to pay off Danish invaders. The problem was that, because the Danes were being given money for going away, they kept on coming back. King Cnut was Danish himself so he did not need to raise taxes to pay himself to go away. He raised Danegeld but used the money for improving defences.

- England continued to be governed in districts known as 'hundreds'.
- England was an important source of cash for William. He needed money to pay his large armies in Normandy and England. The Saxon taxation and coinage system worked well. An example was the raising of a tax known as Danegeld which had been raised in England for a number of years. William continued this method of raising money.
- The system of sheriffs stayed as the important link between local and national government.
- The great city of London, so important to the wealth of England, was granted a Charter by William that allowed it to keep all of its old privileges.
- The Anglo-Saxon kings had consulted their nobles at a meeting of the Witan. William set up the equivalent Great Council which the barons had to attend. All the important archbishops and bishops were required to sit on the Great Council.

Minor problems!

It will be clear that England was, by the early 1070s, very much under William's control. He spent less and less time in England: only a quarter of his time in the end, although there were still threats to his control. Here are some examples.

Scotland: 1072

By the 1070s the only remaining serious claimant to the English throne was a great nephew of Edward the Confessor, Edgar the Aethling. In 1072, King Malcolm of Scotland married Edgar's sister Margaret. William realised that Malcolm might use his forces to back Edgar's claim to the throne. He led his armies north in a show of strength. The two kings met at Abernethy and, amongst other things, Malcolm agreed to expel Edgar from Scotland.

Roger of Hereford: 1075

The greatest threat to William's control of England in the later years of his reign came not from the Saxons but from the next generation of Normans. In 1075, one of William fitz Osbern's sons, Earl Roger of Hereford, rebelled in protest about the loss of rights he felt were due to him as a leading noble in the country. In particular, he felt that he did not have the same power as his father. Roger was supported in his rebellion by Saxon Earl Waltheof amongst others. William had little difficulty putting down the rebellion. Roger was tried for treason under Norman law and imprisoned; Waltheof was tried for treason under English law and beheaded in 1076.

Family problems

William also had trouble from his family.

- One of his sons, Robert Curthose, felt that he had not enough power. Their quarrel ended in battle in Normandy in 1079 which Robert won (with the help of King Philip of France).
- Another member of William's family to cause him trouble was his half-brother Odo. As Earl of Kent and Bishop of Bayeux, Odo had become a very wealthy man, because he was very CORRUPT. Odo had ambitions to become the next Pope and, by 1082, had spent a fortune on a palace in Rome. Most of the money had been raised in England. William disapproved of Odo's dishonesty and corruption and had him arrested.

Domesday Book

The never-ending warfare was very expensive. In 1085 the Vikings led by a new King Cnut (son of Swein) again threatened invasion. This was a more serious threat than William had faced for at least ten years. He returned to England determined to find out how much military service and how much taxation money he could raise. The survey on military service is lost but the survey on landowning, property and tax, later known as the Domesday Book, survived.

Source 14

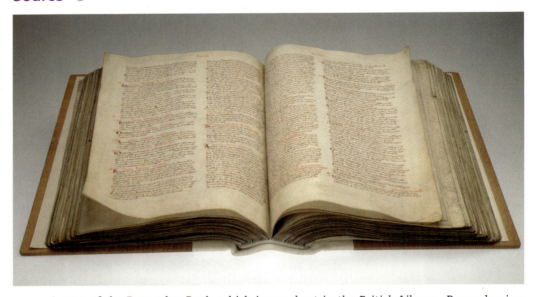

A copy of the Domesday Book, which is now kept in the British Library. Domesday is a nickname. William never called it that. ❓ *Can you think of reasons why this survey might have got the name Domesday? If you are stuck, look at www.domesdaybook.co.uk and go to the FAQ page.*

Did you know?

William had grown fat in middle age. Indeed he was so fat that he did not fit into his coffin. When his servants tried to squeeze his body into the coffin at the funeral, the corpse burst open. The smell was so terrible that the priests who were conducting the funeral ran off. Not a good ending.

The idea of undertaking such a survey was not new. What was different was its size. Royal officials travelled the land collecting information on the size, resources and present and past ownership of every HIDE of land. London was not included because of its complexity.

The book, arranged by county, was presented to William at Salisbury on 1 August 1086. It was an excellent example of William's efficiency as a ruler, as well as one of the most useful sources for historians studying the Middle Ages.

However William is never likely to be remembered primarily as an efficient administrator. His fame is as a powerful and ruthless conqueror.

William died in 1087. He was on yet another military campaign in France and was riding through a burning town. His horse was startled by a falling timber and reared up. William was thrown forward onto the pommel of his saddle which ruptured his kidney. He died several days later of internal bleeding. It was a violent end to a violent life.

Summary task

1 How did William maintain control?
Here are a number of reasons why William maintained control of England 1066–87.

- He built castles.

- He controlled the Church.

- The Saxon opposition was weak.

- He used extreme force.

- He did the Domesday survey.

- He kept some Saxon customs.

- He introduced the Feudal System.

For each one, give an example and explain in your own words **how** this helped William.

2 Working in a small group, choose three reasons from question 1 that you think are more important than the others. Write down your three choices and explain why you chose them.

Filling in the gaps: William II and Henry I

Common Entrance History includes all the monarchs from 1066–1500 but you don't need to know about all of them in the same depth. We have chosen eight kings for the depth studies. That will provide you with all you need to answer Common Entrance questions. Then between the units, this feature – Filling in the gaps – summarises key information about what happened between the depth study kings. You don't need to learn this. But it should help you understand the next unit better if you read it.

William Rufus (1087–1100)

When William the Conqueror died his eldest son Robert was away on Crusade, so his second son William, known as Rufus, became King of England. William II was a bad-tempered and violent man. He faced rebellions from his barons and even his own brother Robert tried to oust him when he came back from Crusade. William had no respect for the Church and in 1097 the Archbishop of Canterbury, Anselm of Bec, was so fed up with William's bullying that he went to France. William Rufus was killed in an apparent hunting accident by a man called Walter Tirel who aimed an arrow at a stag, missed the stag, and pierced the king in the chest. Whether this was an accident or murder is unknown to this day.

Source check

According to William of Malmesbury, William Rufus was:

... thickset and muscular with a protruding belly; a dandy dressed in the height of fashion, however outrageous, he wore his blond hair long, parted in the centre and off the face so that his forehead was bare; and in his red, choleric face were eyes of changeable colour, speckled with flecks of light.

Henry I (1100–35)

William Rufus was succeeded by his younger brother Henry, who was better educated and cleverer. Straight away he made peace with the Church, invited Anselm back to England and issued a Charter of Liberties that promised fair rule. When threatened by his elder brother Robert, Henry invaded Normandy, defeated his brother's army in 1106 and kept him in prison until he died. Henry became Duke of Normandy as well as King of England.

By the summer of 1120, Henry I had every reason to be pleased with himself. He had been ruling England for twenty years. No one questioned his rule. He had worked with the powerful barons and with the Church to govern sternly but well. During his reign, England stayed peaceful and prospered.

What is more he had an heir: a son, William, to be king when he died. Henry knew that nothing weakened a country more than disputes about who should be king.

Everything in England seemed safe and secure. What could possibly go wrong? And then disaster struck.

What is this all about?

Civil War – a bloody one! Between 1139 and 1153, according to the chroniclers, 'All England was in flames' and 'Christ and his angels slept'. It was a dark and desperate time. In this short unit you will examine the reasons for this civil war. Was it all because the barons would not accept a woman to rule England?

Did you know?

Chroniclers wrote that, after hearing about the death of his son, Henry I did not laugh again for the rest of his life.

How a shipwreck changed history

Source ❶

In November 1120 the *White Ship* was making a routine crossing from Normandy to England. In 1106 Henry I had conquered Normandy and there was a lot of traffic between the two countries. There was nothing special about this particular trip, except that on board was William, Henry's only legitimate son. He was part of a large group of about 300 nobles, their wives and sons. Chroniclers say that, because the trip to Normandy had been successful, most people on board were very drunk and persuaded the captain to race the *White Ship* against some smaller ships to see who would reach England first. The sea was calm and the moon was bright. There was no reason to suppose that disaster lay minutes away. No one knows why (maybe the crew were drunk, too) but the *White Ship* hit rocks and sank very quickly. Everyone on board was drowned except one man. And that man was **not** Henry's son!

What ... ?

A CHRONICLER

Someone, usually a monk, who wrote down what he thought were the most important events. The accounts were called chronicles. Some, like the *Anglo-Saxon Chronicle* were written over hundreds of years by many different monks. Others were shorter and written by just one person.

Medieval manuscript showing the sinking of the White Ship and Henry above it, looking sad.

Task

Write a longer caption for Source 1 explaining why the sinking of the White Ship was such a disaster for Henry I. Read the information on page 28 before you start.

What ... ?

LEGITIMATE

Means 'legal'. A king's legitimate children were his children by the woman he was married to. Illegitimate children were his children born to someone he was not married to. Only legitimate children were allowable as heirs.

Henry's problem

Henry was left with a huge problem. He needed to be certain that, when he died, there would be a peaceful handover to his successor. But who was this to be? He had more than 20 illegitimate children but now his only legitimate heir was his daughter Matilda. In 1120 she was a young woman of eighteen, married to the Holy Roman Emperor who was a powerful European ruler. Matilda was a stranger to England, as she had been sent abroad when she was eight years old so that she could be trained in the language and customs of her new home. In 1120 it looked as though Matilda and her German husband would rule England and Normandy after Henry's death. Henry didn't really believe that the powerful English barons would accept a woman as monarch, especially a woman who was thought of as a foreigner.

Why wouldn't the barons accept a woman?

Legally, there was no reason why a woman couldn't rule medieval England as its queen. The problem lay in what medieval people expected of a monarch and in what a monarch had to do to keep the kingdom secure and prosperous. A medieval monarch had to be physically strong enough to travel around the kingdom on horseback, administering justice and quelling rebellions; a monarch had to lead armies into battle; a monarch had to be strong enough to control and gain the respect of powerful barons. For all these reasons, most medieval people believed women could not be monarchs.

Henry's solutions

Desperate for an heir, Henry tried three approaches to the problem:

- His first idea was to produce more sons himself. His wife had died in 1118 and so, three months after William's death in 1120, Henry married again. His second wife was a young woman, Adela of Louvain. But no child was born to them.
- His second idea was to persuade the barons to accept Matilda. In 1125, Matilda's husband died. So she came back to her father's court. Time was running out for Henry. In 1127 he made all his barons swear they would support Matilda as their queen when he died.
- His third idea was to get some grandsons. In 1128, Henry married Matilda to Geoffrey Plantagenet, Count of Anjou. They had three sons (Henry, Geoffrey and William) and so the SUCCESSION seemed secure.

Task

Read about Henry's solutions. Was there anything else he could have done?

However, everything was not as happy as it might have been. Although Henry regarded Matilda, her husband and their children as his heirs, he refused to allow them any sort of power base in England or Normandy. This led to furious quarrels between Matilda and her father. Those barons who were completely loyal to Henry felt they had to oppose Matilda. This was not good news for her, and built up trouble for the years ahead.

Civil war!

King Henry I died on 1 December 1135. Would all the barons keep their promises to Henry and support Matilda as queen? Certainly not! Stephen, Matilda's cousin and the richest baron in England, was on the spot and moved quickly. On 22 December he had himself crowned King of England and then recognised as Duke of Normandy. Many great barons rallied round him. A furious Matilda, stuck hundreds of miles away in Anjou, decided to fight. She concentrated first on Normandy, which her armies invaded in 1136, 1137 and 1138. By 1139 she was ready to take on England.

A bloody civil war broke out. Law and order collapsed. Barons swapped sides and built castles to defend their lands. A chronicler wrote that 'All England was in flames'.

Source ❷

This picture of the Empress Matilda comes from a medieval manuscript. ❓ *What do you think she is holding in her hand?*

— What … ? —

CIVIL WAR
A war between citizens of the same country. It could be a war between barons and monarch, between two powerful families fighting for power or, as happened in England in the seventeenth century, between supporters of the King and supporters of Parliament.

Source ❸

King Stephen is supposed to have been cross-eyed.

31

Matilda had plenty of support in the West Country and made her base in Gloucester. But Stephen controlled London and the wealthier part of what he thought of as his kingdom. Even so, Matilda and her armies advanced steadily eastwards. They gained a tremendous advantage when they defeated Stephen's forces at the Battle of Lincoln in 1141 and captured Stephen himself. At this point many of Stephen's supporters, including his brother, were prepared to abandon him and support Matilda as Lady of England and Normandy. Much encouraged, Matilda advanced on London. A splendid welcome with feasting and the ringing of church bells, to be followed by her coronation, was waiting for her. She then made a major mistake. She angrily turned down the citizens' request to have their taxes reduced, and at a stroke turned the Londoners against her. On 24 June as she prepared to enter the city in triumph, the bells rang out to call the citizens to arms and London's gates were slammed shut against her. The civil war broke out all over again.

In 1153, they finally reached a settlement. The deaths of his wife and his eldest son had depressed Stephen so much that he was prepared to give up. Matilda realised that she really could only ever hope to control the West Country and that she would never be accepted as Queen of England, and was ready to make peace too. So by the Treaty of Winchester (1153) Stephen and Matilda agreed that Stephen should stay on as King of England for the rest of his life. But when he died, Matilda's eldest son Henry would succeed to the throne.

Matilda retired to Normandy. Stephen lived for eleven more months. After fourteen years of civil war, no one was going to argue about Henry's right to succeed. In December 1154, aged 21, he was crowned King Henry II in Westminster Abbey and began his rule in peace.

Did you know?

King Henry II, who reigned after King Stephen, was the first of a long line of *Plantagenet* kings of England. Their name comes from the yellow broom flower (in Latin, *planta genista*) which was the badge of Henry II's father (Matilda's second husband), Geoffrey of Anjou.

Summary task

Read these descriptions of Stephen and Matilda, both written by people living at the time.

A Matilda sent for the richest men in the kingdom and demanded from them a huge sum of money. She demanded, not with gentleness, but with an air of authority. The men complained that they had no money left because of the war. At this, Matilda, with a grim look, her forehead wrinkled into a frown, every trace of a woman's gentleness removed from her face, blazed into unbearable fury.

B When some people saw that King Stephen was a good-humoured, kindly and easy-going man they committed all manner of horrible crimes. And so it lasted for nineteen years while Stephen was King, till the land was all undone and darkened with such deeds, and men said openly that Christ and his angels slept.

Using the evidence of these two sources, explain whether or not you think Matilda would have made a better monarch than Stephen.

Hint: Look back at the good and bad qualities for a monarch you considered on page 4. Make sure you refer to these qualities in your answer.

Henry II

Henry II reigned from 1154 to 1189. He married Eleanor of Aquitaine, which brought him plenty of French territory to add to his empire.

Henry II was a thick-built man, highly educated but with a fierce temper as you will see in his dealings with Thomas Becket (see pages 96–99). He had a number of sons, his favourite being John. However, his sons rebelled against him towards the end of his reign which made him even angrier. But to remember Henry purely as a monarch with a very bad temper is unfair on him.

- He set up a Great Council and governed England well. Especially important were the improvements he made in the running of the legal system and taxation.
- Trade with Germany and Italy flourished, especially the wool trade.
- There was only one revolt – in 1173–74 – and that was easily crushed.
- He introduced strong English rule in Ireland in 1172 and made the Welsh recognise the power of the English Crown.

This statue of Richard I stands outside the Houses of Parliament in London.

Richard I (Richard the Lionheart)

When Henry died he was succeeded by his son Richard. King Richard was a great soldier who was heavily involved in the religious wars between Christians and Muslims known as the Crusades. Indeed Richard led the Third Crusade. You can find out more on pages 128–29. (See also the practice source exercise on page 180.) He was away from England for most of his reign, in fact he only visited England twice. Both times he came simply to raise more money for his wars abroad, especially the Crusades and wars against Phillip II of France.

When Richard was away, the country was run well by Hubert Walter who was, amongst other things, Archbishop of Canterbury. Knights living in the country were given greater responsibility in day-to-day government.

In 1192 Richard was returning from the Crusades when he was taken prisoner by one of his enemies, Duke Leopold of Austria. For two years he was kept prisoner until he bought his release in 1194 using £100,000 of tax money raised in England. He died in 1199 leaving England a much poorer country.

His brother John succeeded him. You are going to examine John's reign in detail in the next unit.

What is this all about?

From Units 1 and 2 it will be clear to you that for a king to control England he needed the support of his barons. That is how William I got control – he gave them land in return for their armies and loyalty. From then on being a strong king meant having a good relationship with your barons. They ran the country for you. They even raised money for you.

In this unit you will study two kings who quarrelled with the barons – John and Henry III. They both ended up waging civil war against them. But they also made some other mistakes. Your job will be to work out what they got wrong and why. At the end you will decide which of the two made the biggest mistakes.

Source ❶

The Angevin Empire. ❓ *If you were a king trying to control all the empire, where would be the best place to live?*

3.1 King John

What did John inherit from Richard I?

When John became king he inherited a large empire. His power stretched all the way from the edge of Scotland to the south of France – see Source 1. It included all of England and much of France. It was known as the Angevin Empire. It had fine farming land, important ports and trade routes, flourishing towns and a growing population.

However, it was not automatically his. To take possession of the French part of the Empire lands he had to promise to serve the King of France. And the current King of France and the French barons did not want John as king. They wanted his nephew Arthur.

Back in England, John was better placed. He had the good will of the barons. They all agreed he was the right person to be the next king.

However, John's brother Richard had left some big problems for John to sort out. Richard had spent much of his reign fighting Crusades in the Holy Land. This meant he more or less ignored England – leaving the barons and the Church leaders to run the country for him. He ran up big debts paying for these wars.

What did King John do?

John's first need was to get himself accepted as king by Philip II of France. Luckily his mother, Eleanor of Aquitaine, helped him. She was French and she persuaded Philip that John should be king, not Arthur. In return John pledged loyalty to Philip and agreed to be his vassal – that is, to serve Philip. So in 1200 John took control of his lands in France and the reign had got off to a good start.

Task

Over the next four pages you are going to examine King John's reign in outline. You are going to find out what he did (and why we think he did it) and you are going to examine the results of each of his actions. As you read each section prepare an 'action' card like this:

ACTION

Action: *He agreed to be Philip's vassal*

Reason: *So the French king would accept him as king*

Result: *+ He got his land in France*
– He was under Philip's control

ACTION

He married Isabella of Angoulême

In 1200 John married Isabella of Angoulême. This was a useful move because control of Angoulême would help John to keep a firm grip on his Angevin empire. But it did not work out well.

- A powerful baron called Hugh, Lord of Lusignan, had already been promised that Isabella would be his wife when she came of age. When Hugh heard that John had married her, he was furious.
- Hugh demanded compensation from John. John refused so Hugh complained about John's behaviour to King Philip of France.
- Philip ordered John to appear before a French court to answer for his actions. He had the power to do this because John was his vassal.
- John refused to appear before the court and, in 1202, Philip ordered that John should lose his lands in France.

ACTION

He murdered his nephew Arthur

Philip made John's nephew Arthur Lord of Aquitaine, Maine and Anjou and declared war against John. At first John was the more successful. He even took Arthur prisoner. What happened next did great damage to John's reputation. In 1203 John ordered that Arthur be murdered. Arthur was stabbed to death, a stone was tied to his body and he was thrown into the River Seine. This murder caused widespread disgust among the barons in both France and England. Many French barons became supporters of Philip in his war against John.

35

ACTION

He increased taxes on the barons

Things now went from bad to worse for John. His mother Eleanor of Aquitaine died so he lost control of Aquitaine. King Philip conquered Norway so he lost that region too. John spent most of his reign trying (and mostly failing) to win back these French lands. He had two big problems:

- Normally the barons could be relied on to provide a king with an army but in this case they refused because they did not trust John and the English barons did not think that the French lands were important. Their land was in England. Normandy was nothing to do with them. It was the king's problem.
- If John could not get an army from the barons then he needed to recruit whoever would fight for him. So he recruited mercenaries (soldiers who fight for anyone who pays them). These mercenaries were expensive and they were not really loyal to John. His armies also needed modern weapons.

To pay these mercenaries, and to pay for these weapons, he decided to tax the barons very heavily.

- He used all the feudal powers at his disposal. For example, any baron who did not provide an army had to pay a tax called scutage instead. John demanded scutage from the barons.
- He also increased inheritance tax and tax on the property of widows.
- He imposed huge fines for crimes committed by barons.
- He sold important positions at court to the highest bidder.

Many barons had to borrow money to pay King John. They resented these taxes greatly and they did not trust John to use the money well.

ACTION

He tried to run the country without the barons

The feudal barons were the 165 most powerful barons who owned much of the land in England. They had supported John when he came to the throne in 1199. Instead of appointing these barons to important jobs John chose to ignore their advice and do things his way. He took a personal interest in running the country. Unlike his brother and father (who were hardly ever in England), after he lost Normandy in 1204, John stayed most of the time in England. He was serious about running England well. The problem was that he was held personally responsible for any mistakes.

ACTION

He quarrelled with the Pope

Kings had to work with Church leaders, not against them. In 1207 the job of Archbishop of Canterbury was vacant. The usual pattern was for the king to propose someone and the Pope to approve them. But Pope Innocent III did not like John's candidate and instead appointed Simon Langton. What happened next?

Did you know?

John did not trust the barons. To force them to do what he wanted he took as hostage the sons of the barons that he thought might rebel against him. He treated the family of one baron, William de Braose, particularly badly. John demanded that de Braose pay a very large fine and when he couldn't do so, John sent him into exile and starved his wife and son to death.

Did you know?

King John had a number of nicknames given to him by people at the time. One was 'Lackland' because he was not given land by his father (unlike his brothers). The other was 'Softsword' because his armies were occasionally defeated in battle. The second nickname is a bit harsh because John was really quite a good general.

Source ❷

This medieval painting shows a monk offering John a poisoned chalice, a drink laced with deadly poison. There is no other evidence this ever happened but it shows the bad feeling between John and the Church.

● John was not pleased with the Pope's choice. He confiscated the land of the Archbishop of Canterbury and banished the monks attached to the Cathedral.
● The Pope retaliated in 1208 by imposing an interdict on England. This meant that all the churches had to shut.
● John responded in fury by confiscating the property of any priest who carried out the interdict.
● In 1209 John was excommunicated from the Catholic Church.

What … ?

EXCOMMUNICATION
This was the most serious punishment that any Pope could hand out. If someone was excommunicated it meant that he or she could not go to church and take part in any church services. This would mean that if you died, you would go to hell.

ACTION ➤ *He tried to recapture Normandy*

One of John's driving ambitions was to regain land in France. In 1206 he had one success – he won back Gascony. He was determined to get Normandy as well. In 1214 he gambled. He allied with the Counts of Boulogne and Otto of Brunswick to launch an attack on Poitou to try to win back Normandy. His armies were totally defeated at Bouvines. The result was he lost credibility as an army leader, and most of the taxes he had raised had been wasted.

Task

You should have made at least six action cards by now. There should be one on:

- marrying Isabella
- murdering Arthur
- raising taxes
- choosing officials
- quarrels with the Pope
- attacking Normandy.

Now do some work with them.
a) Lay them out on a sheet in front of you and discuss with a partner how they are connected with each other.
b) Which of these do you think were mistakes? They would be mistakes if they damaged John or damaged England.
c) Of these mistakes, which do you think did the most serious damage to John? Why?
Keep the cards. You will need them later.

What ... ?

MAGNA CARTA
Translated into English means Great Charter.

Magna Carta

John was in a weak position. To him each of his actions so far might have seemed sensible and fair. To others in England they looked like mistakes. They thought that John was either dangerous or incompetent.

Some of the leading barons met to discuss their grievances against John. They were told of a charter dating from the time of Henry I that spelled out the rights and liberties of the barons. They decided they needed something similar – a new charter, agreed by the king – that would secure their rights and would control the king. Some were prepared if necessary to fight against the king to force him to sign it. In 1215 around 40 barons, mainly from the north and west of England and East Anglia, met in Bury St Edmunds. They chose Robert fitz Walter to lead them.

They sent soldiers to occupy London and John was forced to negotiate. On 19 June 1215, at Runnymede near Windsor, Magna Carta was signed. The rebel barons promised to serve John and it seemed that a peaceful solution to the problem had been found.

What did the charter say?

Magna Carta outlined the feudal rights and liberties of the barons and other groups including merchants, knights and clergy.

- It put limits on the taxes such as scutage that the King could raise from the barons.
- Chapter 14 defined the powers of the Great Council. It said that a monarch had to ask the advice of the barons before he could raise taxes. He did not have to get their approval but he had to discuss it.
- The rights of the Church were made clear.
- The liberties enjoyed by London and other towns were guaranteed.
- The courts were to be improved so that everyone had the right to a fair trial.

Source check

Chapter 39 of the charter stated:

No freeman shall be arrested and imprisoned, or disposed, or outlawed, or banished, or in any way molested ... unless by the lawful judgement of his peers and by the law of the land.

How did John react?

Magna Carta did not stay in force for long. John had signed the charter but he did not accept it. He especially hated Chapter 14. After two months John got Pope Innocent III to declare that Magna Carta was against God's will – nothing could limit the power of a monarch appointed by God.

Civil war broke out again. John's experience and skill as a soldier allowed him quickly to defeat the rebels in all parts of the country except London. It looked as if John might be able to crush the rebels entirely.

In desperation, the London rebels offered the throne of England to Louis of France (son of King Philip) in return for help. Louis landed with his armies in England in 1216. Many barons flocked to join him. The tide of the civil war had turned back in favour of the rebel barons.

At this cliff-hanger moment, John died (of natural causes, probably dysentery). One of the most tempestuous and controversial reigns was over. What do you think happened next?

Did you know?

After John's death in 1216, Isabella of Angoulême returned to France and married Hugh of Lusignan. So he got the promised wife in the end!

Representations of Magna Carta

Source ③

A nineteenth-century painting that now hangs in the House of Lords in the British Parliament. The original is enormous – about 5 metres across.

Source ④

A pottery figurine made in the nineteenth century. Images like this would be mass produced and sold to ordinary people to have on the mantelpiece in the living room.

Source ⑤

An illustration from 1864, since used in school textbooks.

Task

Although Magna Carta itself did not solve the problems between John and his barons, some people see its signing as a key point in history when the power of the monarch was brought under control and the rights of ordinary people were recognised for the first time. As a result there have been many different representations of this key moment. Here are three. Compare Sources 3, 4 and 5, then choose one and explain:

a) what impression you get of the event from this image

b) what you learn about people's attitudes to Magna Carta from the context the image was made for.

3.2 Henry III

Source **6**

A portrait of Henry III painted in 1250.

--- **Did you know?** ---

Henry III was a very religious man. He admired Edward the Confessor and took to dressing like him, wearing simple robes instead of grand expensive ones. Even when on his travels he still insisted on hearing Mass three times each day.

--- **Did you know?** ---

At one point in 1250 there were over 800 people working at the Westminster Abbey building site. Henry insisted that the tomb of Edward the Confessor be moved to the centre of the Abbey. In doing so he created the tradition for England's monarchs to be buried in the Abbey.

Imagine someone suggesting to a younger pupil at your school that they become your monarch. It may sound silly for someone so young to become a country's ruler but it happened in the Middle Ages. In 1216, John's son Henry became king of England at the age of nine, although for the first eleven years that he was Henry III, he was told what to do by his guardians William Marshall and then Hubert de Burgh. All the problems left over from John's reign needed solving:

- Their first task was to end the Civil War. They used the iron fist! The rebel barons were (ruthlessly) defeated at Lincoln and a French fleet was destroyed. Louis returned to France.
- The second task was to solve the problems that had led to the Civil War. Here they used the velvet glove! William Marshall reissued Magna Carta. He was lucky in that one of its biggest opponents, Pope Innocent III, had died. Now the charter was discussed and agreed with the barons and approved by the new Pope. It was finally sealed in 1225 at a public ceremony in front of a crowd made up of both former rebel and loyal barons. It was accepted into English law. It was binding on king and barons alike.

Henry III was still only eighteen. Things had started well. This did not last.

Task

As you study Henry's reign you will prepare action cards just as you did for John's reign. Make one card for each of these actions:

- building impressive churches and cathedrals
- appointing Poitevins to top jobs
- trying to win back French lands
- trying to buy the throne of Sicily
- ignoring the provisions of Oxford.

Henry takes charge

From 1227 Henry began to rule in his own right. Like his father he believed that a king's power had been given to him by God. He distrusted the barons and they distrusted him.

Cathedrals

Henry ordered the building of a large number of churches and cathedrals. The most famous work undertaken during his reign was the rebuilding of Westminster Abbey and the Palace of Westminster. The problem was that such building was very expensive and the money for these projects had to be raised through taxes.

Who ... ?

JUSTICIAR
One of the most important officials at court in the Middle Ages. He looked after all of the king's business.

What ... ?

POITEVINS
People from Poitou in west central France. In the fourteenth century the Poitevins were disliked in the rest of France just as much as they were in England. Peter des Rivaux thought so much of himself that he appointed himself sheriff of 21 counties!

What ... ?

MARK
A weight of gold or silver equal to 8 ounces or 226.8 grams. Now you can work out how many kilograms of gold and silver that Henry paid to the Pope and you can understand why the barons were so annoyed!

Foreign influence

Henry appointed a number of non-English advisers and gave top jobs in the Church to foreigners such as the Frenchman Peter des Roches (who was made Bishop of Winchester). In the winter of 1231–32, foreign church tax collectors started to receive anonymous threatening letters. Henry blamed his English justiciar, Hubert de Burgh, for having something to do with the letters and he sacked him.

Henry replaced Hubert with an Englishman, Stephen of Seagrave. But he was just about the only Englishman in a position of real power. At the Exchequer, a Poitevin, Peter de Rivaux, made a number of changes that gave Henry more power. Sheriffs were given greater power in the regions at the expense of the barons. To make matters worse, most of the English sheriffs were sacked.

In response to this foreign influence some barons, led by Richard the Marshal, attempted a rebellion in 1233. They were easily defeated. Richard was killed in Ireland in 1234.

The rebellion did persuade Henry to sack des Roches and des Rivaux in 1234 but he gave the latter a new job in 1236. Henry's marriage to Eleanor in 1236 brought a fresh wave of foreigners to court.

French wars

Henry was as unsuccessful as his father in his foreign policy.

- In 1229 Henry tried and failed to re-conquer Aquitaine.
- In 1230 his expedition to recover Brittany also failed.
- He was defeated again in 1242 when he tried to win Poitou from the French king, Louis IX.

Henry's wars cost too much money and the barons were not very pleased because taxes were too high.

King of Sicily

In 1254 Henry promised to give the Pope money to fight a war in Sicily in return for choosing his son Edmund as king of Sicily and Apulia. The fee was a huge 135,541 marks plus an annual sum to be paid to the Pope. Henry's idea to make Edmund king of Sicily was not just about prestige. In the fourteenth century Sicily was a rich island. It was also well placed to control the Mediterranean and had been part of the Norman Empire. But this was too much for the barons. One of Henry's formerly distrusted foreign favourites Simon de Montfort emerged as the leader of the disgruntled barons. They met in Oxford in 1258 and drew up the Provisions of Oxford, which limited Henry's power.

Provisions of Oxford

- A Council was to be set up to advise the King. The majority of its members were to be nobles. The King could not make decisions without the Council's agreement.
- The Council was to choose the King's important officials including the Chancellor.
- A regular Parliament would be held every three years. Fifteen members of the Council would meet with a further twelve barons to discuss the issues of the day.
- Henry swore an oath promising to rule according to the points set out by the Provisions.

What ... ?

PARLIAMENT
The word parliament comes from the French *parlemenz* meaning discussion.

At the time Henry had little choice but to accept these proposals. But three years later he decided that he would ignore them. He did not want a regular Parliament. Civil war loomed. King Louis IX of France was asked by both sides and in the *Mise of Amiens*, 1264, he decided in Henry's favour.

Civil war (again)

The barons were not happy with Louis' decision and civil war broke out. For a couple of years the barons had the upper hand. The King's army was defeated at the Battle of Lewes in 1264 and Henry himself and his son Edward were taken prisoner.

In 1265 the barons' leader, Simon de Montfort, called a Parliament. Two knights from each shire and two burgesses from each town were asked to attend. The Parliament met to discuss such issues as tax. This was a much more ambitious Parliament than had originally been proposed under the Provisions of Oxford. Most importantly, for the first time, 'commoners' were invited. Up to now Parliament had only ever included barons. But this Parliament included knights and BURGESSES. With the King and his son still prisoners, and the decisions taken by the barons, this was a radically different form of government from that of the last 200 years. Some of de Montfort's supporters began to feel he had gone too far. When Edward escaped from captivity in 1265 he lead Henry's loyal barons to defeat de Montfort at the Battle of Evesham. De Montfort was killed and the other rebels were savagely pursued and executed. By 1267 the civil war was over and Henry had won.

Parliament did not meet again in Henry's reign. However, the idea that the barons, knights and important townspeople were to be consulted about the issues of the day was here to stay.

Henry's death

Henry had a long reign – nearly 60 years. He survived civil war and rebellion. Yet he gets much less attention than most other kings of England. He died in 1272 and his body was laid alongside that of his hero Edward the Confessor.

Summary task

1 Who made the biggest mistakes?

You have been gathering together action cards for John and Henry. Use these cards to compare their performance. Draw a scale from −5 (big mistake) to +5 (great success). Put John above the line and Henry below the line. Then place each action on the scale.

Now use this plan to help you to compare John and Henry's performance.

a) Did they have any successes?

b) What was John's most damaging mistake?

c) What was Henry's most damaging mistake?

d) Did John and Henry make similar mistakes?

2 Here are two pairs of pictures (right) of John and Henry III, drawn by the same person at different times. In each pair, John is on the left. What impression do you get of each king from the pictures? How is the second pair different from the first?

3 Essay question

Describe the main events that led to the signing of Magna Carta.

Hint: Make sure you look at both the longer term and the shorter term causes. You should mention all the events on your John action cards in your essay.

NB Go to page 179 for a practice source exercise on King John.

Pulling it all together

For each king you have studied so far, fill out a card like this. You might not be able to fill out every row.

King:		
Top tasks for a king	**Score out of 5**	**Reason for score**
Win wars		
Gain territory/keep what you've got		
Get on well with barons		
Get on well with Church leaders		
Keep law and order and peace in the country		
Spend money wisely		
Have healthy sons		
Be a good leader		
Have a good claim to the throne		
Average score		

UNIT 4 Edward I: why was he such a success?

4.1 How did Edward deal with Wales and Scotland?

> **What is this all about?**
> Edward I was King of England from 1272–1307. He learned from his father's mistakes. He surrounded himself with intelligent advisers and made sure that he consulted his leading barons, churchmen, knights and townsmen. Edward also had great success as a war leader – he brought both Wales and (for a short while) Scotland under English control. Edward sounds like a successful king all round!
>
> Through the first part of this unit you will find out how he achieved this reputation.

Source ❶

Edward I.

Task
Make your own copy of this simple diagram. As you work through the unit add notes to it to make your own concept map about Edward's reputation. You can use a different colour for each branch and use pictures as well as words. You could add other main 'branches' if you wish.

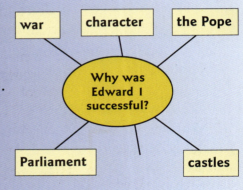

When Edward I became king in 1272 he was 33. He was already an experienced soldier. He had been on Crusade. He had led his father's armies to victory against rebel barons in the civil war. He had a reputation as an ambitious, impatient and ruthless leader. He had ferociously hunted down and punished the king's enemies.

His first big challenge as a king was how to deal with Wales.

Wales

None of the English kings had ever conquered Wales. They had not really tried. It was a country of dense forests, high mountains and poor roads. And as long as the Welsh did not trouble England there was no particular reason to conquer it.

In the 1250s the border areas (see Source 8 on page 52) were run by the Marcher lords who were loyal to the king – but the rest of Wales was under the control of a Welsh prince, Llywelyn the Great of Gwynned. He paid homage to Edward's father Henry. The relationship between Wales and England remained stable.

Llywelyn the Last

Llywelyn the Last was Llywelyn the Great's grandson. He had inherited one third of Wales from his grandfather. The other two thirds had gone to his brothers Owain and Dafydd. He believed that these lands should be united and he fought against his brothers and won. By 1267 he was in control of all Wales. But even this did not change the relationship with English. He promised homage to Henry III and Henry recognised Llywelyn's right to be Prince of Wales. So far the pattern was much the same as in earlier years.

However the situation was about to change. Despite his promise, Llywelyn was not very loyal to Henry. He joined Simon de Montfort's opposition to Henry III (see page 42) and then when Henry died Llywelyn went out of his way to show Edward that he did not think much of him.

- He refused to give homage to Edward I.
- In 1273 he married the daughter of the leader of the rebel barons.
- He started to build a castle at Dolforwyn to resist any English invasion.

It won't surprise you, given Edward's reputation, that he decided to take action. But notice how he did it.

- He summoned Parliament – all the leading knights, citizens and burgesses. They agreed to raise the tax on selling wool and leather. Wool was Britain's most important product at that time.
- He asked Llywelyn once again to pay him homage.
- He raised a strong army of 15,000 men and marched on Wales. This was the largest army ever raised by an English king.

Llywelyn saw that he had no chance and decided to talk not fight. The resulting treaty was not a success for Llywelyn but neither was it a total disaster.

- Llywelyn promised to give homage to Edward but Edward no longer recognised that he was OVERLORD of Wales.
- However, Edward allowed Llywelyn to keep the title of Prince of Wales.
- Edward also realised that it made good sense to be kind and he allowed Llywelyn to keep some of his land around Snowdon.

Wales conquered

However, the Welsh prince was not content. In 1282 Llywelyn and his brother Dafydd attacked Edward's castles at Flint and Rhuddlan. Edward sent another army into Wales. This time the result was decisive. Llywelyn was killed in battle at Irfon Bridge in December 1282. Dafydd was captured and executed. Edward stripped Llywelyn's family of their lands and, by the Statute of Rhuddlan of 1284, Wales was divided up into English-style counties. English laws were applied to Wales.

Edward was determined that the Welsh would not rebel again. In 1283 he ordered the building of three great castles of Conwy, Harlech and Caernarfon. Wales was fully under English control.

Did you know?

Wool was by far the most important commodity produced by farmers in the Middle Ages. English wool was sold across Europe, especially in Antwerp which is now in Belgium. Wool was so important to the English economy that the king's ministers in Parliament sat on woolsacks.

Did you know?

Edward I's nickname was Longshanks, meaning long legs. He was very tall.

45

What about Scotland?

Even more of a potential thorn in any king of England's side was Scotland. Scottish kings had, in the past, given homage to the English kings. However, in 1189 King William the Lion of Scotland bought freedom from homage from Richard I of England. After his success in Wales Edward wanted to have greater control over Scotland. First he tried the marriage route. In 1286 King Alexander II of Scotland died and was succeeded by his four-year-old granddaughter Margaret, Maid of Norway. Edward spotted his chance and arranged the marriage of Margaret to his (then six-year-old) son Edward. Unfortunately, Margaret died on her journey to England in 1290.

'Lord Paramount'

There was no clear successor so the Scottish nobles who feared a civil war between the rival claimants asked Edward to help them judge who had the best claim. This was Edward's great opportunity. He agreed to do this but only on condition that the nobles recognise him as 'Lord Paramount' of Scotland. Caught between the prospect of a civil war in their own country and giving homage to Edward they reluctantly chose the latter.

In 1292 Edward chose John Balliol as King of Scotland. Edward now used his new power to interfere in the running of Scottish affairs. He ordered John Balliol to London and demanded he provide an army for him to pursue a separate war against France. John Balliol's position was impossible and the Scottish nobles jointly renounced their homage to Edward and asked the French for help in fighting a war against Edward! Edward's response was speedy and ferocious. He sent an army to capture Berwick-on-Tweed who slaughtered everyone in the town. He captured John Balliol and forced him to ABDICATE. Then his army continued north and totally defeated the Scottish army at Dunbar in 1296.

Enter William Wallace!

William Wallace was the leader of a group of outlaws. Following the humiliation at Dunbar Wallace decided it was a time for the Scots to rise up in full scale revolt against the English. Through 1297 he led his men as they swept across Scotland attacking the English wherever they could find them. Wallace's gang of outlaws had turned into a successful guerrilla army. They killed the sheriff of Lanark, supposedly because he had killed Wallace's sweetheart. Although totally outnumbered they seized Lanark, Glasgow and Scone. More Scots flocked to join Wallace's army including the future king of Scotland Robert Bruce.

Source ❷

A map showing the battles between England and Scotland.

Did you know?

During the wars in Wales Edward I became aware of the efficiency of the Welsh longbow – deadly weapon up to six feet long. It was probably the decisive weapon at the Battle of Falkirk and was later used with great success against the French cavalry at battles such as Crécy in 1345 and Agincourt in 1415.

Task

Essay writing

Use the information on pages 44–47.

1 Describe how Edward extended royal control in England and beyond.

2 Explain why you think Edward was successful in extending royal control.

You might make use of the following points:

- use of Parliament
- ability to raise taxes
- the Church
- reform of government
- military strength

The Battle of Stirling Bridge

Edward was alarmed by the news of Wallace's success and sent an army of 40,000 foot soldiers and 300 horsemen north to deal with the threat.

However, an approaching English army was not the only problem facing Wallace in the late summer of 1297. Many Scottish lords who had joined up with Wallace were uneasy and changed sides. Despite this setback, Wallace managed to push the English armies south of the River Forth and his armies laid siege to Dundee. In early September 1297, Wallace's spies informed him that an English army led by the Earl of Surrey was advancing on the Abbey of Cambuskenneth. Wallace called off the siege of Dundee and rushed to face the English. His army caught the English soldiers attempting to cross the river at Stirling Bridge on 11 September. The battle was a disaster for the English and a triumph for Wallace.

'Hero of Scotland'

The English were utterly defeated and Wallace was now the hero of Scotland. He was made regent (which means taking charge) while the real king John Balliol was a prisoner in England. He did not wait for a very angry Edward to get another army together; instead he decided to invade England. Wallace's army got as far south as Newcastle before hearing of an English army of 100,000 foot soldiers and 8,000 cavalry coming his way.

The Battle of Falkirk

Wallace did not want a fixed battle. He knew he was outnumbered and that was not how he had succeeded in the past. He tried to organise a surprise attack more in the style of the Battle of Stirling Bridge but he was betrayed by two Scottish nobles and Edward found out about his plans. Instead Wallace retreated from the English forces, operating a 'scorched-earth' policy – destroying all food and supplies that Edward's army could use. Edward's army did begin to suffer – food was short and morale was low.

Finally the two armies met face to face at the Battle of Falkirk.

The battle was a disaster for Wallace. His army was outnumbered three to one and one of his most important allies, Comyn, Lord of Badenoch, led his men off the battlefield halfway through the fight. Wallace's army was beaten but he managed to escape capture by fleeing to Stirling and then to France.

Conclusion

Edward ordered that Scotland come under English rule although it could keep its own laws. Scottish nobles and knights could sit in the English parliament but had to give up their forts and castles. This was not the end of the story. English control did not last (see page 56) but for now it was another resounding success for Edward.

Source 3

A statue of William Wallace in Dryburgh in the Scottish Borders.

What happened to William Wallace?

Wallace tried to get Philip, King of France, to support the Scottish cause. He failed and returned to Scotland in 1303 to carry on fighting the English.

Edward offered a reward of 300 marks for the capture of Wallace. This was a very large sum of money for the time. Eventually, one of Wallace's servants, Jack Short, betrayed Wallace to the Scottish baron John Monteith, who captured him and took him to Dumbarton Castle, and then to London. On 23 August 1305 Wallace was tried in Westminster Hall, accused of treason against Edward. Wallace denied the charges. He argued that he could not be guilty of treason against Edward because Edward was not King of Scotland and had no right to send an army there.

Wallace was found guilty and condemned to death. He was dragged through the streets of London to Smithfield. He was then hanged, drawn and quartered. His head was put on a pole on London Bridge, his right arm was sent to Newcastle, his left arm to Berwick, his right leg to Perth and his left leg to Aberdeen. It was a horrible death.

Task

Work in pairs to write two plaques to go with the statue in Source 3 explaining what Wallace achieved. One of you be positive: emphasise Wallace's heroism and successes; the other be negative: emphasise his criminal past and his failures.

Source 4

Edward I presiding over Parliament. ❓ *Use the internet to find a picture of Parliament today. What similarities and differences do you see?*

Edward and Parliament

There was more to Edward's success than his war record. He was only able to win his wars against the Welsh and the Scots because he kept the support of people in England. In particular he knew how to work with the barons in Parliament.

Edward's wars and castles cost a lot of money. Magna Carta had stated that no monarch could raise taxes without 'the common consent of the people'. This did not mean that the king had to ask everyone's consent and it certainly did not mean that he had to ask the poorer people what they thought. But it was a check on the king's power and Edward was the first king to know how to handle it. He used his Great Council (selected group of advisers) well. You have already seen how he summoned Parliament before he started his conquest of Wales. In 1295 he called another Parliament known as 'The Model Parliament' with the aim of seeking advice before he embarked on his Scottish campaigns.

Did you know?

As part of his money raising Edward I taxed Jewish moneylenders. When they could no longer pay, they were accused of disloyalty and Edward abolished their right to lend money at interest. He decreed that every Jew over seven years old had to wear a yellow badge on his clothes. Later he arrested all the heads of Jewish households: 300 were taken to the Tower of London and executed. Others were killed in their own homes. In 1290 the King banished all Jews from the country.

Did you know?

When Edward's wife Eleanor died in 1290 Edward was devastated. She had born him 16 children – most of whom had died as babies. Her body was taken from Lincoln to London. The journey took 12 days. Edward ordered that a stone cross be built at each point that her funeral procession stopped for the night. The final stop was at Charing Cross in London and a replica of the Eleanor Cross still stands outside Charing Cross station today.

NB See page 181 for a practice source exercise on Edward I.

This was a very different attitude from his father's. Even so things were not all plain sailing for Edward. When the barons and many merchants did not like his plans for high taxes in 1297, they made Edward agree to the Confirmation of the Charters. This said that Edward could not raise taxes without Parliament's approval. This was a change. Before, they had given advice; now, they had to approve. Edward agreed to the Confirmation because he was, at the time, at war with both France and Scotland.

Edward's strength was that he understood that, if he was going to govern effectively and have the money he needed, then he would have to give ground occasionally. For example, in 1303 Edward I gave merchants the right to trade freely in return for accepting a new taxation system.

Edward and the Pope

Edward dealt with the Church far better than most of the previous kings. Again, he learned from the mistakes of others. In 1296, Pope Boniface VIII thought that he would try and impose his authority on Edward I. In a letter called *Clericis laicos* he told all of the priests in England that they should not pay tax to Edward without his permission. Edward was not pleased and threatened to take the lands of any clergy who did not pay tax. Importantly, he got the support of the people through the Great Council and Parliament for his stand. The Pope backed down and Edward had won the day.

Edward died as he had lived – fighting a war. In 1306 there was a new Scottish rebellion and despite ill health Edward joined the campaign. But he died en route to Scotland in 1307. On his tombstone it says: 'Here lies Edward I, Hammer of the Scots.' This is what they chose to remember at the time. Do you think that is how Edward should be most remembered?

Summary task

You should have now compiled a diagram summarising the different elements of Edward's achievements. Add to it as you study Unit 4.2 with details about castles. Then use it to help you write an essay:
'Why was Edward successful in extending royal control in England and beyond?'

In your essay you will first need to **describe how** Edward extended royal control. You will need to mention Wales, Scotland, the relationship with the barons and the Pope.

Then you will need to use your own judgement to **explain why** he was able to do this. Your chart will give you many ideas to work with but make sure you consider how each of the following helped him succeed:

- His skills as a military leader
- His character
- The way he worked with Parliament.

4.2 How and why did castles change?

> **What is this all about?**
> Through the previous units there have been many references to castles. In Unit 1 they were vitally important to the Normans in their conquest of England. In this unit they were equally important to Edward in conquering Wales more than 200 years later. However Edward's castles were very different from William's. Between 1066 and 1300 castles had changed significantly. Find out how and why.

Stage 1: Motte and bailey

The Normans used castles to establish their authority in England. The first motte and bailey castles were built in strategically important locations such as river crossings or crossroads. They were constructed mainly of wood, were very easily burned down and could not be built very tall. Their purpose was to act as a base for groups of soldiers who were controlling a region. The more troublesome a region, the more castles were built.

Source 6

Rochester Castle. In the foreground is the curtain wall. In the background is the tall stone keep. Building this castle cost one third of the king's annual income.

Source 5

An artist's impression of the building of Chichester castle in 1068.

Stage 2: Stone keep castles

After the 1069 rebellion, William decided that he needed to build more permanent reminders of Norman power. Stone keep castles were built to last. The most famous of these castles were the White Tower at the Tower of London (page 18) and Rochester Castle in Kent (Source 6). With a stone keep, there was no need for a mound of earth. Instead a keep was built with strong foundations and could be built high. The defenders could spot attackers several kilometres away which gave time to prepare their defences. There was still a bailey but it too was surrounded by a stone wall. The front door of the keep was on the first floor so if attackers penetrated the outer walls the defenders could lift the wooden steps inside, making it near impossible for the attackers to get into the keep.

As attackers found ways to damage a stone keep the design evolved. Rochester originally had square towers with sharp corners. Miners were able to undermine these corners and the edges could be damaged by rocks fired from a trebuchet. You can see from Source 6 that one tower has been rebuilt as a round tower. This was much stronger. They still served the same purpose as motte and bailey castles to house a garrison but they were also able to withstand a long siege.

Source ⑦

An aerial view of Beaumaris Castle.

Stage 3: Concentric castles

Castle building reached its peak with the CONCENTRIC castles built in Wales on the orders of Edward I. The most famous are at Harlech, Beaumaris (above), Caernarfon and Conway. They are called concentric because of the way the heart of the castle was defended by a series of curtain walls. But Edward's castles had many other improvements.

- **Gatehouse** A concentric castle had a very heavily defended entrance. Guarding the gatehouse was a **drawbridge** that could be raised when attacked. The entrance was also defended by a series of **doors** and huge iron gates called **portcullises**.
- **Curtain walls** The outside curtain walls were lower to allow archers to see an approaching enemy. The curtain wall nearest the castle was higher to give the defenders the best possible opportunity to defend their castle.
- **Towers** Towers were a variety of shapes. For example, at Caernarfon, there were towers within towers. The greatest of Caernarfon's towers is the Eagle Tower, which has walls 5.4 metres thick.
- **Double walls** The walls were made from two walls with the hollow between them filled in with rubble. This was to give them extra strength.
- **Arrowslits** Slits were built into the walls so that archers could fire at attackers from different angles.
- **The sea** Most castles were built by the sea which allowed large boats to supply the castle and made a siege virtually impossible.
- **The town wall** Outside the castle the town was also surrounded by a strong wall.

┌─ **Did you know?** ─┐

The portcullis became the symbol of the Royal Exchequer (where they kept the royal money). If you look at a modern one-penny piece you will see a picture of a portcullis on the tails side.

┌─ **Did you know?** ─┐

At the bottom of the keep's wall was a slope called a batter, which helped water, oil, etc. dropped by the defenders to splash over the attackers.

51

Source 8

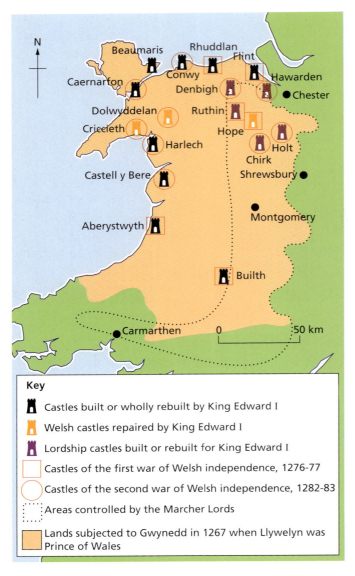

Castles in Wales.

Key

🏰 Castles built or wholly rebuilt by King Edward I

🏰 Welsh castles repaired by King Edward I

🏰 Lordship castles built or rebuilt for King Edward I

▢ Castles of the first war of Welsh independence, 1276-77

◯ Castles of the second war of Welsh independence, 1282-83

⋯ Areas controlled by the Marcher Lords

▢ Lands subjected to Gwynedd in 1267 when Llywelyn was Prince of Wales

Source 9

A medieval illustration showing castle building.

Did you know?

Edward's castles in Wales were not just built for conquest. They were designed so that English families could come and settle there, with the full protection of the castle walls. They were also built as home and office for Edward's officials in Wales such as Sir Otto de Grandison who became constable of Caernarfon in late 1285.

Task

Study Source 9.

1 What job is being done at A, B, C and D?
2 What tools are being used? Make a list.
3 Which of these tools are still used today?
4 For each tool not still in use, how would this job be done today?

Source ⑩

Case study: How was Caernarfon built?

An artist's reconstruction of Caernarfon Castle and the walled town.

Edward I employed Master James of St George to build Caernarfon. He probably met him in Savoy (which is on the borders of Italy and France) on his way back from the Crusades. Master James had huge experience building castles across Europe.

Building was often distracted by events elsewhere. The craftsmen who built Caernarfon were also needed to help Edward fight his wars in Scotland and France. Their skills were much in demand in sieges, battles and when putting up forts to secure a conquest. In 1293 work came to a stop on the castle as workmen travelled to Gascony; in 1302–3 little work was done because of the war in Scotland.

Because the castle was not finished for so long it was open to attack; in 1294 rebels led by Madog ap Llywelyn stormed the castle walls and burned whatever they could find. Caernarfon Castle was virtually finished by the time that Edward I died in 1307 but it had cost £27,000 to build, the equivalent to a king's normal revenue for a year. It is no wonder he needed to raise all those taxes.

Edward had seen at first hand how useful the castles built by Crusaders in the Holy Land had been. He asked Master James to copy some of their best features. Master James brought a small but highly skilled staff of STONEMASONS and engineers with him from Europe, backed up with labour from across England. Master James needed carpenters, diggers and woodcutters as well as labourers. Building a castle in hostile territory meant that he also needed a large group of soldiers to protect his workforce.

First the site of the castle would be completely cleared and the ground plan was marked out. The foundations were dug down to bedrock and filled with rubble so the ground could take the weight of the castle walls. Most castles were built of high quality blocks of limestone, sandstone, granite or marble. Rubble was used to fill in the thickness of the walls between facings of stone blocks. Much of the stone was cut to size at the quarries rather than at the building site, although any intricate carving would be done at the site. The stones were lifted into place in baskets, in wheelbarrows, on shoulders or by crane. Plumblines were used to make sure the walls were level and straight. In winter, the tops of unfinished walls were covered in thatch for protection. The higher the castles went, the more scaffolding was needed. Holes were left in the walls for poles to hold the scaffolding.

Did you know?

Edward I was the last great castle-building king. From this time on castles were less important.

- England became more settled. In the troubled border areas people still needed castles to protect them but through much of England there was no need.
- Kings and nobles wanted to live in comfortable palaces or manor houses not austere castles.
- The development of gunpowder meant that not even the strongest castles could withstand attack.

Life in a castle

Castles were also homes. Inside the castle, the people could eat, garden, work, pray, play or be entertained. These pictures show some of the activities that might be going on in a normal day.

Morning

Task A

Look closely.

First work with a partner to identify all the activities taking place in each picture. Notice **who** is involved: lords, ladies, servants or soldiers. Notice **where** it is happening.

Task B

Write a story.

Your story should include at least three of the characters that you see in the illustrations. It should take place in a single day. And it should all take place inside the castle walls. If you like, you could try to illustrate your story like a medieval manuscript.

Evening

Filling in the gaps: Edward II and Edward III

Edward II 1307–27

Edward II was not like his father. He did not like wars and when he did have to lead his army he was a very poor general. He also made mistakes in choosing his advisers. He had favourites to whom he gave too much power and influence. Put the two together and you have a recipe for disaster, or at least a bad reign.

As you have already read, Edward II's father put a huge amount of effort into conquering Scotland although he was never securely in control. Edward managed to undo all of his father's work in a relatively short time. In 1313 the Scots again rose against English rule, led by Robert Bruce. Edward's response was to send an army to Scotland but it was defeated by Bruce and the Scots declared their independence from England. By the end of his reign, Gascony had also been lost to the King of France.

Edward's choice of advisers did not go down well with the barons. He gave top jobs to his favourite people whether they were well-suited to them or not. His first favourite was Piers Galveston. It is believed Edward had a homosexual relationship with him. Edward made him regent when he had to leave the country. Galveston was bold and witty but he was an incompetent ruler.

Later in Edward's reign his favourite was Hugh Despenser, who was arrogant, cruel and treacherous and who made many enemies. In 1321 Parliament tried to exile Despenser. Edward's response was to raise an army, and capture and kill the leader of the anti-Despenser group.

In the end it was Edward's wife Isabella who brought him down. In 1325 she went to France, supposedly to arrange the marriage of their son Edward (they were not original when it came to naming him). She then returned to England but with an army! She quickly captured London, arrested and hanged Despenser, forced her husband to abdicate and had him thrown into prison. Eight months later he was brutally murdered, reportedly impaled on a red-hot poker.

Edward III 1327–77

Edward III was different again. Unlike his father he was a brilliant soldier and an excellent king. Edward allowed and encouraged Parliament to develop. The House of Lords and House of Commons emerged as distinct Houses of Parliament. In the country, the Justices of the Peace were given greater powers to run their local regions.

He was king for 50 years and a couple of other important things happened in his reign that we deal with in other units. In 1337 a series of wars that were later to be called the Hundred Years War broke out between England and France. Some events of the wars are covered in Unit 6. In 1348 the most terrible plague, known as the Black Death, killed almost half the people in England. It is covered in detail on pages 154–159.

Source A

A drawing of Geoffrey Chaucer in a medieval manuscript.

Task

Tabloid newspapers did not exist in the Middle Ages but if they had, what headlines might they have written for the events on these two pages? Choose two 'stories' from the reign of Edward II or Edward III and write headlines to accompany them.

Edward's reign is also famous for developments in literature and religion.

- **John Wycliffe** A professor at Oxford University, Wycliffe produced the first Bible to be written in English (up until then they had been written in Latin or Greek). He also criticised some of the ideas of the Catholic Church. His ideas were popular and he soon had a following of people known as LOLLARDS.
- **Geoffrey Chaucer** One of the most famous writers in the history of the English language, Chaucer wrote the *Canterbury Tales* about a group of PILGRIMS on their way to visit the tomb of Thomas Becket at Canterbury Cathedral. The story is about much more than the pilgrims; it paints a vivid picture of life in medieval England.

However, Edward's reign did not end happily. In 1376 his son Edward, the Black Prince, who was a great soldier, died. He had lost his heir. And on a warm summer night in June 1377, Edward III himself died. He was alone, deserted by his friends. Even his mistress, Alice Perrers, fled, first slipping the rings from his fingers and pocketing them. So the crown of England passed into the hands of his grandson Richard, a ten-year-old-boy.

UNIT 5 Richard II and the Peasants' Revolt: was he brave or devious?

What is this all about?

In 1377 Richard II became King of England. He was only ten years old. He inherited a kingdom that was outwardly successful, but serious problems were festering beneath the surface.

For four years he was king in name only. Others made decisions for him – sometimes very bad ones. Then suddenly, faced by a new challenge – thousands of angry peasants and villagers were marching to London to see him – the boy-king took control. How well did he do? You decide.

Task

On the next two pages the text describes the different problems that were brewing in England in the fourteenth century.

1 Work in pairs. One of you make a list of the concerns of the peasants. The other make a list of the concerns of the king and his advisers.

2 Compare your lists. Which is longer? Is there anything that comes on both lists?

Source ❶

This portrait of the young King Richard II was painted by an anonymous contemporary artist.
? *How old do you think Richard is in this painting?*

In 1381 the peasants were angry for many different reasons. Some were long-term – problems that had built up over many years. Others were short-term and had occurred, more or less, during the reign of Richard II.

The Black Death

The Black Death hit England in the 1340s. Between one third and one half of the population of England died. As well as personal tragedy, the Black Death caused big changes in English villages. Peasants formed the bulk of the population and so, inevitably, most of the people who died were peasants. This led to a serious labour shortage. The peasants who survived were in great demand. Those who were free got higher wages from landowners. Some even started leaving their lords to look for higher wages elsewhere. Serfs, who were not free, wanted to buy their freedom and worked for the landowners for cash. Or they simply ran away to another place. The feudal structure that had held English villages together for hundreds of years appeared to be collapsing.

The Statute of Labourers 1351

The government stepped in to try to stop the huge increase in wage bills and the changing relationship between peasant and lord. The Statute:

- set the maximum wage payable at the 1346–47 rates;
- arranged for runaway peasants to be returned to their lords;
- reaffirmed the right of lords to claim certain services from their peasants.

For a while this worked. But by the time Richard II came to the throne, the peasants were becoming restless again and many were refusing to serve their lords, demanding an end to what they saw as slavery.

Who ... ?

JOHN BALL

In 1366, the Church banned him from preaching, but he clearly never stopped because the Archbishop of Canterbury had him imprisoned three times. His sermon made to the rebels at Blackheath on 13 June 1381 inspired them to continue their rebellion.

Source check

'When Adam delved [dug] and Eve span Who was then the gentleman?'
This was part of a poem written in the early 1300s by Richard Rolle de Hampole. 'Gentleman' refers to the upper class. Its message was that all people were equal. John Ball used it as the basis of much of his preaching.

Religious ideas

Some priests within the medieval Christian Church began criticising accepted beliefs. Travelling preachers, in particular a priest called John Ball, taught that everyone was equal before God. To the peasants, this was an extremely attractive idea. It linked in with their growing resentment that they had to give up to two days a week unpaid labour to the Church. Abbots and bishops claimed that, because their estates belonged to the Church, they should not rent them out or give the peasants their freedom. Old customs, they said, should not be interfered with in any way. The peasants, on the other hand, wanted to be free of a burden they believed made the Church rich and themselves poor. Priests like John Ball gave them a religious argument for wanting this freedom.

War with France

The Hundred Years War with France started in 1337. Initially, England was very successful with tremendous victories at Crécy in 1346 and Poitiers ten years later. Money seized from the war was invested in building splendid manor houses and churches and the peasants could see the positive side of war. But by 1377 a series of military disasters resulted in French raids on the English coast. People began to fear for their homes, their jobs and their lives.

The Poll Taxes

For the peasants, this was the final straw. Money had to be found to pay for the war with France.

● In 1377, the year Richard II came to the throne, the first Poll Tax was imposed. Everyone over fourteen years old, rich and poor, had to pay four pence to the government. This clearly hit the poor far harder than the rich.

● In 1379 another Poll Tax was introduced but this time an attempt was made to link the tax to income. The poor still paid four pence while barons paid £2 (120 times as much). This didn't raise enough money.

● In 1380 a third Poll Tax was imposed. The rate was three times that of 1377 – 12 pence – and the same for everyone! This was both unfair and an intolerable burden on the peasants.

Poor government

Richard II himself cannot be blamed for all these problems but his council can. The boy-king did not rule alone. He was too young. Instead, he was 'guided' by a council of nine of the greatest barons in the country, led by his uncle, John of Gaunt. The council didn't rule particularly well; they spent a lot of time arguing amongst themselves as they struggled to control the king in their own interests. This lack of a strong king certainly allowed these social and political problems to fester.

It's quite clear that young King Richard and his advisers were sitting on a powder keg of trouble. The Peasants' Revolt, when it broke out in 1381, challenged medieval ideas and concepts about society and people's position within it. As such, it was a serious and concerted attempt by thousands of peasants to limit the power of the Crown. It, too, reflected dangerous new ideas about the ways in which society should be organised and the Church structured. How well did Richard II, then aged 14, cope with the crisis?

Those were the causes. The following were the events that finally sparked the revolt. Although the revolt affected areas as far apart as Hampshire, the Wirral and the Scottish Borders, most of the action came from peasants in Kent, Essex, Suffolk and Norfolk.

In May 1381, a tax collector arrived in the Essex village of Fobbing to find out why villagers there hadn't paid their poll tax. He was thrown out. So were the soldiers who were sent to restore law and order. The Essex villagers organised themselves. Rebellion spread and riots and demonstrations became common. Men sharpened scythes and sickles and dusted down the longbows they had fought with in France.

The peasants march to London

In early June 1381, rebels from Kent, led by Wat Tyler, captured Canterbury, seized the sheriff and made a bonfire of all his records. They opened up Maidstone prison and released John Ball, who had been imprisoned for preaching that all men were equal. Joined by the Essex rebels, they marched on London. Their aim was to put their demands before the King. They claimed they had no quarrel with him; in fact, they seemed to look on Richard II as their only true leader. Their quarrel was with the council of nobles, Church leaders and tax collectors. Thousands of peasants from all over the country downed tools and joined the rebels from Kent and Essex. Many tradesmen, priests and outlaws joined, too. As they marched, they destroyed tax records and tax registers, and burned buildings that housed government records. They attacked manor houses and destroyed documents that gave details of labour services that the peasants owed to their lord or to the Church. By 12 June around 60,000 rebels were camped outside the walls of the City of London: the Essex contingent at Mile End and those from Kent at Blackheath.

King Richard and his advisers took refuge in the Tower of London, which was a royal palace as well as a fortress. Soldiers guarded them, but the troops were not used. The rebel forces, massed in two huge groups, were too great to be challenged. Then the rebels sent word that they wished to talk with the King.

It's quite clear that young King Richard and his advisers were sitting on a powder keg of trouble. The Revolt challenged medieval ideas about society and people's position within it. It challenged the power of the king and his council. It reflected dangerous new ideas. How would Richard II cope with the crisis?

Who ... ?

WAT TYLER

The leader of the Kent section of the Peasants' Revolt. Everything we know about him was written by his enemies – the ruling classes – and in particular by a French chronicler called Jean Froissart. But even they are all agreed about his intelligence, eloquence and charisma.

The crisis deepens

Richard decided to meet with the rebels. The very next day, accompanied by his closest advisers, he was rowed down the Thames towards Blackheath. Unfortunately the two advisers Richard had chosen to accompany him were Simon Sudbury (his Chancellor and also the Archbishop of Canterbury) and Robert Hales, his Treasurer. These two were, of all Richard's advisers, the men the rebels hated the most, linking them with the Poll Tax and the imprisonment of John Ball. As soon as they saw who was on the barge, the rebels began chanting 'Traitor, traitor' and 'Kill them, kill them.' Fearing the worst, Richard's attendants refused to moor the barge to let him land, and rowed smartly away to loud jeers and insults from the rebels.

Source

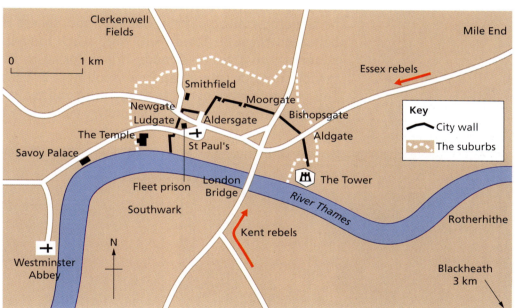

The routes taken by the rebels into the City of London.

Source check

In June 1381, the English poet John Gower watched the rebels pouring into London. He wrote that *... savage hordes approached the city like waves of the sea and entered it by violence. At their head a peasant captain urged the madmen on. With cruel eagerness for slaughter, he shouted in the ears of the rabble, 'Burn! Kill!'*

That night, Richard watched from the windows of the Tower as flames leapt from the Savoy Palace, the London home of his uncle, John of Gaunt. Chanting rebels surrounded the Tower, demanding to meet the King. How had the rebels got into the City? The answer was simple: the people of London had opened the city gates to the rebels. Once in, they went on the rampage. As well as ransacking and firing the Savoy Palace, they broke open the Fleet prison, attacked lawyers and burnt down the Temple where the legal records were kept. London was in the hands of the rebels and they seemed out of control.

Meeting at Mile End

It was clear to Richard that he had to meet face-to-face with the rebels. The following day he rode out, with an escort of nobles and soldiers, to Mile End. There, he faced Wat Tyler. Allowing Tyler to kiss his hand, Richard listened to the rebels' demands. They wanted an end to serfdom, the abolition of all labour services, the death of all 'traitors' (defined as the King's advisers) and pardons for all those taking part in the rebellion. Richard immediately agreed to all these demands, except the one concerning 'traitors', saying that only the law courts could decide who was a traitor. To show he meant business, Richard had 30 clerks ready to write out charters of freedom so that the rebels could take them back to their lords as proof of Richard's promises.

So far, so good. However, some of the rebels, not liking what Richard had said about the 'traitors', decided to take matters into their own hands. They stormed the Tower of London, found the two men they considered to be the arch-traitors, Simon Sudbury and Robert Hales, and promptly beheaded them on Tower Hill. They stuck their heads on poles and mounted the poles on London Bridge for all to see. That night there were terrible riots in London and more killings. But Richard kept his promises. The peasants were given their charters and many of them went home. But a sizeable body remained, demanding more from the King.

Source ❸

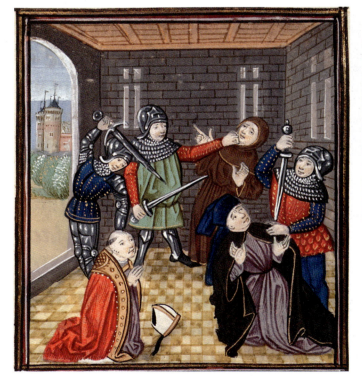

This is a fifteenth-century painting of the murder of Simon Sudbury, the Archbishop of Canterbury, and Robert Hales, the Treasurer.

Task

1 Look at Source 3. This is clearly a very inaccurate picture. Use the text and your own knowledge to suggest three things that are wrong.
2 What do you think was the attitude of the artist to
   a) the rebels
   b) the villains?
3 Can this source still be useful to a historian studying the Revolt?

Meeting at Smithfield

A further meeting was arranged. On the evening of 15 June King Richard met again with Wat Tyler, this time at Smithfield, a market and fairground outside the city walls. The choice of meeting place was the idea of the Lord Mayor of London, Sir William Walworthe. He wanted to get the rebels as far away from the city as possible, fearful that any attempt by the troops to attack the rebels in the city would result in either the city burning to the ground or the rebels vanishing into its alleyways, courtyards and twisting back streets.

Once at Smithfield, the King and Tyler greeted each other politely. This time, Wat Tyler's demands were even more extreme. He asked for all lords' estates to be reduced in size and for all Church lands to be divided among the peasants. Once again, Richard agreed. Suddenly there was a scuffle between Wat Tyler and Sir William Walworthe. Tyler fell from his horse, a dying man. No one knows whether this assassination was planned or was the result of a misunderstanding. But as soon as the peasants realised what had happened, they raised their bows. The royal party were within seconds of being massacred.

It was the boy-king Richard who saved the day. He rode toward the peasant army shouting 'Sirs, would you shoot your king? I will be your chief and captain. Follow me and you will have what you seek!' Confused but by nature loyal, the peasants followed their king, who led them away from the city, towards open farmland at Clerkenwell. There, Richard repeated the promises he had made to Wat Tyler at Mile End. The peasants believed him. Leaderless, but with their main demands met, they set off for home.

Broken promises

Once the peasants had dispersed, Richard broke all his promises. Any peasants remaining in London were rounded up and killed. All London householders had to swear loyalty to the King. Wat Tyler's head was cut off and stuck on a pole on London Bridge. With London secure, royal troops then had to subdue the countryside. They moved through Essex and Suffolk, putting down minor rebellions and hanging peasants who were involved. In Chelmsford and Colchester, batches of rebel leaders were hanged on the roadsides as a dreadful warning to others. A royal army restored the abbot of St Albans, who had been forced to grant a borough charter and they hanged John Ball, who had been taken to St Albans from the Midlands for trial. Troops restored order in Cambridge, where a college that owned land had been burned and a judge beheaded. Everywhere peasants were fined or imprisoned, and there was much work for the hangman. The charters granted by the King were shown to be worthless. Perhaps Richard II showed his true colours at Waltham, where he told the peasants 'Villeins you are and villeins you shall remain'.

What ...?

VILLEIN
A peasant who was entirely subject to his lord and kept on the lord's manor.

Task

1 King Richard II had one attempted meeting with the peasants and two actual meetings with them. It seems that these meetings were his own idea and against the wishes of his advisers. Do you think this makes him:

brave   stupid   stubborn   foolish sensible?

Choose the words that you think best describe Richard's actions and explain why.

2 Use what you know about medieval kings to explain how likely it was that the meeting at Smithfield was a put-up job and Wat Tyler was deliberately killed.

Who won?

By the autumn of 1381 the Peasants' Revolt was over. Hundreds of peasants had been killed or injured in the fighting or had been hanged as a punishment. Their leaders were gone – hanged or in hiding. The royal promises had been broken; the charters granted to them by Richard II had been withdrawn; and the peasants were forced back into their old ways of life.

In the short term it looked very like a defeat for the peasants. But there is a different way of seeing it. Richard and his council had been given a big scare.

- Just months later the Poll Tax was withdrawn.
- Within ten years Parliament abandoned all attempts to control wages.
- Eighty years later, artists were interpreting the revolt in the style of Source 4, right.
- Just over a century later all peasants were free.

Source 4

This picture, painted in about 1460, shows John Ball (on the horse), Wat Tyler (wearing a black hat on the left) and their peasant supporters. ❓ *What moment in the Revolt do you think this is supposed to show?* ❓ *How likely is it that this is a true record of what happened?*

Summary task

Overall, and bearing in mind what you know about medieval kings, how well do you think King Richard II handled the Peasants' Revolt? Score Richard on a scale of −5 to +5 and write some paragraphs to explain your score.

Postscript: what happened to Richard?

Richard II survived the Peasants' Revolt but his reign did not end well. He was inconsistent – first working with Parliament but then trying to rule without. In the end, Richard's reign turned nasty, taxes went up and his enemies were thrown into prison. A group of barons, led by Henry of Bolingbroke, forced Richard to abdicate and threw him into the Tower of London where he was murdered. In 1399 Henry Bolingbroke became Henry IV.

Task

The only medieval English king we have not told you anything about in this book is Henry IV. Do some research of your own to write a 'Filling in the gaps' feature. You have a maximum of 200 words to sum up his whole reign, which was 1399–1413. If you are stuck for ideas you can start with www.wikipedia.org.

THE PEASANTS' REVOLT OF 1381: WHY DID IT HAPPEN?

Source A

Many believed that the thoughtlessness of the Archbishop and his provincial bishops was responsible, because in their care lies the faith and stability of the Christian religion. Certainly they allowed John Wycliffe and his followers to behave shamefully, and preach throughout the whole country to corrupt the people. It seems to me that these evil times are the result of the sins of the people of the earth, especially the friars. Nowadays there is a saying 'This is a friar and therefore a liar.'

Written at the time by Thomas Walsingham, a Benedictine monk at St Albans Abbey.

Source B

A foolish priest called John Ball used to preach to the people as they came away from Mass on Sundays:

'My friends, the state of England cannot be right until everything is held in common and there is no difference between nobleman and peasant and we are all as one. Why do nobles lord it over us? We are all descended from our first parents, Adam and Eve, so how can they be better men than us?'

Written at the time by the French historian Jean Froissart. He worked in England for the wife of Edward III. He wrote Froissart's Chronicles which told the history of Europe 1326–1400. He interviewed people who were present.

Source C

In the year 1379 King Richard II held his parliament in London. It granted the King a tax so wonderful that no one had even seen or heard of its like before. This is the way it was to be paid:

Each earl	£4
Each baron or knight	40s
Each squire	6s and 8d
Each Justice of the Bench	100s
The Mayor of London	£4
Merchants	13s and 4d
	OR 6s and 8d
	OR 3s and 4d
Each archbishop	£6 13s and 4d
Each married man and his wife, over sixteen years of age	4d
Beggars do not have to pay anything.	

From a contemporary account of the second Poll Tax, which was introduced in 1379. There were 20 shillings (s) in a pound and 12 pence (d) in a shilling.

QUESTIONS

1 Read **Sources A** and **B**.
Whom do the authors blame for the Peasants' Revolt?

2 Now read **Source C**.
How might Richard II's advisers explain why the Poll Tax was a fair one?
How could this source be used to explain why the peasants were angry?

3 Study **Sources A–C**.
Which source would be the most useful to a historian trying to find out why the Peasants' Revolt happened?

4 'The main reason for the Peasants' Revolt in 1381 was the Poll Tax.'
Explain whether or not you agree with this opinion.

UNIT 6 Who was the real Henry V?

What is this all about?

Henry V was king from 1413 to 1422. He has been described as 'the greatest man ever to rule England'. This reputation rests largely on his famous victory over the French at the Battle of Agincourt in 1415. You are going to study this battle first and ask some difficult questions: was it really a great victory? Was Henry responsible for the victory? Have writers like William Shakespeare made him look better than he really was? Then you are going to look at some other information about him before finally deciding whether or not he was a good king.

Did you know?

The Hundred Years War lasted longer than 100 years: from 1337 to 1453.

Background: England v. France

The Battle of Agincourt took place during The Hundred Years War between England and France. See if you can work out why this war started.

William the Conqueror already owned lands in France when he won the Battle of Hastings in 1066 and became King of England. This meant that later English kings controlled large areas of France – more in fact than the French king!

However, in 1204 King John managed to lose much of this territory. This was a blow to England's prestige and meant that England now had a powerful rival on its doorstep. It soon caused other problems as well. Trade was important to England. Wine was imported from France but this trade was now under threat from French pirates. The French also stopped the cloth merchants of Flanders from buying English wool. Nothing much was done about this until Edward III became King of England in 1327.

In 1328 the King of France, Charles IV, died. He had no sons, and all his brothers were dead. He did have a cousin, Philip, and a sister, Isabella. Philip quickly grabbed the throne. This greatly annoyed Edward because he was Isabella's son – she and his father, Edward II, were married. Edward thought this gave him the right to be King of France.

The situation got worse in 1337 when Philip announced he was going to conquer Guinne, a part of France still under English control. Edward decided to invade France. The Hundred Years War had started.

The Hundred Years War before Henry V

Edward III had much success in France. In 1346 he had a great victory at the Battle of Crécy where the English archers played a crucial role. His son the Black Prince became a living legend – a brilliant general, brave and heroic. In 1356 he won an equally brilliant victory against the French at Poitiers. Edward and the Black Prince died within a year of each other in 1376–77 and the French won back some land. In 1396 peace was agreed

Task

List as many reasons as you can why Edward III decided to invade France. Remember, some of these reasons might go back a long time before Edward. Number your reasons, starting with 1 for the most important.

and that is how it stayed until Henry V started the fighting again in 1415. He was determined to win back the lands in France that he thought were rightfully his.

Source ❶

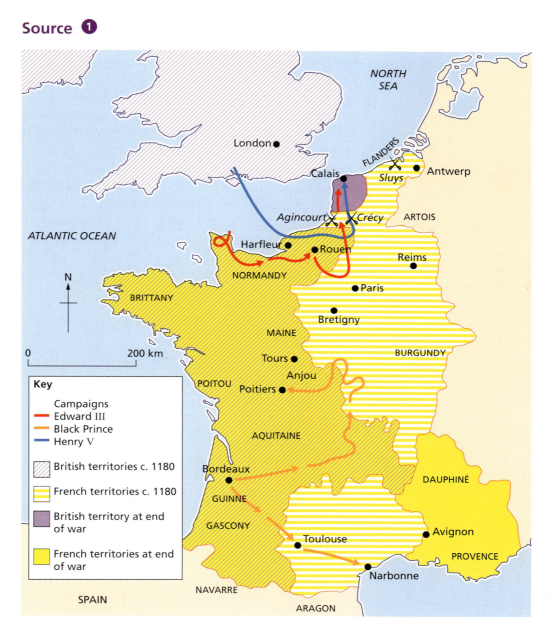

France during the Hundred Years War.

The Battle of Agincourt, St Crispin's Day (25 October) 1415

On 11 August 1415 Henry set sail for France. He took with him 6,000 archers and 2,500 knights on horseback. In September, after a month's siege he captured the town of Harfleur. But the siege left his army weakened by disease and hunger. He knew he was not strong enough to fight the French army and tried to retreat to Calais. However, the French army, led by the DAUPHIN, barred his way near the castle of Agincourt.

The English army was not in good shape. Many of the soldiers were suffering from dysentery and rations were low. The night before the battle Henry ordered total silence in the camp, so that everybody could get a good night's sleep. It was so quiet that the French thought they had crept away! Morale in the English camp was low. They were worn out, hungry and outnumbered by the many-skilled, heavily armoured French knights.

In Shakespeare's play *Henry V*, written nearly 200 years later, Henry makes a speech to his troops on the evening before the battle. Shakespeare shows Henry rallying his troops, lifting their spirits, and showing great leadership qualities. This speech has become famous.

Source ❷

He that shall live this day, and see old age,
Will yearly on the vigil feast his neighbours,
And say 'To-morrow is Saint Crispian.'
Then will he strip his sleeve and show his scars,
And say 'These wounds I had on Crispin's day.'
Old men forget; yet all shall be forgot,
But he'll remember, with advantages,
What feats he did that day: then shall our names,
Familiar in his mouth as household words
Harry the King, Bedford and Exeter,
Warwick and Talbot, Salisbury and Gloucester,
Be in their flowing cups freshly remember'd.
This story shall the good man teach his son;
And Crispin Crispian shall ne'er go by,
From this day to the ending of the world,
But we in it shall be remember'd;
We few, we happy few, we band of brothers;
For he to-day that sheds his blood with me
Shall be my brother; be he ne'er so vile,
This day shall gentle his condition;
And gentlemen in England now a-bed
Shall think themselves accurs'd they were not here,
And hold their manhoods cheap whiles any speaks
That fought with us upon Saint Crispin's day.

Henry V, William Shakespeare. ⍰ *Why do you think this was such a good speech?*

Source ③

Kenneth Branagh as Henry V in a film from 1989.

The two sides face each other!

It rained for most of that night, just as it had for the previous two weeks, turning the ground sodden with ankle-deep mud. Both armies rose before dawn and assembled for battle. The English had 5,000 archers and 900 MEN-AT-ARMS. The French army was about 25,000-strong.

The English

The English formed a single line to the south. There were no reserves. The line was divided into three groups of men-at-arms. Each of these groups was made up of the advance, the main body and the rearguard, each about four men deep. Between each of these groups of men-at-arms and on each flank (side) were the archers with longbows. They were protected by large pointed stakes.

The French

The French formed three lines to the north. The front two lines were made up of dismounted men-at-arms. In the third line the men were on horseback. Cavalry was placed on each flank. Between the first and second lines were archers and crossbowmen.

The site

The sides were about 800 metres apart, separated by a gently rolling recently ploughed field crossed by two roads. A slight dip in the field meant that they could clearly see each other. Either side of the field was a forest. The field narrowed to only 800 metres where the armies would meet.

⎡ Did you know? ⎤

The longbow was made of wood from either the yew or ash tree and was six feet high. The bow-string was made of linen and the arrows were made from birch. Each archer carried about two dozen arrows under his belt and a variety of points for different purposes, such as penetrating armour. The arrows were deadly at up to 350 metres. The French crossbow required less skill to use but was very powerful. However, a longbow could shoot twelve arrows in the time it took to fire one crossbow bolt.

Task

Use the information above to complete and label this plan of the battle at the start.

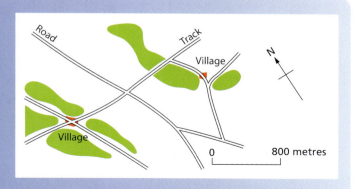

THE BATTLE OF AGINCOURT

THE ENGLISH ADVANCE

For four hours the two armies stared at each other. The English did not want a battle and the French did not fancy wading through the mud! It was sensible for them to wait for the English to attack as this would put them, with their inferior numbers, at a great disadvantage. Or perhaps they were just going to wait until the English starved and they would win without having to fight.

Henry knew that without food his troops would get weaker, so at about 11 a.m. he ordered his men to advance. They moved forward steadily until the French were just within the range of their longbows. If the French had attacked while the English were advancing and before they had reset their positions the English would have been in trouble. Henry then ordered the archers to drive their stakes into the ground at an angle that would ensure the French horses were impaled by the stakes.

Henry planned to provoke the French into attacking. He ordered the archers to fire. The English archers could fire ten flights a minute and the air was thick with arrows which poured down on the French like rain. Henry's plan worked and the French cavalry on the flanks attacked the English archers on the flanks. It was a disaster.

THE FRENCH ATTACK

The cavalry charged at about 12 miles an hour and flight after flight of arrows hit them. The arrows were not strong enough to penetrate the knights' armour but the horses were not so well protected. Wounded horses threw their riders into the mud. Others crashed into the English stakes.

As the survivors retreated they crashed into their own men-at-arms who were advancing. Everything was now going wrong for the French! Their horses had churned the mud up making it harder for later attacks. The forest narrowed the field, squeezing the French against each other and preventing them from outflanking the English.

The attack was chaotic. The French noblemen all rushed like an undisciplined mob to be in the front line. They were jostling with each other and they had no room to lift their weapons! And all the time the English archers were firing at them. The French had so little room that they even failed to fire their artillery (bombards), which because of the chaos would have probably killed as many French as English.

By the time the French reached the English lines they were exhausted by the mud, the crowding and the arrows. Soon the English lines were protected by a solid wall of French bodies! The French men-at-arms were pushed out towards the English archers. These archers finished the French off: two of them would attack a French knight from the front while a third archer slashed at the unprotected parts behind the knee. They would kill the knight by thrusting their sword through the grille of his faceplate. Many of the French knights were simply stuck in the mud and were trampled on.

THE END

After only half an hour the first two French lines had been destroyed. The English soldiers started to take prisoners for ransom and strip valuables from the dead. This was a normal thing to do in those days. Henry, however, wanted all his men ready for a French counter-attack: there were still more soldiers in the surviving French third line than in the whole of the English army. He ordered that all prisoners be killed. More French soldiers were killed then than were killed in the fighting. The French counter-attack failed and the Battle of Agincourt was over. Six thousand French soldiers had been killed and many more were taken prisoner.

Source ❹

A fifteenth-century French painting of the battle.
❓ *This is clearly not a very accurate picture. What has the artist got wrong?*

Task

Write an essay to answer the question: 'Why did the English win the Battle of Agincourt?'

Make sure you do not simply tell the story of the battle – this has already been done for you. You have to **explain why** they won.

Planning

In planning your essay you need to organise the reasons for the English victory into the following groups:

- reasons that show Henry was a good leader
- reasons that show the English were good fighters
- reasons that show the French made mistakes
- reasons that show the English were lucky and the French were unlucky.

Writing

You could start your essay by briefly explaining why, before the battle, the French were favourites. Then you need to write about the different kinds of reasons for the English victory. Use a separate paragraph for each type of reason. You should finish your essay with a conclusion explaining which you think was the most important type of reason for the English victory.

Was Henry V a great king?

The historian Holinshed wrote in 1577:

> This Henry was a king, of life without spot, a prince whom all men loved, and none disdained, a captain against whom fortune never frowned, nor mischance once spurned, whose people him so severe a justicer both loved and obeyed (and so humane as well) that he left no offence unpunished, nor friendship unrewarded; a terror to rebels, and suppressor of SEDITION, his virtues notable, his qualities most praiseworthy.

Shakespeare used Holinshed's book when he wrote his play *Henry V*. You can see the similarities between Holinshed's and Shakespeare's Henry V.

Was Henry so perfect? On these two pages you will find some more information about Henry. You also need to look at the pictures of Henry carefully.

HENRY THE LAD

When he was about twenty years old Henry chose some unsuitable friends and spent much time in taverns and brothels. He was involved in drunken brawls and generally enjoyed himself.

HENRY THE SOLDIER

He was fighting against the Welsh when he was only 14 years old. He successfully led his father's army in the Battle of Shrewsbury, 1403, against the Percys who wanted to overthrow Henry IV. He won many victories over the French and many people see him as a military genius, a patient and brilliant strategist.

SON OF A USURPER

Henry's father, the Duke of Lancaster, USURPED the throne from Richard II in 1399 and became Henry IV. Not everyone accepted him as king and there were several risings by Richard's supporters. There was disorder in England for the rest of Henry IV's reign leaving questions about Henry V's right to the throne in 1413.

A STRONG KING

When Henry V became king he dealt with the dangers he faced. He put down a rebellion by the Lollards and had one of the leaders, his old friend Sir John Oldcastle, executed.

Source 5

Henry V – a portrait painted almost 200 years after his death.

STRATEGIC THINKING

His decision to invade France was a way of exporting the violence of the nobles to another country. (Having a foreign war is always a good way of diverting people's attention away from problems at home!) After Henry's victory at the Battle of Agincourt he was a national hero and no one dared to challenge him.

HENRY COULD NOT BE TRUSTED

There are many examples of Henry deserting his friends. He turned on Harry and Thomas Percy at the Battle of Shrewsbury in 1403 and had his old battlefield and drinking partner Sir John Oldcastle burned to death.

Source 6

Henry V's marriage to Catharine of France in 1420.

FRANCE WON AT LAST?

In 1417 Henry led another expedition to France and won more victories. In 1420 in the Treaty of Troyes he agreed to marry Catherine of Valois, the daughter of the French king, Charles VI, who recognised Henry as his heir as King of France. However, worn out by the fighting, Henry died of dysentery during a third expedition to France in 1422. Charles VI died soon after him. If Henry had lived for a couple more months he would have been King of France.

LEFT PROBLEMS FOR HIS SON, HENRY VI

Perhaps Henry spent too long in France. He was certainly obsessed with winning the French lands. But the wars put him and England into greater and greater debt. There were discontented rumblings back in England. Many people had opposed Henry's third expedition to France and there was always the danger of other noble families claiming the throne. This is exactly what happened after Henry died.

THE WAR AFTER HENRY: HAD HE REALLY ACHIEVED ANYTHING?

The war went disastrously for England after Henry's death. Henry VI was only a baby and the Duke of Bedford took over command. Helped by Joan of Arc, the Dauphin gradually pushed the English back and by 1450 all that England had left was the port of Calais. The war was over; English dreams of conquering France were at an end.

Summary task

Work in pairs. Turn back to pages 4–5.
1 Using the information about what qualities a medieval monarch needed, design an application form for the job of being a medieval king.
2 Imagine you are Henry V and complete the form.

UNIT 7 The Wars of the Roses: an overview

What is this all about?

The Wars of the Roses is the name given to the civil war between the supporters of the two powerful families, the House of Lancaster and the House of York. It was not called this at the time. We use this name because of the badges of the two sides – the Red Rose of Lancaster and the White Rose of York.

Both families were descended from Edward III and so they both had claims to the throne. The struggle for power between them eventually led to more than 20 years of civil war.

In this unit we give an overview of the causes and the main events.

Task

The information on this page suggests several causes of the Wars of the Roses. Can you add to the list below?

- More than one person was descended from Edward III and could therefore claim the throne.
- Margaret of Anjou's treatment of Richard of York.
- Groups of nobles had grown more powerful during Henry VI's reign.

1 Draw a diagram to show all the causes are linked.
2 Circle the most important cause, that is, if you took this away the Wars of the Roses would not have happened.

When Henry V died the throne passed to his baby son Henry. Henry VI's reign was not a success. While he was a child, unpopular nobles ran the country for him. They lost nearly all the land won by Henry V in France. You can't blame Henry VI for that. But when he did grow up, Henry VI was a weak king. He did little to stop people breaking the law and he allowed powerful nobles to build up private armies. Henry was religious, generous, peace-loving and liked to live simply. While these can be seen as very good things, it was not what was expected from a king at the time.

In 1450 around 30,000 people marched on London to protest about Henry's government. This was known as Cade's rebellion. The marchers fought a pitched battle with the King's soldiers on London Bridge. They were beaten but it was a sign of how unhappy many people were.

Henry's advisers

One of Henry VI's greatest failings was his choice of advisers. He relied on a small group of favourite advisers and did not consult his ambitious cousin Richard Duke of York, probably the most powerful man in the country. Richard himself had two claims to the throne! Both his father and mother were descended from Edward III. Henry's lack of consulation led to resentment from Richard and his allies. Through this period, the nobles were gradually dividing into two groups: the Lancastrians who supported Henry VI, and the Yorkists led by Richard.

Richard's opportunity

In 1453 Henry suffered from the first of a series of periods of mental illness. A Council of Regency was set up to run the country, led by Richard.

The war starts

In 1455 Henry was well enough to rule again although it was his wife Margaret of Anjou who was really in charge. She exiled Richard from the royal court. So Richard raised an army, fought against the King's supporters and took the King prisoner at the Battle of St Albans. Richard claimed he only wanted to remove 'poor advisers' from Henry's side. The Wars of the Roses had started.

The main events

Task

1 Draw a simple timeline from 1455 to 1487.
   a) Write on your timeline what you think are the five most important events of the Wars of the Roses.
   b) Highlight red the times when the Lancastrians were on top. Leave white those periods when the Yorkists were on top.
2 During the Wars of the Roses there were some weak monarchs and some strong ones. Who do you think was the weakest monarch? Who was the strongest? Write a few sentences explaining your choice.
3 Towards the end of the timeline (right) there are some clues about why the Wars of the Roses ended. Write two paragraphs explaining why the Wars of the Roses came to an end.

Dates	Battles	Developments
1455	Battle of St Albans	Defeat for the Lancastrians, Somerset is killed.
1455 –59		When Henry VI has another period of mental illness, Richard is appointed Protector and Margaret is side-lined.
		Arguments erupt about who should succeed Henry: Richard, or Henry's son, Edward.
		Disorder spreads across the country while the nobles quarrel. Margaret persuades Henry to send Richard to Ireland. One of Richard's allies, the Earl of Warwick, nicknamed 'the Kingmaker', becomes more powerful.
1459	Battle of Ludford Bridge	Lancastrian victory. Richard's son, Edward, and Warwick flee to Calais. Lancastrians back in control.
1460	Battle of Northampton	Warwick invades southern England, marches north and defeats Henry at Northampton. Warwick captures Henry.
1460		The Act of Accord: the two sides agree that Henry should remain king and Richard is recognised as next in line to the throne. Richard is made Protector to govern in Henry's name. However, Richard is killed in battle later in the year.
1461		Edward of York (Richard's son) declares himself as King Edward IV.
	Battle of Towton	The biggest battle of the war so far. Edward wins and Henry VI and Margaret flee to Scotland.
1464		Edward IV marries Elizabeth Woodville without Warwick knowing. Warwick's influence over Edward begins to wane.
1469		Warwick turns against Edward.
1470		Warwick invades England and Edward has to flee the country. Warwick announces that Henry is king again.
1471	Battle of Barnet Battle of Tewkesbury	Edward invades England and defeats Warwick and the Lancastrians in both battles. Henry is murdered shortly afterwards and Edward becomes king again!
1483		Edward IV dies. His heir is the 12-year-old Edward V. Edward IV's brother Richard Plantagenet puts the boy Edward and his younger brother in the Tower of London 'for protection'. Richard declares the boys are illegitimate and announces himself as King Richard III.
1485	Battle of Bosworth	Henry Tudor invades England and defeats Richard who is killed in the battle. Henry becomes Henry VII. He marries Elizabeth of York, the daughter of Edward IV. She is the surviving Yorkist with the strongest claim to the throne. The Houses of Lancaster and York are united.
1487	Battle of Stoke	Henry executes all possible other claimants whenever he can. In 1487 he defeats Lambert Simnel who is claiming to be the young Earl of Warwick with a claim to the throne. Henry VII is a very strong king. He controls the nobles and brings peace to England.

In Unit 8 you will investigate the last part of the story, 1483–87, in greater detail.

What is this all about?

King Richard III, the last Plantagenet king of England, reigned for only a little over two years. Yet more books, articles, novels and plays have been written about him than just about any other English monarch. He is probably the most controversial ruler England has had.

- Some see him as a ruthless murderer of his young nephews and as a wicked ruler.
- Others see him as a loyal brother (to King Edward IV), who would have made an excellent monarch, but whose reputation has fallen victim to relentless Tudor propaganda.

Even today, historians argue about which interpretation is correct. In this unit you will decide what you think.

What is this?

PROPAGANDA
The spreading of selected information and rumour in order to support a particular idea or viewpoint.

What's the problem?

The problem in reaching any agreement about the sort of man, and the sort of king, Richard was lies with the evidence. There are hardly any sources from Richard III's time that give us reliable insights into his character and motives. We have to rely heavily on chronicles written in early Tudor times – during the years when anyone with any sense would support the new king, Henry VII, and criticise the king he had defeated in battle, Richard III.

The two men writing nearest to Richard's time are both critical of Richard but their evidence is problematic.

Dominic Mancini was an Italian cleric who came to England in the summer or autumn of 1482, probably as part of a diplomatic mission. He should, therefore, have been in an excellent position to know what was going on. But he spoke no English, never travelled anywhere outside London and his writing is full of factual mistakes. Indeed, he left England shortly after Richard's coronation in July 1483. Much of what he was writing about from then on did not come from first-hand knowledge, but gossip. He names just one person, Dr John Argentine, who was PHYSICIAN to the boy-king Edward V, as one of his informants. He does not

Source 1

This portrait of King Richard III was painted by an unknown artist in the sixteenth century. It was almost certainly copied from a portrait painted of Richard while he was still alive. ❓ *What impression does it give you of Richard? Choose some adjectives.*

give us any clues as to where he got the rest of his information, either while he was in London, or later.

The anonymous author of the continuation of the *Crowland Chronicle* wrote between 1459 and 1486. Because we don't know who the person was who continued the *Chronicle*, we can't reach a judgement on how likely he was to have been objective about Richard. He suggests that, in southern England at least, Richard was disliked and mistrusted. But perhaps the author was a southerner. Richard's power base was in Yorkshire. Maybe a chronicler in the north would have written differently. We shall never know unless an as yet unsuspected chronicle is discovered. There is an additional complication in that much of the original *Chronicle,* as written down during Richard's life, was destroyed by fire in 1731 and historians are forced to use a much later 1684 copy.

So, with all these reservations, let's get on with the story.

Richard's background

Stage 1: the baby of the family

At the time of his birth at Fotheringhay, Northamptonshire, on 2 October 1452, no one could have predicted that some 30 years later, Richard Plantagenet would have the crown of England within his grasp. True, his father (the Duke of York) may well have had ambitions for one of his sons to be king but Richard was the seventh son and was hardly likely to succeed to the dukedom, let alone the crown. Although three of Richard's elder brothers died in infancy, this still left him the youngest of four boys.

When Richard was born, his brother Edward was ten, Edmund was nine and George was three. There were girls, too. Anne was thirteen years old, Elizabeth eight and Margaret six. The last child, Ursula, was born when Richard was three years old. It was in this sprawling family that Richard grew up. His two elder brothers, Edward, Duke of March and Edmund, Duke of Rutland had household governors and tutors at Ludlow Castle in the Yorkist heartland of the Welsh Marches. They were the important sons. As a small boy Richard was probably brought up with George and the girls at Fotheringhay under the watchful eye of Cecily, their mother.

> **Who ... ?**
>
> Richard Plantagenet, Richard Duke of Gloucester and King Richard III are all the same person! Don't get confused.

> # Task
> The story of Richard III is quite complicated. We will be telling it in detail. To help you keep track of events and to help prepare you for your final task:
> 1 Draw your own timeline of Richard's life 1452–85. Add information as you work through the chapter.
> 2 a) Above the line note evidence that shows Richard was loyal, kind, good or brave.
>   b) Below the line note evidence that shows Richard was treacherous, ruthless, evil or cowardly.

What ... ?

USURPER
A person who unlawfully seizes another person's position or authority.

Stage 2: childhood influences

Disaster, however, was to strike the Yorkist family. Richard, Duke of York was killed at the Battle of Wakefield in 1460 along with his second son, Edmund, who was then seventeen years old. Cecily thought it sensible to send the two younger boys, George and Richard, abroad into the care of Philip the Good of Burgundy. Only her eldest son Edward remained to fight for the Yorkist cause against the Lancastrians. But George and Richard's stay abroad was a short one. Political fortunes in England changed. The Lancastrian King Henry VI was deposed and Parliament declared the last three Lancastrian kings to have been usurpers. Edward was proclaimed King of England as Edward IV. Richard returned to England with George so that they could take part in their brother's coronation on 28 June 1461. Edward was just eighteen years old, George was eleven and Richard eight. As the nearest KINSMEN to the king, they played important parts in the elaborate ceremony of the coronation. George was made Duke of Clarence on that day and in the autumn, a month after his ninth birthday, Richard was made Duke of Gloucester.

In common with all young boys of his standing, Richard was sent away from home to live in another great lord's household. Nothing much is known of his whereabouts during his early adolescence. It is possible that Richard, along with George and Margaret, were in Greenwich under the general care of the royal household. What is certain is that in 1465 he was formally placed in the care of Richard Neville, the powerful Earl of Warwick (see box). The young Richard of Gloucester would have spent his time in the great Warwick castles of Middleham and Sheriff Hutton.

Who ... ?

Richard Neville, Earl of Warwick, was known as 'Warwick the Kingmaker'. His wealth and power meant that whenever he switched sides during the Wars of the Roses, the side he backed (Lancastrian or Yorkist) was the side that produced the king.

Source ❷

A modern photograph of Middleham Castle, North Yorkshire, one of the grand estates owned by the Earl of Warwick.

These years Richard spent in the north of England were influential. Here he met Anne, the younger daughter of the Earl of Warwick; here he made friends with the young Francis, Lord Lovell, who was brought up by the Earl of Warwick and who was to become one of Richard's most loyal supporters. Most importantly, he was accepted into the close-knit circle of rich and powerful northern noblemen and gentry who were to provide him with his power base in later life.

Early in 1469, Richard was recalled to his brother's court. Although he was just sixteen, he was created Constable of England and given important responsibilities in Wales. All, so far, just the sort of progress you would expect to see in the younger brother of a fifteenth-century English monarch. But, as you would also expect in these turbulent times, yet more disaster was about to strike the Yorkists.

Did you know?

What happened to Richard's other brother, George, Duke of Clarence? He wanted to be king too! He first supported Edward, then plotted against him. After a rigged trial in Parliament, George died in mysterious circumstances in the Tower of London, probably being drowned in a barrel of malmsey wine.

Stage 3: a loyal brother to the king?

The years 1469–71 were years of crisis. The Earl of Warwick changed sides and challenged the authority of the Yorkist king, Edward IV. Edward was forced to flee to Burgundy. Richard went with him and, unlike the shifty middle brother George (see box), shared Edward's months of exile. They returned to England together in the spring of 1471 and set about re-establishing Edward's position.

The official Yorkist account of what happened, *Historie of the Arrivall of Edward IV*, shows Richard in full support of his brother:

> The King landed within Humber, on Holderness side, at a place called Ravenspur. The King's brother Richard, Duke of Gloucester, and, in his company, 300 men, landed at another place four miles from thence.
>
> The King, full manly, set upon the Lancastrians at Tewkesbury and so also the King's vanguard, being in the rule of the Duke of Gloucester.

Richard of Gloucester, as Constable of England, presided over the trial and execution of a number of leading Lancastrians. Some said that he was involved in the murder of Prince Edward of Lancaster (King Henry VI's son) although it seems pretty certain that the prince was killed during the Battle of Tewkesbury. It is far more likely that Richard was involved in the murder of the Lancastrian Henry VI (who had been held prisoner in the Tower of London since the Battle of Tewkesbury), either on the direct orders of his brother Edward or on his own initiative.

Did you know?

For much of his reign Henry VI was mentally ill. The stress of kingship added to his condition. For the final years of his reign he was a pawn, controlled by others. Whoever held the King as prisoner was in charge. Henry was king only in name.

Task

Use these last two pages to add further events and evidence to your timeline.

What ... ?

PATRONAGE
Giving support or protection to someone, usually by putting them into positions of influence.

Source check

Even Dominic Mancini, Richard's main critic, had to admit that Richard did a good job:

Richard kept himself within his own lands and set out to acquire the loyalty of his people through favours and justice. The good reputation of his private life and public activities powerfully attracted the ESTEEM of strangers. Such was his renown in warfare that, whenever a difficult and dangerous policy had to be undertaken, it would be entrusted to his discretion and his generalship. By these skills Richard acquired the favour of the people.

Stage 4: a northern lord

Richard was well rewarded for his loyalty. Edward IV gave him tremendous power in the North, a sign of his absolute trust in his younger brother. Edward made Richard:

- Warden of the west march against Scotland (1470)
- Chief steward of the northern estates of the Duchy of Lancaster (1471)
- Keeper of the forests beyond the Trent (1472)
- Steward of Ripon (1472)
- Sheriff of Cumberland (1475)
- Lieutenant of the North (1480)

Not everything Richard had came from royal patronage. Richard worked hard to get hold of the former Earl of Warwick's lands, and he succeeded. Gradually Richard acquired the lordships of Middleham, Sheriff Sutton, Penrith, Barnard Castle, Durham, Scarborough, Skipton, Richmond and Helmsley. But Richard wasn't just acquiring land and castles, he was acquiring power and support. He controlled an area greater than that previously controlled by Warwick the Kingmaker. And he ruled it well, providing sound government, peace and stability.

Then came unexpected and horrifying news. On 9 April 1483, Richard's brother, King Edward IV, died aged 41, after an illness lasting ten days. He left a wife, Elizabeth Woodville, and seven legitimate children. Two of these were boys: Edward, aged twelve and Richard, aged nine. So twelve-year-old Edward was the heir to the throne and would soon be crowned Edward V. What was Richard, Duke of Gloucester, uncle of his brother's orphaned sons and daughters to do? This was his situation:

- He was the most powerful man in the kingdom: he had a huge power base in the North and he was the only surviving brother of a dead king and the uncle of a boy-king.
- Edward, his nephew, would need a Council or an individual – a PROTECTOR – to rule for him for at least four years until he was old enough to rule by himself. In his will, Edward IV had asked for Richard to do that job.

However, there was a rival for the job of Protector.

- Anthony Woodville, the Earl Rivers, was also uncle to the boy-king Edward. The Woodville family had become very powerful. Edward IV had given them good jobs. To keep their power base they also needed to control Edward V.

Richard had no time for the Woodvilles. He owed them no loyalty and certainly did not want them to challenge his power in England. But if Woodville became Protector it would definitely reduce Richard's power.

- Edward IV and his sons enjoyed a great deal of support from the nobility and the people in general. There was no faction pushing for an alternative claimant. The succession looked clear.

Task

What should Richard do now?

Richard has the biggest opportunity of his life. Power beckons. But there are threats. The boxes below summarise the situation at this time.

Sort through the information in the boxes then discuss, in the light of this information:

1 What do you think that Richard is **most likely** to do?
  a) Take the job of Lord Protector, or
  b) Seize this opportunity and try to become king himself.
2 What would you **advise** Richard to do and why?

a) Richard was ambitious

b) Richard's brother Edward IV had successfully seized the throne by force although his claim was weak

c) Richard did not like or trust the Woodvilles

d) Richard was the most powerful person in England

e) Richard was the dead king's younger brother

f) The King's Council might appoint Woodville Protector instead of Richard

g) Richard's brother wished him to be Edward's Protector until Edward was older

h) Earl Rivers wanted to become Lord Protector

i) Richard's guardian the Earl of Warwick had murdered his political rivals and never been charged with any crime

j) Richard liked to be in control. Rather than let others do things to him he liked to do things to them. That was how he had become powerful

k) Whenever he had been weak it had ended in trouble for Richard – for example he and Edward IV had been twice exiled from England by their rivals

l) Edward IV had been a strong king and the powerful nobles were quite happy that the young Edward should become king now

Source ❸

This stained glass window in the church of St Matthew, Coldridge, Devon, shows the boy-king Edward V.

The short 'reign' of King Edward V

In a time of such chaos and rivalry the chances of twelve-year-old Edward establishing himself as king depended on what all the other players in the game of power decided to do.

- The royal council started to organise a coronation for Edward V.
- William, Lord Hastings, who had been one of Edward IV's closest and most loyal supporters, gave firm backing to Richard of Gloucester as the best way of establishing Edward V on the throne.
- Richard dispatched letters to Elizabeth Woodville, Edward IV's queen, and to the royal council, expressing sorrow at his brother's death and expressing loyalty to Edward V.
- Richard presided over a commemoration service to Edward IV held in York, attended by all the northern nobility and gentry, at which he publicly swore loyalty to the new king.

Events then moved swiftly.

When Edward IV died, Richard, Duke of Gloucester, was in Yorkshire. The boy-king Edward V was in Ludlow with his other uncle, Anthony Woodville, the Earl Rivers. Both men immediately left for London. Earl Rivers took Edward with him, plus a small retinue. Richard marched south with a large retinue, including armed guards. The two groups met at Stony Stratford, where Richard lavishly entertained the Woodville contingent. The following morning he then had Anthony Woodville arrested and sent to the northern stronghold of Pontefract. Richard took the young Edward V into his care and together they proceeded to London. This wasn't such a rash move as it might at first seem. He had some powerful people on his side. The anonymous author of the *Crowland Chronicle* tells us:

> The more far-sighted members of the Council thought that the uncles and brothers of Edward V on his mother's side should be absolutely forbidden to have control of the person of the young man until he came of age.

The barons met to decide what should happen. It was agreed that government should be in the hands of a group of nobles including Richard. Dominic Mancini, no fan of Richard, tells us what happened next:

> [Richard] wrote to the Council declaring that he had been loyal to his brother Edward at home and abroad, in peace and war, and would be, if only permitted, equally loyal to his brother's children. This letter had great effect on the minds of the people who now began to support him openly and aloud; so that it was commonly said by all that the Duke [Richard] deserved the government.

On 10 May, Richard Plantagenet, Duke of Gloucester, was formally appointed Protector of the Realm.

What ... ?

RETINUE
People in the service of an important person who usually accompanied that person on his or her travels.

Richard of Gloucester, Lord Protector

Richard lost no time in rewarding his supporters. Lord Howard, Viscount Lovell, the Earl of Northumberland and the Duke of Buckingham were the four who received most, as a reward for past services and a guarantee of future support. This was entirely normal. But he also made sure that there was continuity with Edward IV's reign. John Russell, Bishop of Lincoln, passionately loyal to Edward IV (and possibly the author of the *Crowland Chronicle*), became chancellor. Most of Edward's household remained in their jobs and there were very few changes made to those who actually governed at local and national level. This included William, Lord Hastings, the sensible, steady and staunch supporter of Edward V and his brother. There was nothing here to surprise or alarm anyone.

Then things got nasty.

On 10 June, Richard wrote to the city of York asking for military assistance to root out a Woodville plot to murder himself and the Duke of Buckingham. This was readily given. On 13 June at a council meeting, Richard had Lord Hastings arrested and, without any trial, summarily beheaded on Tower Hill. Also removed were two other staunch supporters of Edward V: Thomas Rotherham, Archbishop of York and John Morton, Bishop of Ely. Elizabeth Woodville (Edward V's mother) was persuaded to allow her second son, Richard, to go to the Tower of London for his own safety and to be company for his brother, Edward V.

By 21 June, London was flooded with northern supporters of Richard of Gloucester.

Did Richard of Gloucester really suspect a Woodville plot against him? Or was he simply inventing it as an excuse to get rid of the most powerful of Edward V's supporters, so he could make his own bid for the crown? We don't know! However, the sources agree about what happened next.

- On Sunday 22 June, Dr Ralph Shaw preached in St Paul's Cathedral, London. In the congregation were the Dukes of Gloucester and Buckingham. What Dr Shaw had to say was startling indeed. He questioned the dead King Edward IV's right to have ruled, on the grounds that he was illegitimate. He was not, so Dr Shaw said, the legitimate son of Richard of York. The only legitimate son of Richard of York who was still alive was Richard, Duke of Gloucester. It was Richard of Gloucester who should be king.
- On Tuesday 24 June the Duke of Buckingham addressed the leading men of London in the Guildhall. He said that Edward IV, when he was a very young man, had married a woman called Lady Eleanor Butler. He had never divorced her. This meant that his marriage to Elizabeth Woodville was invalid and that the boy-king Edward V and his younger brother Richard of York were both illegitimate (as were their sisters) and so could not rule.

Task

Use these last four pages to add further evidence to your timeline.

In this climate of uncertainty, more soldiers from the north, supporters of Richard, began to march to London under the command of Sir Richard Radcliffe. On their way they killed Woodville and his two main supporters, Lord Grey and Lord Vaughan, where they were in prison in Pontefract Castle.

Meanwhile, in London, a group of influential nobles hastily presented Richard of Gloucester, Protector of the Realm, with a petition, begging him to accept the Crown. He did. A magnificent coronation was held on 6 July 1483 for King Richard III and his wife, Queen Anne.

And if you are wondering what happened to Edward V, turn to page 89. He'd never even been crowned king and, after Richard's coronation, he was never seen again!

Source ❹

A contemporary picture of King Richard and Queen Anne, dressed for their coronation. ❓ *What do you make of their expressions? Are they devious, cunning, noble or innocent?*

Task

Time to take stock again. Using all the information you have so far, do you think Richard III had all the time planned to seize the Crown? Or had he just exploited opportunities as they arose?

Jot down your ideas and discuss them with a partner.

Remember that we do not know the 'right' answer. It all depends on how you interpret events and how you use the information to back up your ideas.

Did you know?

William Shakespeare put Richard III in his play *Henry VI Part Three* and even wrote a whole play about him called, of course, *Richard III*. In these plays, Shakespeare variously describes Richard III as a 'bottled toad', 'a rooted hog', a 'hell-hound' and a 'lump of foul deformity'. We can guess that he didn't like him much!

King Richard III of England

After his coronation, Richard III and his court began a major tour of the country – a royal progress – to show himself to the people as their king and so gain their support. Richard III, as was normal and to be expected, richly rewarded his supporters. Most of these were northern lords. Indeed, when Richard got to York on 29 August, he was entertained on a grand scale. His son Edward was invested as Prince of Wales in York Minster and he told the city of York that they needed only to pay half the taxes they owed to him. Richard was consolidating his power base in the north. Meanwhile in the south, a different story was emerging.

Buckingham's rebellion, October 1483

In October 1483 word reached Richard that many powerful people, including some whom he thought were his supporters, had turned against him. They had raised an army and were plotting to depose him.

Most alarmingly for Richard the rebellion involved Henry Stafford, the Duke of Buckingham, his most loyal supporter. Although he was a Lancastrian he had backed Richard. Together the two men had swept to power. When Richard became king, Buckingham had been richly rewarded. Yet within four months, he had betrayed Richard.

This rebellion was serious. It spread throughout the southern counties of England, the south west and Wales. It was backed by large numbers of the gentry who would usually be expected to support the monarchy and who had initially supported Richard. Something had gone very wrong for Richard.

The rebels' objective was to free Edward V and make him king. Then when they discovered that Edward was missing and probably dead, they pinned their hopes on Henry Tudor to be king instead of Richard III. Henry had already set sail from France.

Richard's response was typically ferocious. Sweeping down from the north, Richard and his loyal supporters easily put down the rebellion. Henry Tudor, sailing from France to take part in the rebellion, turned back. Richard showed no mercy to Buckingham. Without trial, Richard had him executed on 2 November 1483.

Why did Buckingham change sides? Maybe he thought Henry Tudor would be a better king. Maybe he wanted to be on the winning side. Maybe he had set his own sights on the crown. Maybe he suspected Richard had killed his two nephews. We do not know.

So Richard won but Buckingham's rebellion had been a terrible shock. It proved to Richard that he had failed to inherit Edward IV's support and it had identified a new rival in the shape of Henry Tudor.

Did you know?

John Rous wrote *A History of the Kings of England*. He began writing it in Richard III's reign. During the reign of Henry VII, John Rous altered a lot of what he had written about Richard. He said that Richard had been in his mother's womb for two years instead of the usual nine months (medically impossible!) and that when he was born he had teeth in his mouth and hair down to his shoulders.

Did Richard III rule England well?

Richard ruled for only two years. These were his main actions.

- Richard's only Parliament passed measures to help the poor and make the courts fairer for them and justice more accessible to them.
- Richard set up the Council of the North in July 1484 under the control of his nephew, John de la Pole, Earl of Lincoln, to govern the north of England. This arrangement worked well, was popular and was continued for another 150 years.
- Edward IV had left the treasury almost empty. Richard made strenuous attempts to improve royal finances.

However, Richard seems to have spent most of his brief reign trying desperately to ward off threats to his throne.

- Richard's first move, after Buckingham's rebellion, was to reward those who had shown him loyalty. He gave them powerful jobs and money.
- Northerners were generally more loyal to him than southerners, so he moved many northerners down to the south and put them in positions of power and influence. This caused a lot of resentment amongst the southern gentry, many of whom lost their jobs.
- He made sure that Elizabeth Woodville and her daughters lived comfortably and in a manner suitable to their rank. Maybe he was just being kind; more probably he was hoping to end the Woodville threats to his position.
- He needed too to make sure that when he died he had a son to succeed him. So he was frantic when his only child Edward died in April 1484. He named his nephew John de la Pole as his successor. But he also continued his efforts to have a son. His wife Anne was too old to have any more children. She died in March 1485 and there were rumours that she had been poisoned. Free to search for another wife, Richard reportedly wanted his niece, Elizabeth Woodville.

Henry Tudor arrives in England

However, none of Richard's measures could deal with the one of most worrying threats of all to his throne – the Lancastrian claimant to the English throne – Henry Tudor. He had failed to land his small fleet in England during Buckingham's rebellion. But back in France he was building up a bigger army, with the help of the King of France and some soldiers and supplies from Scotland as well. In the summer of 1485 he decided that now was his moment to launch another bid to seize the throne from Richard. He landed on the west coast of Wales at Mill Bay and marched through Wales. Although the people of Wales had usually backed the House of York, Henry himself had Welsh ancestry and that helped him to gather soldiers as he marched. Eventually Henry arrived in England with an army of around 5,000 soldiers.

Task

Use these last four pages to add further evidence to your timeline.

Did you know?

We have several reports about the Battle of Bosworth which contradict each other and don't tell us clearly and exactly what happened. They even disagree as to the whereabouts of the battlefield!

Did you know?

There were four categories of soldier. In order of pay:
- The **foot soldiers** who carried a spike and a hook with which they would try to attack the enemy and pull the knights off their horses.
- Skilled **archers** who would use the longbow to deadly effect.
- **Men-at-arms** wore heavy armour and carried deadly weapons including hammers, battleaxes and clubs.
- Cavalry – **knights** mounted on horses.

Key

- Royals (K=King Richard III, Nk=Norfolk, Nd=Northumberland)
- Rebels (HT=Henry Tudor)
- Stanleyites
- Swampy ground
- Hill

The Battle of Bosworth Field

When Richard III and Henry Tudor faced each other on Bosworth Field on 22 August 1485, Richard seemed to have everything going for him. He was a king defending his own land and he had a fighting force three times greater than that of Henry Tudor. But it was not as simple as that.

Richard's forces included soldiers commanded by the Duke of Northumberland who could not be relied on. He was suspicious of Richard. Even more of a problem for Richard were the Stanleys. They had brought a large army but in the past they had changed sides more than once to suit their own purpose, and Henry was Stanley's stepson. So to make sure that Stanley stayed loyal, Richard had taken his son hostage. This was a high-risk strategy.

Henry's army was smaller but he had 3,000 professional French soldiers with him. He also had some loyal followers: while he had been waiting in France, a steady stream of English exiles had joined him. Henry had, too, picked up a following of about 200 men as he marched his troops from Milford Haven towards Nottingham. Henry's weakness was that he had very little experience as a military leader. Henry's luck was that Richard had made enemies and he couldn't even rely on his own supposed supporters.

Source 5

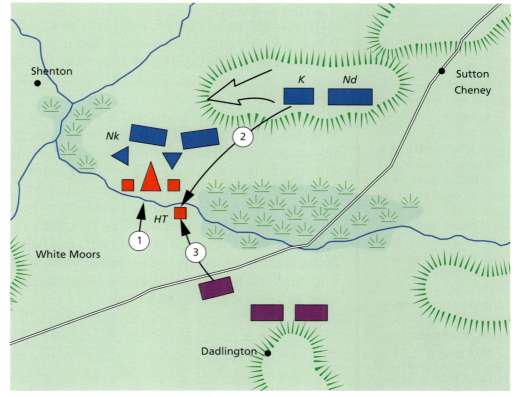

A map of the probable site of the Battle of Bosworth Field.

The battle begins

The first attack came from Henry's forces led by the Earl of Oxford (1 on the map, Source 5 on page 87). As their foot soldiers charged towards Richard's armies they were met by troops commanded by the Duke of Norfolk. The fighting for the next hour was bloody in the extreme. The foot soldiers, using any weapon at their disposal, stabbed, hit and slashed each other. An hour of such close hand-to-hand combat resulted in the death and injury of many of the soldiers. One casualty of the fighting was the Duke of Norfolk. It was noticeable that Stanley and Northumberland had not got involved. First blood to Henry.

Richard's charge

But all was not lost for Richard. He remained at the top of Ambion Hill away from the chaos that was happening down below. As the battle became ever more desperate, Richard spotted across the battlefield that Henry and his closest supporters had become cut off from the main body of their army. This was his chance to see off Henry once and for all. Richard rallied his cavalry of 1,500 knights and charged across the battlefield towards Henry's position (2).

It must have been a terrible sight for Henry. His faithful knights formed a protective guard around their leader and waited for the worst. Richard and his cavalry crashed across the battlefield, cutting down everything in their way. Henry's flag bearer, Sir William Brandon, was cut down to the ground. It is said that Richard got to within a sword's length of Henry, although we can't know for sure. Just imagine how close Richard was to keeping his throne. But a surprise was in hand. At this moment, seeing Henry close to defeat, Stanley decided to join in – but on Henry's side!

The end of Richard

With a battle-cry of, 'A Stanley, a Stanley!' Stanley's soldiers charged into Richard's army forcing them into the swampy ground (3). Richard sent urgent orders to Northumberland asking him for help. But none came. Northumberland either could not or did not want to come to Richard's help. Now Richard was in a hopeless situation.

Despite the most desperate attempt to fight his way out of trouble, Richard was eventually surrounded by soldiers who killed first his horse and then rounded on Richard himself. In Shakespeare's play *Richard III*, Richard says the now famous line: 'A horse, a horse, my kingdom for a horse!' which meant that if he could have held on to his horse, he might have escaped and won the battle.

> **Did you know?**
>
> Richard was the last English king to die in battle. He is also the only English king who has no royal tomb. After Bosworth, Richard's body was taken to the Franciscans in Leicester. On Henry VII's orders, Richard's body was on display so that anyone who wanted to make sure he was dead could go and have a look. Some years later Henry gave £10 for a coffin into which the Franciscans could put Richard's bones. When the Franciscan monastery was closed 50 years later, the bones were thrown out and the stone coffin became a horse-trough outside a local inn.

Task

Every year, in some newspapers, a notice appears on 22 August in the *In Memoriam* section. It reads 'In memory of King Richard III, treacherously slain on Bosworth Field'.

1 Explain why someone might believe that Richard III was 'treacherously slain'.
2 Do you agree?

But there was no horse. Richard was cut to the ground. Even chroniclers hostile to him commented on his courage. Polydore Vergil reported:

> Alone, he was killed fighting manfully in the press of his enemies.

No fifteenth-century battle continued once the leader of one side was killed – so it was with Bosworth. With Richard dead the battle was over. Legend says that one of Henry's men found Richard's crown nestling in thorn bush, and Henry was crowned King of England, there on the battlefield by his new friend Lord Stanley.

Richard's body was stripped, thrown onto a horse and taken from the battlefield. The last Plantagenet ruler left Bosworth as a naked corpse. Henry left it as King of England.

The rule of the Tudors had begun.

Postscript: The mystery of the missing princes

One of the most damning accusations made against Richard III was that he murdered his two nephews, Prince Edward (Edward V) and his younger brother Prince Richard, while they were in his care in the Tower of London. For hundreds of years people have argued about the evidence and interpreted it in different ways. Now it is your chance to join the debate.

These are the facts on which everyone agrees.

- In May 1483 Prince Edward arrived in London and went to stay in the royal apartments in the Tower of London. This was the most important royal palace in London.
- Prince Edward was soon joined by his brother, Prince Richard. The boys were seen playing together in the Tower gardens.
- Arrangements were begun for Prince Edward's coronation as Edward V in June.
- Suddenly, it was declared that Edward had no right to become king because his parents were not legally married.
- Parliament declared that Richard, the boys' uncle, should be king in Prince Edward's place. He was crowned King Richard III on 6 July 1483.
- After Richard's coronation, the Princes were not seen again. Rumours began circulating that they had been murdered.
- Richard III was killed at the Battle of Bosworth in August 1485. When the victorious Henry Tudor rode into London, he took over the Tower. No mention was made of the two Princes.
- In 1502, Henry announced that as far back as 1483 Sir James Tyrell had confessed to murdering the Princes. Tyrell said he did it on Richard's orders.

Turn over for the source investigation and see what you think happened.

THE CASE OF KING RICHARD III AND THE MISSING PRINCES

The evidence against Richard

The first two pieces of evidence come from Dominic Mancini and the anonymous author of the continuation of the *Crowland Chronicle*. They were writing about Richard earlier than anyone else.

Source A

After June 1483 Prince Edward's servants were kept from him. He and his brother Richard were taken to rooms further inside the Tower. They were seen behind the windows and window bars, but less and less often, until finally they were seen no more. I have seen men burst into tears at the mention of Prince Edward's name, for already some people suspected he had been done away with. I have not discovered if he has been killed, nor how he might have died.

From a book written by Dominic Mancini in 1483 called How Richard III Made Himself King. *See page 76 for more information about Mancini.*

Source B

For a long time the two sons of King Edward remained under guard in the Tower. Finally, in September 1483, people in the south and west began to think of freeing them by force. The Duke of Buckingham, who deserted King Richard, was declared their leader. But then a rumour was spread that the Princes had died a violent death, but no one knew how.

From the anonymous author of the Crowland Chronicle, *writing in 1486.*

QUESTIONS

1 On what do **Sources A** and **B** agree?

2 Is there any **evidence** here that the Princes were murdered?

Source C

After his coronation in July 1483, King Richard decided he must kill his nephews. This was because as long as they were alive, people would not think him the true king. He wrote to Sir Robert Brackenbury, the Constable of the Tower, asking him to put the children to death. Sir Robert refused. Then his page suggested Sir James Tyrell. Tyrell agreed and Richard sent him to Brackenbury with a letter commanding Sir Robert to deliver up the keys of the Tower to Tyrell for one night.

Tyrell decided that the Princes should be murdered in their beds the next night. He chose Miles Forest and John Dighton to do the job. Forest was one of the Princes' guards and had murdered others. The two men pressed feather beds and pillows on the children's faces until they stopped breathing. Tyrell had the Princes buried at the foot of the stairs, deep down under a pile of stones. But King Richard wanted them to have a better burial and so they were dug up and buried secretly in another place.

This story is well known to be true because when Sir James Tyrell was imprisoned in the Tower in 1502 for treason against King Henry VII, he and Dighton confessed that they had done the murder in the way I have described.

From a book written by Sir Thomas More in 1513 called The History of King Richard III. *More was only five years old when Richard came to the throne. He got most of his information from John Morton. John Morton was an enemy of Richard's, who had invited Henry Tudor to invade England and become king in Richard's place.*

Source D

During the Mayor's year of October 1482–October 1483, the children of King Edward were seen playing in the garden of the Tower at various times. After Easter 1483 people began whispering that King Richard had put the Princes to death, but there were many opinions about how they died. Some say they were suffocated between two feather beds. Some said they were drowned in wine. Others said they were poisoned. Tyrell was reported to be their murderer, but others thought it was an old servant of King Richard's.

From The Great Chronicle of London *written in 1513 by Robert Fabyan. He was a London draper 1483–85. During the reign of Henry VII he became an* ALDERMAN *in the City of London. He was interested in history but was not always very accurate.*

QUESTIONS

3 What does Thomas More say in **Source C** about Richard's motive for murder?

4 What proof does Thomas More give to show that his story is true?

5 Do you believe More's story? Why?

6 In what ways is Robert Fabyan's story in **Source D** different from that of Thomas More?

7 Why do you think their stories are different? (Hint: think about whether they were in a position to know what they were writing about.)

The case for Richard's defence

Source E

In 1484, after strong persuasion from Richard, Queen Elizabeth Woodville sent all her daughters to Richard's court at Westminster. Christmas Day that year was celebrated with great splendour in the Great Hall at Westminster. There was far too much dancing and fun. King Richard presented Queen Anne (his wife) and Lady Elizabeth (the Princes' sister) with a set of new and fashionable clothes each. This caused a lot of gossip.

From the anonymous author of the Crowland Chronicle *writing in 1486.*

Source F

Richard decided to try all he could to make his peace with Elizabeth Woodville. He sent messengers to her and after a time she forgot her troubles and sent her daughters to stay with Richard at court. After this she wrote secretly to the Marquis of Dorset advising him to forget Henry Tudor and return quickly to England where he would be sure to be treated well by King Richard.

From The History of England *written by Polydore Vergil in 1517. Vergil was an Italian writer and churchman. He came to live in England in 1507. Henry VII gave him a good position in the Church and asked him to write a history of England.*

QUESTIONS

8 How far do **Sources E** and **F** agree?

9 How likely do you think it would have been for Elizabeth Woodville to let her daughters go to Richard's court for Christmas if she believed he had murdered her two sons?

Source G

There is no **proof** that Richard murdered the Princes. On what is the accusation based? It is based on rumours, on hearsay evidence and on statements from unreliable and inaccurate witnesses. The Duke of Buckingham had the same opportunity and stronger motive. As Constable of England he could get into the Tower and to the Princes. Remember he didn't go with Richard on his tour after the coronation in 1483. Instead he stayed behind in London and caught up with Richard at Gloucester. Then Buckingham went to Wales and began plotting to overthrow Richard. His motives for murdering the Princes were stronger than Richard's. They were in his way because he wanted to claim the Crown himself, or help Henry Tudor claim it. By murdering the boys and then spreading a rumour about their death he could blacken Richard's character. Looking at the facts, Buckingham appears much more likely to be their murderer than Richard.

From Richard III *by Professor Paul Kendall, published in 1955.*

Source H

I do not doubt for one moment that the Princes were alive when Henry VII came to London in August 1485. He issued a proclamation, giving all Richard's supposed crimes and this list did not include the killing of the Princes. That to my mind is definite proof that the Princes were not even missing. They must still have been in the Tower. Richard had no reason to kill them: Henry had every reason. If they lived, all he had fought for would be useless because Prince Edward had more right to be king than Henry Tudor. Henry was capable of such a crime, so the boys were quietly but efficiently murdered. Elizabeth Woodville, the boy's mother, was locked into a nunnery. Henry spread the word that Richard had done the killing. Henry Tudor, murderer and liar – it's time the truth was known!

In 1972 Philip Lindsay, a historical writer, wrote an article in the magazine Argosy. *This is an extract.*

Task

Use the sources and your answers to the small questions to answer the big one: 'Did King Richard III kill the Princes in the Tower?'

You have a choice of three verdicts: 'guilty', 'not guilty' or 'not proven'.

Remember to back up what you say with evidence from the sources or your own knowledge.

QUESTIONS

10 When does Professor Kendall (**Source G**) think the Princes were murdered?

11 Why does Professor Kendall blame the Duke of Buckingham for the Princes' death?

12 When does Philip Lindsay (**Source H**) think the Princes were murdered?

13 Why does Philip Lindsay blame King Henry VII for the Princes' death?

Summary task

Over the past 19 pages you have been gathering evidence about Richard III. You are now going to use that evidence to help you write an essay:

'Was King Richard a wicked uncle or a loyal brother?'

To help you focus you can use this outline.

Paragraph 1
Explain the question in your own words.

Paragraph 2
Describe at least two of Richard's actions that show him to be treacherous, ruthless, evil or cowardly.

Paragraph 3
Describe at least two of Richard's actions that show him to be loyal, kind, good or brave.

Paragraph 4 (optional)
Explain the problem we have in using evidence from the time about Richard.

Paragraph 5
Your overall conclusion. Explain which way the balance falls for you – wicked Richard or loyal Richard? Include your strongest reason to support this view.

Pulling it all together

Through Section 1 you have been compiling record sheets like this. Complete three more sheets now for the monarchs Richard II, Henry V and Richard III.

King:		
Top tasks for a king	**Score out of 5**	**Reason for score**
Win wars		
Gain territory/ keep what you've got		
Get on well with barons		
Get on well with Church leaders		
Keep law and order and peace in the country		
Spend money wisely		
Have healthy sons		
Be a good leader		
Have a good claim to the throne		
Average score		

Now it is time to draw some conclusions. Work in groups to compare your charts and decide between you:
a) Who was the best monarch and why?
b) Who was the worst monarch and why?
c) Who was it easiest to agree about and why?
d) Who provoked most disagreement and why?
e) Who would you most like to find out more about?
f) Which of the king's jobs on page 5 do you now think was the most important, that is, the one the king had to get right to be a success?

Religion in the Middle Ages

WELCOME TO CANTERBURY!
Look at this massive cathedral. This is more than just a church. It is a statement. It is one of the grandest buildings in England. Not even a king gets a palace like this. It shouts out to all who see it that God is important and magnificent. And it proclaims that the Church is powerful.

If you are going to understand the Middle Ages you have to understand the power and significance of the Christian religion. In our time religion is a matter of personal preference: some people are religious, others are not; some go to church, most do not. In the Middle Ages it was very different.

- Religion was a matter of life or death – for almost everyone.
- Religious leaders – the leaders of the Christian Church – were as powerful as kings.
- The leader of the Church – the Pope, who was based in Rome – was probably the most powerful individual in Europe.
- The Church was rich. It owned masses of land and earned a lot of money. Tens of thousands of people worked for the Church.
- Every village in England had its own outpost of the Christian religion – a parish church, with its own priest, where once a week all the people came for Mass, to be told how to live, and to take one more step – so they hoped – on their road to heaven.

It was powerful stuff!

Unlike the previous section which told a single story from the beginning of the Middle Ages to the end this one is thematic. The stories here overlap each other and they overlap with the stories in Section 1. You will need to use the timeline on page 3 to keep your bearings. Each unit focuses on one topic or depth study which will add a particular dimension to your understanding of religion in the Middle Ages.

- In the previous section you will already have seen how important it was for a king to work well with Church leaders. Some of the most spectacular failures were the kings who fell out with the Pope or with the Church leaders. In **Unit 9** you are going to examine one of the most famous fallings-out between a king and the Church, which led to the murder of Archbishop Thomas Becket. You will consider what this tells you about the importance of religion in the Middle Ages.
- In **Unit 10** you will find out more about cathedrals – with a particular focus on Canterbury. You will find out what to look out for on your own site visit to a cathedral.
- In **Unit 11** you will investigate monasteries and convents – with a special focus on Fountains Abbey in Yorkshire. You will think about why so many people wanted to become monks or nuns and what life was like for them in the monastery or convent. You will also see how important the monasteries were by the end of the Middle Ages.
- In **Unit 12** you will study how religion affected the lives of ordinary people in villages – the peasant farmers, who formed the vast majority of the English population. You will join them as they try to get to heaven.
- Finally in **Unit 13** you will shift focus and scale entirely and look at the ways that religion helped to cause a series of wars between Christians and Muslims – known as the Crusades – that lasted for over 200 years. What do these chilling events tell us about religion in the Middle Ages?

Task

You won't need to study all these units, but whichever topics or depth studies you follow throughout the section, your challenge will be to create your own spider diagram or concept map to sum up what you have found about religion in the Middle Ages. See page 131 for ideas.

UNIT 9 Church and State: Henry versus Becket

What is this all about?

Henry II was King of England from 1154 to 1189. He was one of the most powerful and successful kings of the Middle Ages. His reign was one of peace and stability in England. He ruled a vast European empire known as the Angevin Empire that spread across France and the British Isles. He introduced a number of changes in how England was run so more money could be raised to pay for the upkeep of the empire.

You can see a suitably 'king-like' portrait of him on page 33. Yet Source 1 on this page shows him in a very different situation: humiliated, and at the mercy of the monks of Canterbury. In this unit you find out what this tells us about the struggle for power between king and Church in the Middle Ages.

Source 1

Henry is whipped by monks at Becket's tomb.

Task

Source 1 is a stained glass window. Write the text for a plaque to go beneath this window explaining what it shows and what this event tells you about the power of the Church at this time. You have a limit of 200 words.

Thomas Becket was the son of a merchant. He did not come from a noble family. He worked as a clerk and archdeacon at Canterbury Cathedral. When Henry was looking for a new Chancellor, Archbishop Theobold recommended Becket and in 1155, Henry appointed him. Soon they became close friends. In 1162 Henry needed a new Archbishop of Canterbury and he wanted Becket.

Control of the Church

Henry thought that, with Becket as Archbishop of Canterbury, he would have greater control over the Church. In particular, he would be able to get all the churchmen to swear an oath of allegiance to him rather than the Pope. However, as soon as Becket was appointed, it became clear that he was not going to do what Henry wanted. There was one issue above all others which was to prove to be a battleground between them.

What ...?

THE CHANCELLOR
Had to deal with the day-to-day government of the country as well as act as the king's AMBASSADOR. In 1158 Becket went to Paris for Henry with eight five-horse wagons and 24 changes of clothes. To impress his hosts he gave away all his gold and furs.

Did you know?

Before Becket's exile in 1164, he and Henry used to have huge rows. It was reported Becket once said to Henry: 'We ought to obey God rather than men.' To which Henry responded: 'I don't want a sermon from you. Are you not the son of one of my peasants?'

Did you know?

One hundred years before Becket, Anselm, the then Archbishop of Canterbury, spent roughly half his time in exile. This was because he believed he should obey the Pope over the king, much to the annoyance of William II. Becket's problem was not new.

Henry did not like the fact that priests and members of religious orders were not being tried in the King's courts but in Church courts. Henry believed that this undermined the power of the King.

Constitutions of Clarendon, 1164

At the meeting of the Great Council at Clarendon in 1164 Henry demanded that Becket, the bishops and barons accept a king's rights to try priests. In short, Henry insisted that royal justice should rule. The agreement at the end of the meeting, known as the Constitutions of Clarendon, also gave the King the right to appoint archbishops and bishops. Becket initially agreed to the King's points but then refused to add his seal to the agreement.

Becket flees

Henry was now out to get Becket. In 1164 he put Becket on trial on a number of charges. Becket fled into exile in France. In 1169 he met Henry in France but they failed to resolve their differences. They met again in France in 1169, the outcome being that Becket agreed to return to England in December 1170. However, immediately on Becket's return rumours spread round Henry's court that Becket was bullying bishops and looking for revenge against Henry.

Becket is murdered

When these rumours reached Henry he exploded with rage. Four knights decided to teach Becket a lesson. They travelled to Canterbury Cathedral to find him. They first met him unarmed but an argument followed, the knights failed to arrest him and they stormed out. They returned fully armed and determined to arrest Becket. A struggle followed and Becket was murdered in the cathedral (see next page).

Becket the Martyr

When Becket's body was prepared for burial it was discovered that he was wearing underclothes made of horsehair, a sign of penance. A number of people began to claim that miracles were taking place because of Becket. A blind woman called Britheva claimed to be able to see again after some of Becket's blood had been put on her eyes. Thousands travelled to Canterbury in hope of a miracle. A shrine was built for Becket and, in 1173, Becket was made a saint.

Henry's penance

Henry was forced to back down over Church courts and in 1174 he did PENANCE at the shrine of Thomas Becket. This involved him walking barefoot into the cathedral, lying on the floor of Becket's tomb, being whipped by the monks and the bishops and sleeping on the ground by the tomb without food.

THE MURDER OF THOMAS BECKET

There are different accounts of Becket's murder. Here are four of them. See if you can work out from the sources what actually happened.

QUESTIONS

1 Some points of information are mentioned or shown in every source. Read through the sources and pick out three of these **common** points.

2 Some points are mentioned in only one source. Pick out one point from each source that is **unique** to that source.

Source A

The knights entered the cathedral with swords drawn, shouting in a rage:
   'Where is Thomas Becket, traitor of the King and kingdom?'
   No one responded and instantly they cried out more loudly,
   'Where is the archbishop?'
   Becket descended from the steps to which he had been taken by the monks who were fearful of the knights and said in an adequately audible voice:
   'Here I am, not a traitor of the King but a priest.'
   The MARTYR Becket sensed he would be killed and with his neck bent as if he were in prayer and with his joined hands he prayed to God, St Mary and St Denis. He had barely finished when one of the knights, fearing Thomas would be saved by the people and escape alive, suddenly set upon him and cut off the top of Becket's head. The lower arm of the writer [Edward Grim] was cut by the same blow. Indeed the writer stood by Becket, holding him in his arms – while all the other priests and monks fled. Becket was hit on the head again and with the third blow he bent his knees and elbows and fell.

The third knight then struck Becket; and with this blow he shattered the sword on the stone and his crown [the top of his head] separated from his head so that the blood turned white from the brain yet no less did the brain turn red from the blood. A clerk who came in with the knights placed his foot on the neck of the holy priest and precious martyr and (it is horrible to say) scattered the brains with the blood across the floor, exclaiming to the rest, 'We can leave this place, knights, he will not get up again.'

From Edward Grim The Life of St Thomas, Archbishop of Canterbury. *Edward Grim was a witness at the murder and is mentioned in a number of the stories.*

Source B

And these four knights came to Canterbury on the Tuesday in Christmas week. They came to Saint Thomas and said that the king commanded him to apologise for his mistakes and reverse the excommunication on the bishops. Thomas said that he could not do that. The knight Sir Reginald said that if he didn't do as he was told it would cost him his life.

Then one of the knights hit him on the head as he kneeled before the altar. Sir Edward Grim put his arm out with the cross to defend Becket. The sword hit the cross and nearly cut Grim's arm off. Grim then fled in fear as did all the other monks. The knights then each hit Becket, they cut off a great piece of the skull of his head, that his brain fell on the pavement. They were so cruel that one of them broke the point of his sword against the pavement. And when he was dead they stirred his brain and then stole his goods and horse.

The Golden Legend or Lives of the Saints, *compiled by Jacobus de Voragine, Archbishop of Genoa, 1275.*

Source C

The servants of the devil [the knights] had no respect for either Becket or the Cathedral. They attacked the dignified Becket as he stood in prayer before the holy altar. Even though it was Christmas time, these evil men most inhumanly murdered him.

    Having done the deed, they left triumphant and full of joy.

William of Newburgh, 'Becket and Henry', selections from Book II of his History *(c. 1200).*

Source D

QUESTIONS

3 How does **Source A** differ from **Source B** in its account of Grim's reaction? Why do you think there were these differences?

4 How is the tone of **Source C** different from the other sources?

5 What would make a historian think that the artist who drew **Source D** based his ideas on Edward Grim's account (Source A)?

6 Using **all** the sources and your own knowledge, write what you think is an accurate account of Becket's murder.

A contemporary picture of the murder of Becket.

UNIT 10 A visit to Canterbury Cathedral

What is this all about?

The most powerful person in the English medieval Church was the Archbishop of Canterbury. When William I conquered England he got rid of the Anglo-Saxon Stigand from this job and appointed his loyal friend and adviser Lanfranc. Archbishop Lanfranc appointed many other Normans to the key roles in the Church and together they began a huge programme of cathedral building. Many of these cathedrals are still standing today. In this unit you are going to visit one of them.

What is a cathedral?

England was divided into areas called dioceses, each of which had a bishop. Each bishop had a throne. The word cathedral comes from the Latin word *cathedra* which means 'bishop's throne'. So a cathedral is simply a church with a bishop's throne in it.

So far it is quite simple. However there were two types of cathedral in England:

- Monastic cathedrals such as Canterbury or Winchester were run by monks. These cathedrals were really part of a monastery.
- SECULAR cathedrals such as York or Exeter were run by priests.

A cathedral had other functions too. It was like administrative centre – a place from which to organise and run a diocese. It was also a symbol – a cathedral was a symbol of the power of the Church just as a castle was a symbol of the power of the king or the barons, so it needed to be impressive.

In 1072 the King's Council at Windsor ordered that all cathedrals be placed in towns or cities. Some bishops were told to move; for example the Bishop of Dorchester moved to Lincoln and the Bishop of Selsey moved to Chichester.

Every diocese was divided into areas called archdeaconries and every archdeaconry divided into groups of parishes called deaneries. This gave the Church a much better structure.

Who ... ?

LANFRANC

Born in Italy in around 1005, he taught as a monk at the monastery of Bec in France where he prepared young men for a life in the Church (including the future Pope Alexander II). He was well known for having an excellent understanding of the Bible. He became a loyal adviser to Duke William of Normandy. He served as Archbishop of Canterbury from 1071 until his death in 1089.

Task

Source 1 shows you the styles of church windows and doors in the Middle Ages.
1 Which do you like the best?
2 Canterbury Cathedral has been added to over the years. Which of these styles best fits the photo on page 94?
3 Next time you visit a cathedral, see if you can tell, from the windows and doors alone, in which period it was probably built.

Canterbury Cathedral

Since the Archbishop of Canterbury had the most important job in the Church, the cathedral there was also the most important in the country. There had been a cathedral in Canterbury since Anglo-Saxon times. The Anglo-Saxon building had been badly damaged by a fire in December 1067. In 1070 Lanfranc ordered that Canterbury Cathedral be rebuilt from scratch in the Normans' favourite 'Romanesque' style and took a personal interest in the plans. From 1071 to 1077 the rebuilding of the cathedral took place at breakneck speed.

We have been left an account of the rebuilding of the cathedral by a monk, Eadmer. He tells of a number of problems that needed to be overcome before the cathedral could be rebuilt. One problem was that people were buried in the old cathedral. Eadmer tells us that the bodies in the east end of the cathedral were dug up and stored in the west end until the east end was rebuilt, then the bodies were reburied.

Source

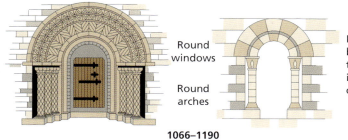

ROMANESQUE

Round windows

Round arches

Most cathedrals and churches built between the tenth and twelfth centuries were built in this style. It is sometimes called Norman.

1066–1190

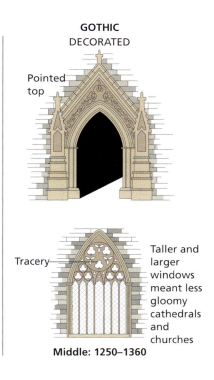

EARLY ENGLISH

Pointed arches were stronger than round arches

Lancet windows

Early: 1170–1290

GOTHIC

DECORATED

Pointed top

Tracery

Taller and larger windows meant less gloomy cathedrals and churches

Middle: 1250–1360

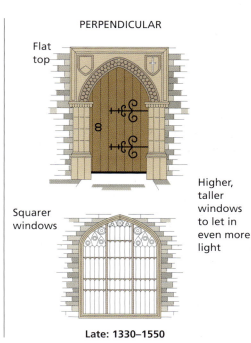

PERPENDICULAR

Flat top

Squarer windows

Higher, taller windows to let in even more light

Late: 1330–1550

Main features

This plan shows Canterbury Cathedral as it is today. Some of the features date back to the Normans. Some are more recent. Parts of the cathedral would be used for different things. All around were small chapels and shrines. The cathedral was also a monastery so many of the features relate to the daily life of the monks.

Source 2

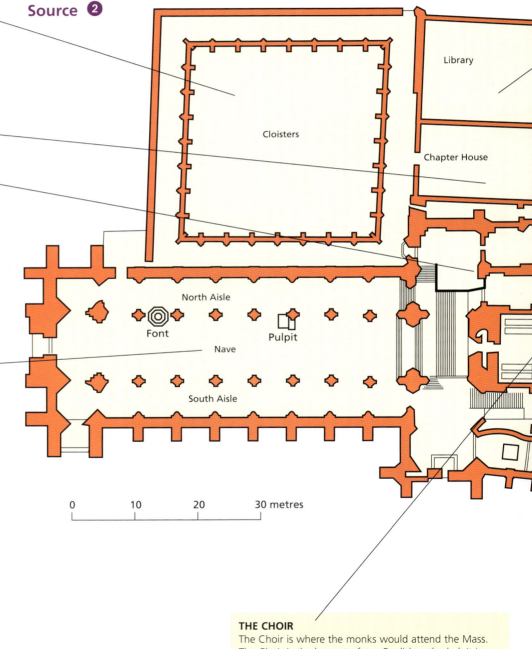

THE CLOISTER
The Cloister was the centre of daily life in the monastery. This was where the monks lived and where Lanfranc set up a school for local children. It was also where the monks were trained.

THE CHAPTER HOUSE
This was where the monks would meet to hear a Chapter of the Rule of St Benedict read to them. They would then deal with the business of the monastery.

MARTYRDOM
A small altar marks the spot where, on 29 December 1170, Archbishop Thomas Becket was murdered. It is called the Altar of the Sword's Point because it used to house the tip of Richard de Brito's sword which broke on the pavement as he attacked the Archbishop (see pages 98–99).

THE NAVE
The Nave is at the centre of the cathedral. The present Nave was finished in 1405 and is an example of Perpendicular architecture. It replaced the Nave built by Lanfranc.

THE CHOIR
The Choir is where the monks would attend the Mass. The Choir is the longest of any English cathedral. It is also noted for its height. It was built in the Gothic style by William of Sens, and was finished by 1184.

Source check
The rebuilding of Canterbury Cathedral was done so quickly that a writer at the time called William of Malmesbury commented: *You do not know which to admire more, the beauty or the speed.*

LIBRARY
Lanfranc built a large library. At the beginning of Lent, each monk in the monastery was given a book to read. By 1170 the library contained nearly 600 volumes, a vast number for those days.

EASTERN CRYPT
For 50 years after his death, Becket's body rested in a tomb in the crypt. This is where the first pilgrims to St Thomas Becket came to pray.

SHRINE OF ST THOMAS
There is now an inscription on a brass plate and a burning candle to mark the point where St Thomas' shrine used to be. The shrine was destroyed on the orders of King Henry VIII who was involved in his own struggle with the Church.

Water tower (monastery water supply)

N

CORONA
This little chapel originally contained a part of Becket's skull which was cut off when he was murdered.

Treasury

Choir

Archbishop's throne

Position of high altar in Middle Ages

A plan of Canterbury Cathedral.

TOMB OF THE BLACK PRINCE
Edward, Prince of Wales (1330–1376) was known as 'The Black Prince' because of the colour of his armour. He was the son of Edward III and led the English in one of their greatest military triumphs against the French at the Battle of Poitiers in September 1356. He is buried in a magnificent shrine in the cathedral.

ST AUGUSTINE'S CHAIR
This marble throne was originally made for the chapel dedicated to St Thomas. It is now the throne of the Archbishop of Canterbury.

Task

Research project
If you are lucky enough to be taken on a trip to a cathedral, try to collect as much information as you can. This information might include the following:

- a booklet or leaflet about the cathedral's history
- postcards or pictures
- plan of the cathedral.

When you get home or back to school, write a project about the cathedral. Try to include the following points:

- When was the cathedral built and who by?
- What style is it built in?
- What has been changed in the cathedral since it was first built?
- Which individuals and stories are associated with the cathedral?

What is this all about?

Many men and women decided to dedicate their lives to the service of God. The men joined monasteries or abbeys and the women went to convents or nunneries. They separated themselves from ordinary people. They followed strict rules. They spent hours in prayer. This might sound a hard life but in the Middle Ages it was very popular. By the 1300s there were thousands of monks and nuns. What was the attraction and what was life really like for them?

The rule of St Benedict

The basic idea of separating yourself off from the world in order to focus on God came from early Christian times. Men would go off into the desert, on their own or in groups, to meditate and to fast. The idea gradually spread to western Europe, where the monks followed rules set down by St Benedict who lived 480–547.

All monks and nuns had to make three vows. They had to keep these solemn promises throughout their lives:

- **Poverty**   No monk or nun could own anything at all. Whatever they owned when they joined a monastery or convent had to be given up to the community and used for the good of all.
- **Chastity**   No monk or nun could get married or have sex with anyone at all, ever. This showed that they put God first, above everything.
- **Obedience**   Monks and nuns had to obey the head of their monastery or convent at all times and without question.

St Benedict built on these vows by writing a detailed set of rules. These rules were really a code of behaviour that covered all aspects of a monk's day. St Benedict's rules included what clothing the monks should wear, what the sleeping arrangements in dormitories should be, the sort of food that could be eaten, how guests were to be looked after and how the sick were to be cared for. Monks who followed the Rule of St Benedict were called Benedictines. Here are some extracts.

- Idleness is the enemy of the soul. The brothers should have set times for manual work and for reading prayers.
- A mattress, woollen blanket and pillow are enough for bedding.
- All monks should take turns to wait on each other so that no one is excused kitchen work.
- Above all, care must be taken of the sick.

What ... ?

MEDITATE
To think deeply and quietly about something.

FAST
To go without food.

What ... ?

HABIT
The garment a monk or nun wears.

The thinking behind this code was that if there were rules that had to be followed, monks could then focus their time on worshipping God and not on petty squabbles like what to wear.

Source ❶

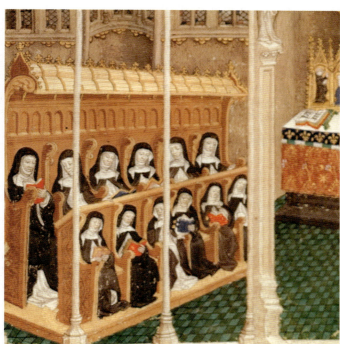

Monks and nuns at prayer. Benedictine monks wore black habits with a cowl hood that they could pull over their heads if they wanted to. The nuns wore headgear called wimples that covered their hair and hid most of their faces. Both monks and nuns had girdles round their waists with three big knots tied in them to remind them of the three vows they had made.

Did you know?

At Canterbury, food was to be basic and only the very sick were allowed to eat meat. Only on certain occasions and times of the year were the monks allowed the luxury of eating lard. The abbot (who at Canterbury was also the archbishop) had to eat at the same table as his monks.

In the Middle Ages there was a great boom in the number of people wanting to dedicate themselves to God and enter monasteries and convents. It has been estimated that in 1066 there were around 1,000 monks in Britain; by the beginning of the 1300s this number had risen to 13,000. By this time, one man in every 200 was a monk. In addition, there were about 30,000 people who were connected to the life of monasteries because they worked there as servants. This meant that monasteries (and to a lesser extent, convents) had a tremendous impact on their local communities and on Britain itself.

What ... ?

LAY BROTHER

The Cistercian order had lay brothers who made vows and worked in and for monasteries, but were not full monks like the choir monks. They attended fewer church services and were allowed to mix with the outside world.

CHOIR MONK

A novice who made his vows and became a full monk, usually in the Cistercian order.

How did boys become monks?

In the early days, families sometimes gave a boy to a monastery to be trained as a monk. This was supposed to show that the family was deeply religious. We don't know what any of these boys thought about being given away like this, but some of them can't have been too impressed! By the 1100s this practice had died out, and all boys and young men going into a monastery did so voluntarily.

Task

In 1141, Orderic Vitalis wrote a book called *History of the Church*. In it he described how his parents sent him off to become a monk. Read what he wrote carefully (below), and try to work out whether Orderic's father sent him away because of his love for God or because of his love for Orderic.

> When I was five years old I was sent to school in the town of Shrewsbury. There, Siward, a priest, taught me to read and write and instructed me in the psalms and hymns. Then, O glorious God, you inspired my father to put me under your Rule. So, weeping, he gave me, a child of ten, into the care of the monk Reginald. My father sent me away for love of you and never saw me again, for he promised me in your name that if I became a monk I should go to heaven after my death.

Boys could go into a monastery from the age of ten. If they went in that young, they could change their minds and leave at any time before they took holy orders. However, most young men decided to take up the religious life when they were about fifteen. They were welcomed into monasteries as trainee monks, called novices. They would work alongside the monks learning how to do different jobs and singing in the choir. They would also be taught how to read and write. All the novices would be supervised by the Master of Novices for at least a year. He would watch them carefully and try to work out if they really were suited to the religious life and, if they were, when it would be appropriate for them to become fully fledged monks. To become a monk would mean taking the three vows of poverty, chastity and obedience. The novices would have to leave all their old life behind and become obedient to God and to the rules of the monastery. They wouldn't even be able to leave the monastery without the abbot's permission. This sort of life didn't suit everyone and some did leave after having a 'taster' as a novice.

Once a novice was ready, he took the three vows that committed him to the monastic life and was given a tonsure (a special haircut). Then the really serious learning would begin. The young monk would have to learn what was expected of him at the different services and at all the different stages of a monk's day. He would need to train, too, to be a useful member of the religious community as, for example, an illustrator or a cellarer (see page 112) or an infirmarian, who cared for the sick and dying.

Did you know?

A monk had the top of his head shaved so that he had a bald patch. This was called a tonsure. The ring of hair that was left was supposed to represent Christ's crown of thorns.

What … ?

A TITHE
One tenth of what everyone produced – barley, hay, flour, eggs, for example – had to be given to the Church.

Did you know?

Some orders required their monks and nuns to take a vow of silence. So they developed sign language to ask for what they wanted. If, for example, a nun wanted some more fish for her dinner, she would wiggle her right hand sideways, like a fish moving through the water; if a monk wanted bread he would make a circle with both thumbs and the next two fingers.

And he would have to take his share of the everyday jobs that keep a community going. All this while being obedient, chaste and poor!

Was it the same for girls?

Not quite. There were far fewer convents than monasteries. Between 1250 and 1540, well over 100 convents were set up, but only four had more than 30 women in them and 63 had fewer than ten. By 1200 there were about 3,000 nuns in Britain compared to 13,000 monks. Why was this?

It is true that many nuns believed they had a calling to give up the world and enter a religious order. But there were others who saw entry into a convent as a sensible career move. It meant they were spared the necessity of getting married and would be educated and gain experience in living within and managing an organisation. But this applied only to girls from wealthy families. Convents had less money than monasteries, and families often had to pay to send their girls there. Poor families could not afford this, and, besides, their daughters had to work to bring in much needed cash.

Convents were separated from monasteries so that nuns and monks could not meet and be tempted into relationships. But convents still depended on monasteries. Local abbots and bishops usually gave them tithes, and sometimes wealthy men and women would leave them money in their wills, but they did not attract the funding that monasteries did. Many convents took in paying guests – usually wealthy widows and wives – for short breaks from the stresses of life. This wasn't always a good thing as this sort of contact with the outside world made many nuns wish things were different for them.

Task
a) List the various reasons why someone might join a monastery or convent.
b) Highlight in different colours those that apply to just men, just women and both men and women.

Source ❷

Source ❸

Source ❹

Source ❺

Task

Work it out
Using the information on pages 104–107, work out what is happening in each of these four pictures. (For answers, see page 190.)

Different orders

The Rule of St Benedict was a hard Rule to follow. It wasn't surprising that, over the years, little by little, many monks and monasteries slid away from parts of it. Then, gradually, breakaway groups founded new religious orders, trying hard to get back to what they saw as the purity of St Benedict's Rule. More and more religious orders were founded, all of which adapted the Rule of St Benedict to meet their needs and beliefs. There were so many that, in 1215, the Pope banned any new orders. New monasteries had to adopt the rules of the existing ones.

Not all religious orders expected their members to spend all their time in isolation. Some went out into the world and taught ordinary people about Christianity. They were called friars.

Order	Where was the Order founded?	When did the Order arrive in Britain?	What were the aims of the Order?	Did you know?
Benedictine	In 525 by Benedict in Italy.	597. Led by Augustine who founded a monastery at Canterbury and became the first Archbishop of Canterbury.	To follow St Benedict's Rule that would enable them to lead a godly life.	Called the 'black monks' because of their black habits, which they wore over white gowns.
Cluniac	In 910 when William of Aquitaine gave land for a new monastery at Cluny in France.	1077. First monastery built at Lewes in Sussex.	To lead a strict and holy life.	Followed St Benedict's Rule but spent more time praying and in church services than the Benedictines.
Cistercian	1098 by Robert de Champagne at Citeaux in France.	1131. First monastery built at Rievaulx in Yorkshire. Became the most popular Order in England.	To follow a strict interpretation of St Benedict's Rule.	Built monasteries in remote areas. Supported choir monks (full monks) and lay brothers who were not educated but who took vows and worked as labourers. Became skilled sheep farmers. Made their habits from the grey/white wool of their sheep and were called 'white monks'.
Carthusian	1084 by St Bruno at Chartreuse in France.	1178. First monastery built at Witham in Essex.	To lead a solitary life while keeping strictly to the Rule of St Benedict.	Lived in individual cells and hardly ever spoke. Ate one vegetarian meal a day. Strictest of all the Orders. Wore white habits.
Dominicans (Friars)	1216 by St Dominic in Spain.	1221.	To teach ordinary people about Christianity.	Better educated than most priests and very good teachers. Inspired by the ideas of St Francis.
Franciscans (Friars)	1209 by St Francis of Assisi in Italy.	1224.	To teach ordinary people about Christianity.	Travelled the country, without any possessions or money, teaching and preaching to ordinary people.

Case study: Fountains Abbey

Fountains Abbey was a large Cistercian monastery founded in North Yorkshire in 1132. It began when a breakaway group of Benedictine monks decided their life in York Abbey had become too soft. They wanted to get back to the strictness of the Rule of St Benedict and persuaded the archbishop to let them have some land in Skelldale, a remote corner of north Yorkshire. There they planned to build a monastery and join the new order of Cistercians.

One of these monks was Brother Hugh. In 1206 he remembered what he had been told of these beginnings, and he wrote about them in the *Fountains Chronicle*:

> The land was thick with thorns, lying between the slopes of mountains and among rocks jutting out on both sides. It was more suitable as the home of wild beasts than the home of human beings.
>
> Here the holy men gathered to seek shelter, keeping off the harsh winter as best they could, with straw and grasses thrown over them. At night they usually sang psalms according to the Rule. By day they worked: some weaving mats, others using young trees to build a chapel and some cultivating gardens.

Before long, the monks had built a huge church from stone. Each year, they added new buildings and extended existing ones. They gradually extended the land they owned, too, until Fountains Abbey was the largest landowner in north Yorkshire. The lay brothers became highly successful sheep farmers and the Abbey itself ran many farms (called granges) scattered throughout northern England. Important churchmen, merchants and pilgrims visited Fountains and were entertained in the guest rooms. Fountains wool became famous, not just in the local markets but throughout England and northern Europe. The choir monks and lay brothers were good at what they did. Fountains Abbey became very rich and very powerful.

Not everyone approved of the Cistercians! At the end of the 1200s, Walter Map wrote:

> The Cistercians work so hard that they have become very rich, but they are mean and do not like to spend their wealth. They are happy to borrow farming equipment from others, but they will not lend anyone their ploughs. Their Rule does not allow them to work as parish priests, so when they are given new lands they destroy any villages there and throw out the people who live there.

Fountains Abbey, like all the English medieval monasteries, now lies in ruins. You can find lots of photos of what it looks like today on the internet, for example at www.fountainsabbey.org.uk. The artist Alan Sorrell drew the picture below. How could he have worked out what the abbey looked like?

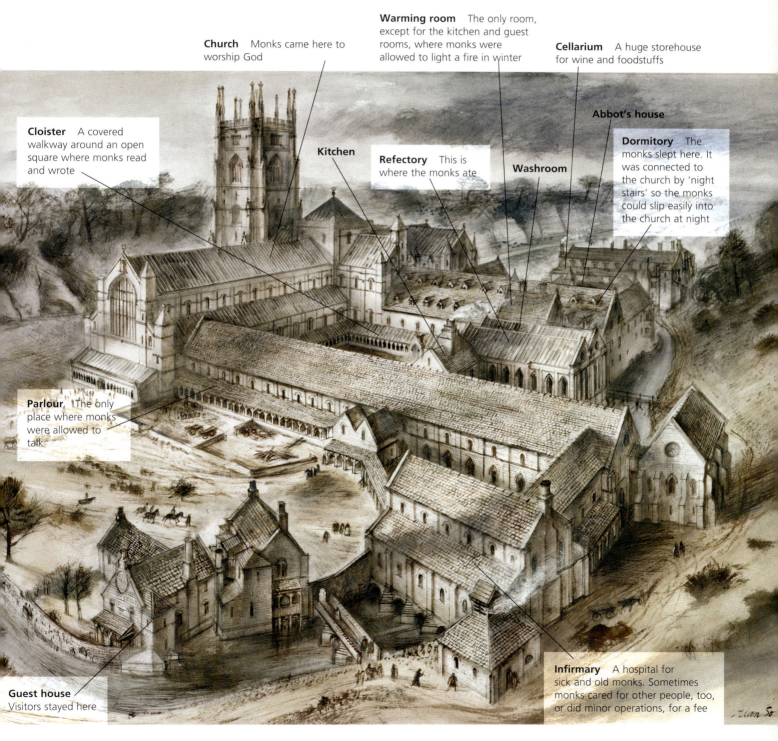

Warming room The only room, except for the kitchen and guest rooms, where monks were allowed to light a fire in winter

Church Monks came here to worship God

Cellarium A huge storehouse for wine and foodstuffs

Abbot's house

Cloister A covered walkway around an open square where monks read and wrote

Kitchen

Refectory This is where the monks ate

Washroom

Dormitory The monks slept here. It was connected to the church by 'night stairs' so the monks could slip easily into the church at night

Parlour The only place where monks were allowed to talk

Infirmary A hospital for sick and old monks. Sometimes monks cared for other people, too, or did minor operations, for a fee

Guest house Visitors stayed here

What did the monks do?

At its peak, Fountains Abbey probably housed about 50 choir monks and around 200 lay brothers. The Abbey was a highly organised unit.

I'm in charge here. I've entertained the King and many noblemen.

I'm responsible for the church services, the music, and the choir books. I teach the monks to sing and how to read aloud clearly.

I look after the valuable linen, the embroidered robes and banners and the gold and silver plate on the altar.

I'm responsible for all the goods stored in the cellarium. I deal with tradesmen from outside.

Abbot

Precentor

Sacristan

Cellarer

I'm in charge of the refectory and the serving of food. I have to make sure there are fresh rushes on the floor and that lamps are lit on dark days and in the evenings.

I look after all the clothes and bed linen. I have to make sure the fire in the warming room is well stoked and that there is enough hot water.

The young novices are my responsibility. I have to care for them, educate them and decide whether or not they're suited to life in the monastery.

I see to the distribution of food and clothing to the poor when they come to the monastery gates every morning.

Refectorian

Chamberlain

Novice master

Almoner

When?	What?
0200 hrs	*Vigils* The night service, followed by reading and prayers until dawn
Dawn	*Lauds* A short service
0600 hrs	*Prime* A short service followed by Mass
0700 hrs	*Chapter* Monks listen to readings from the Rule of St Benedict, confess where they have broken the Rule and are disciplined, discuss the work for the day and sort out their duties The monks then worked in the workshops or gardens
0900 hrs	*Tierce* A short service
1000 hrs	Reading and writing
1200 hrs	*Sext* Short service after which the monks had a wash and then Prandium, the main meal of the day After the meal, another wash and a rest
1500 hrs	*Nones* A short service, then a drink and more work
1800 hrs	*Vespers* A short service followed by supper
1900 hrs	*Collation* Where one monk read aloud to the others
2000 hrs	*Compline* The last service of the day
2100 hrs	To bed

Daily schedule

The day at Fountains Abbey followed a set pattern, but the timings shifted slightly between summer and winter. The labels on page 111 tell you where these things would take place.

Impact on the community

Fountains Abbey provided:

- food and clothing for the poor
- employment for ordinary people
- health care for local people.

Monasteries were important for other reasons:

- Monks kept chronicles recording the events of the time.
- Monks copied out old books and saved old learning from being lost.
- Infirmarians who looked after the sick became expert in medicine and basic surgery.
- Monasteries were healthy places. They developed systems to supply hot water, drainage and sewage. Monks washed, used lavatories and cared for the sick in buildings away from the main body of the monastery.
- Some monasteries taught local children how to read and write.

Task

On page 112 are some of the different responsibilities monks had in Fountains Abbey. List them in order of importance
a) to the smooth running of the monastery
a) to the community outside the monastery.
Now compare your lists with a partner. Where are they different? Where are they the same? Discuss why and see if you can arrive at a list with which you both agree.

Summary task

What good did monasteries do, and for whom? Write an essay explaining your answer.

WHAT WAS LIFE REALLY LIKE FOR MONKS AND NUNS?

Source **A**

Before I came here I could never have kept silent for so long and given up the gossiping I loved so much. I used to do whatever I liked, laugh and chatter with my friends, go to rich feasts, drink much wine and sleep late in the mornings.

Now how different it is! My food is very little and my clothes are rough. I sleep on a hard mat, tired out with work. Just when sleep is sweetest, the sound of the bell wakes me up.

I can only talk to three men. I obey my master like an animal. Yet here there are no grumblings and quarrellings. Here everything is shared equally and 300 men cheerfully obey one master.

A novice monk in about 1200 wrote what he felt about his life at the monastery of Rievaulx, a big Cistercian monastery in Yorkshire.

Source **B**

I am tormented and crushed by the length of the services at night. I am often overcome by the hard work I have to do with my hands. The food sticks to my mouth. The rough clothing cuts through my skin. I am always longing for the delights of the world and sigh for its pleasures.

In about 1200, another novice monk wrote what he felt about his life at the monastery of Rievaulx.

Source **C**

A monk copying out a manuscript. Before the invention of printing, all books were made this way.

Source **D**

Nuns caring for the sick at the Hotel Dieu in Paris.

Source

A monk sampling wine.

Source F

Archbishops and bishops were shocked that nuns wore golden hairpins and silver belts, jewelled rings, laced shoes, slashed tunics, low-necked dresses, costly materials and furs. Bishops regarded pets as bad for discipline and tried to turn the nuns' animals out. The nuns just waited until the bishops went and whistled the dogs back again. Dogs were easily the favourite pets, but nuns also kept monkeys, squirrels, rabbits and birds. They sometimes took animals to church with them.

An extract from a book called Medieval Women *written by Eileen Power, published in 1975.*

QUESTIONS

1 Study **Source A**.
   What does Source A tell you about this novice monk?

2 Study **Sources A** and **B**. These novices were living and working in the same monastery at roughly the same time.
   How far are their accounts similar and how are they different? Can you suggest reasons for this?

3 Study **Sources C**, **D** and **E**.
   What can you learn from these three pictures about the work of monks and nuns?

4 Study **Sources D** and **F** or **Sources A** and **E**.
   These sources give very different views of nuns/monks.
   Does this mean that one of them must be wrong? Explain your answer.

5 Study **all** the sources.
   Which one do you think would be the most useful to someone trying to find out what life was like for people who had taken religious vows?

6 'Monks and nuns led a comfortable life and did no good for anyone but themselves.'
   Use all the sources and your own knowledge to explain how far you agree with this statement.

What is this all about?

In the early Middle Ages most of the people in England were poor peasant farmers. They lived and worked in the same village most of the lives. They lived in simple homes, had simple lives, ate simple food. What did religion mean to them? In this unit you will explore how the Church affected the lives of ordinary men, women and children.

What ... ?

A PARISH
Part of a diocese that has its own church and priest to whom tithes were paid.

The parish church

The most important building in a medieval village was the church. It was usually built of stone and had a tall tower, or steeple, pointing skyward. It was a constant reminder to the peasants of the presence of God in their everyday lives. They heard the church clock strike the hours throughout the day and night when they were working in the fields or trying to get to sleep at home. At times of celebration, the church bells rang out joyfully. It paced their lives.

The hub of village life

The church was more than a building and bells. Peasants went to the parish church for all the important events in their lives.

- They took their babies there when they were only a few weeks old so that the parish priest could baptise them. In medieval times many babies died before their first birthday, and a baby that wasn't baptised couldn't be buried in consecrated ground and didn't stand a chance of getting to heaven.

Source ❶

What ... ?

BAPTISM
The ceremony by which people became part of the Christian Church, usually by being sprinkled with holy water.

CONSECRATED GROUND
Ground set apart by the Christian Church for holy purposes, like the burial of the dead.

A medieval parish church in Aylesford, Kent today. Notice how it towers over the houses in the village.

- Men and women were married in the parish church or, more usually for villagers, in the church porch.
- It was in the parish graveyard surrounding the church that they were buried when they died.
- It was to the parish church that villagers went every Sunday and holy day for Mass.
- They went to confess their sins to the priest and to receive, through him, God's forgiveness for the wrongs they had done.

Parish churches were not just religious buildings. They were open to everyone throughout the week and were usually very busy places. They were like modern community centres. Without pews or any sort of fixed seating, church buildings were sound, weather-proof spaces where markets were held and people swapped information and news. Churches might be used as theatres where travelling actors performed plays and entertained the villagers with music and dancing. Feasts and fairs were held in churches and churchyards.

Feast days, festivals and fun

Religious festivals were also the focus of fun. The church reserved certain days as special feast days or festivals, called holy days. In theory no one worked on these days but there were over fifty a year. The lord would not like that so the Church chose a few specific festivals that would be holy days (holidays) for everyone.

Source ❷

Activities inside a medieval parish church. These would not normally all be happening at the same time. ❓ *How many can you name?*

The parish priest

The parish priest was the direct link between ordinary people and the vast and powerful organisation that was the Catholic Church (see Source 4). The parish priest was chosen by the lord of the manor and in the early Middle Ages the lord would choose someone from among the villagers.

Source 3

Source 4

A medieval parish priest conducting a burial.
❓ *What do you think is the message of the 'flying bones'?*

The structure of the medieval Catholic Church.

Spiritual duties

The central and most important work of the priest was to conduct services in the parish church on Sundays and other holy days. The most important of church services was the Mass. Here the priest read the service (which was in Latin) or, if he could not read, recited it from memory. Then he blessed some bread and wine and offered them to God. The Church taught that, at that moment, God miraculously changed the bread and wine into the body and blood of His son, Jesus Christ. This is called transubstantiation. The priest would then drink the wine and eat the bread on behalf of the people, in the belief that this would bring them close to God. Peasants watching this familiar ceremony, week in and week out, would come to believe in the presence of God in their lives.

Priests also had to care for the sick, the troubled and the dying, hold church services and give spiritual advice to their parishioners. These were his spiritual duties.

Temporal duties

Through the Middle Ages the work of a parish priest became more and more complicated. He had to collect TITHES, keep records of births, marriages and deaths in his parish, write wills, teach the children and sometimes check that feudal dues were being properly paid to the lord (his temporal duties). These duties demanded someone who was intelligent and educated. Increasingly the lord was likely to choose a man who could read and write and who had some understanding of the world beyond the parish. By about 1400 many priests were educated men from rich families.

Celibacy

Only men could be priests. In the early Middle Ages priests could be married and have families. By about 1400, nearly all priests were unmarried and were supposed to stay that way. The Church regarded them as being 'married' to their parish. They were supposed to treat everyone equally, which obviously they couldn't do if they were married.

Source check

A GOOD PRIEST

In 1386, Geoffrey Chaucer wrote about a parish priest in his *Canterbury Tales*. This is part of what he wrote:

He truly knew Christ's gospel and would preach it
Devoutly to his parishioners.
He much disliked extorting tithe or fee,
Nay, rather he preferred beyond a doubt
Giving to poor parishioners round about
From his own goods and Easter offerings.
Wide was his parish, with houses far ASUNDER,
Yet he neglected not in rain or thunder,
In sickness or in grief, to pay a call
On the remotest, whether great or small.
His business was to show a fair behaviour
And draw men thus to heaven and their saviour.

Source check

A BAD PRIEST

In 1397, the Bishop of Hereford collected evidence about priests in parishes under his control. These are some of the complaints:

- *The priest puts his horses and sheep to pasture in the churchyard.*
- *The priest was away for six weeks and made no arrangement for someone to take his place.*
- *The priest spends his time in taverns, and there his tongue is loosed to the great scandal of everyone. He is living with a woman called Margaret, and he cannot read or write so he cannot look after his parishioners' souls.*

Discuss

1 The 'good priest' source comes from a poem. The 'bad priest' source comes from an official church record. Which source do you think is most useful for telling us what parish priests were really like?

2 The text 'Temporal duties' describes how the role of the priest changed during the Middle Ages.

  How do you think those changes might affect the ordinary villagers?

Getting to heaven

Death was an everyday reality for medieval peasants. Many babies and children died young. Peasants would be considered old by 30 and many died before reaching 40. Plagues and famines, as well as ordinary diseases such as measles and flu, created havoc and, in times of epidemic, killed thousands of men, women and children. Death was ever present.

The Christian Church helped here too. The Church taught that after death there was eternal life. No matter how grim and short life was on Earth, eternal life in heaven was waiting. Or was it? Eternal life was waiting only for those who lived good lives, avoided sin and followed the teachings of the Catholic Church. And even then it wasn't that easy.

- Some people, those who never asked for forgiveness for their sins, went straight to hell.
- Everyone had sinned. No one was good enough to go straight to heaven. So the souls of the 'maybes' went to purgatory. This was a pretty dreadful place, but not as grim as hell. Souls stayed there for possibly hundreds of years until their sins had been burned away and they could enter heaven. It was possible to speed up this process if friends and relatives said prayers for them, lit candles in church for them, visited holy places for them or bought pardons for them from travelling pardoners.

Medieval people were keenly aware of the terrors of hell and eternal damnation and the paradise of heaven, and the Church surrounded them with reminders. There were three main methods.

1 Paintings

Source ❺

This painting is from the Queen Mary Psalter, c. 1300. Paintings like this would be found on the walls of churches. The righteous are being welcomed into heaven; the wicked are being pitched into the fiery cauldron of hell.

Discuss

Which of the three methods do you think would have most impact on the peasants?

Rich people could see the paintings in books, like the Psalter below. However, most peasants could not read, so the walls of parish churches were decorated with large detailed paintings as well. Children would see them every time they went to church and eventually their message would become as familiar as breathing. Very few of these wall paintings have survived, but those that have are the 'doom' paintings that reminded people about heaven and hell.

Source 6

This window shows angels visiting shepherds to tell them of the birth of Jesus.

2 Stained glass

The Church also got its message across through stained-glass windows. Many of the windows in parish churches were not made from plain glass, but were rich with colour and each one had a message. Some windows told part of the story of the life of Jesus Christ; others showed people what they should, or should not, do.

Source 7

This window shows a Christian visiting prisoners, one of the 'acts of mercy' encouraged by the Church.

3 Sermons and stories

Some priests told stories to their peasant parishioners to try to get them to remember the teaching of the Church on various different matters. For example:

> There was once a worthy woman who hated a poor woman for more than seven years. When the worthy woman went to church, the priest told her to forgive her enemy. She said she had forgiven her. When the church service was over, the neighbours went to her house with presents to cheer her and to thank God. But then the woman said 'Do you think I forgave her with my heart as I did with my mouth? No!' Then the Devil came down and strangled her there in front of everybody. So make sure that when you make promises you make them with the heart, without any deceit.

Pilgrimage

A pilgrimage is a journey to a place believed to be holy. People went on pilgrimages for all kinds of reasons in the Middle Ages. They went to give thanks for something good that had happened to them; they went in hope of a cure for an illness; and they went to ask God for a special favour. They went, too, to show the world how holy they were.

- The most special place of all to go on a pilgrimage to was the Holy Land where Jesus lived and died.
- After that came Rome, where many saints were buried and where the Pope lived.

Such pilgrimages took time and money. They were out of the question for a poor person. So what could a peasant do if he or she wanted to make a pilgrimage?

Relics and shrines

The answer was, of course, to visit a local shrine or holy place. Relics of a saint – hair, bones or toenails, for example – would be kept in a special box. People believed that these shrines and relics had miraculous powers that could cure diseases.

People left offerings such as wax images of limbs at shrines as a 'thank you' to the saint for favours and miracles granted.

Task

Source 8 shows sites of pilgrimage in England. Choose the one most local to you and use an internet search to find out:
a) when the saint lived
b) what made him or her famous
c) a story associated with that site.

Source 8

A map of major pilgrimage sites in England.

Source ❾

The head reliquary of St Oswald, who was King of Northumbria and died in 642. Reliquary means a container for relics. There is a head inside this casket. It is supposed to be St Oswald's.

Attitudes

Running through all the information on the past seven pages has been an attitude. People felt themselves to be in the hands of God. God made them ill or healthy. God made the weather good or bad. God also made them rich or poor.

Summary task

What impact did the Church have on the lives of peasants?
(**Hint:** this is an essay question. You should look at different aspects of a peasant's life and at the involvement of the Church in them, then reach a balanced conclusion.)

UNIT 13 What do Crusades tell us about the power of religion in the Middle Ages?

What is this all about?

The Crusades is the name given to a series of wars that started in 1095 and that lasted for over two centuries. At the heart of these wars was the battle between Christian and Muslim armies for control of Jerusalem. However, that struggle was only one part of the story. The same fervour that drove Crusader knights also led thousands of young children to join the Children's Crusade, and yet others to murder Jews in Germany and England. It was a complex and strange time. We have focused on three stories. See what they suggest about the power of religion in the Middle Ages.

Background Europe

Christianity was easily the most important religion in England. It was also the main religion in the rest of Europe. However, it was not the only one. In areas of southern Europe and the Middle East, Islam was much stronger.

For 300 years, Muslims and Christians mostly lived in peace with each other. From the middle of the eleventh century this began to change. Fearful of being completely overrun, the emperor of Byzantium, Alexius Comnenus, appealed in 1095 to Pope Urban II for help in defeating the Seljuk Turks. The Pope appealed to the Christian world to join the battle.

Source ❶

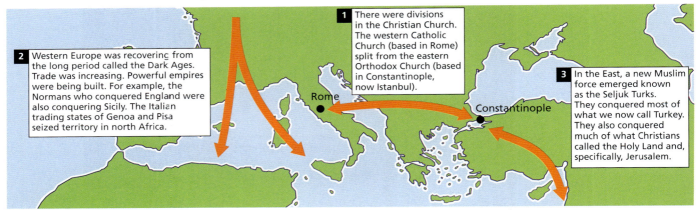

1 There were divisions in the Christian Church. The western Catholic Church (based in Rome) split from the eastern Orthodox Church (based in Constantinople, now Istanbul).

2 Western Europe was recovering from the long period called the Dark Ages. Trade was increasing. Powerful empires were being built. For example, the Normans who conquered England were also conquering Sicily. The Italian trading states of Genoa and Pisa seized territory in north Africa.

3 In the East, a new Muslim force emerged known as the Seljuk Turks. They conquered most of what we now call Turkey. They also conquered much of what Christians called the Holy Land and, specifically, Jerusalem.

Rome

Constantinople

The pressures building in Europe in the eleventh century.

Background Jerusalem

To Christians: The hill of Calvary in Jerusalem was the place where Jesus Christ was crucified. It was in Jerusalem that he was resurrected and went to heaven. From the fourth century Christian pilgrims from all over the world flocked to visit the holy sites of Jerusalem. In 1076 Jerusalem fell under the control of the Seljuk Turks who were less willing to allow Christian pilgrims into Jerusalem.

To Muslims: Jerusalem was the place where the Prophet Muhammad had ascended to heaven from the el-Agra stone in the centre of the city. The mosque that was built on the site became the third holiest place in the Muslim world.

Source ❷

A horrible race has violently invaded the lands of the Christians. They have destroyed the churches of God and even changed them into churches for their own religion. Jerusalem is now the prisoner of the enemies of Jesus Christ. These people don't even know how to pray to God. Everyone going to fight to free Jerusalem will be forgiven their sins.

Pope Urban II speaking in 1095.

Story 1: The First Crusade 1095–99

In 1095 Pope Urban II appealed to the Christian world to join a battle to drive back the Seljuk Turks (see Source 2).

In those days communication was not as easy as it is now. So Urban travelled around preaching this message many times and also sent other bishops, priests and travelling preachers round Europe to preach the same message. It worked. The response was overwhelming. Tens of thousands of men and women, rich and poor, young and old, peasants and professional soldiers flocked towards Constantinople.

In the so-called Peasants' Crusade, about 12,000 peasants led by Peter the Hermit and Walter the Penniless, were the first group to reach Seljuk territory. They were massacred on 21 October 1096.

But others followed. You can see their routes in Source 4. Many of the crusaders were French including probably the most effective military leader, Boemond of Tarranto. Their journey to Constantinople was bloody. In Germany, Crusaders attacked and killed hundreds of Jews.

They had various **motives**. Many believed that if they fought and recaptured Jerusalem they would go to heaven. They were told that fighting in a holy war resulted in any sins that they had committed being forgiven. For some the Crusades were a chance to get rich. And Crusaders were excused taxes because, by taking part in a Crusade, they were officially pilgrims.

Source ❸

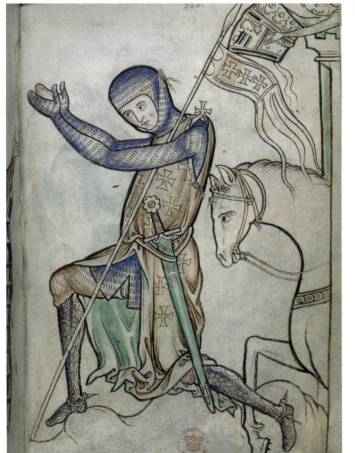

A Crusader knight. ❓ *What is he doing? What impression does this give you? Is he noble, peaceful or warlike?*

What ... ?

CRUSADES

Those who first volunteered to go to the Holy Lands on crusade cut out red crosses and sewed them onto their tunics. The French word for crosses is croisades which turned into Crusades. Those who 'took the cross' were blessed by a priest before they departed for the Holy Land. The Muslims called the Crusades the 'Frankish Invasion'.

Source 4

A map of the Crusaders' routes.

Crusader successes

The Crusader force was 30,000 and was divided into a number of smaller armies. There was no single leader and division was later to weaken the Crusaders. But at this stage the Crusaders were lucky because the Seljuk Turks had been divided too since the death of their powerful leader Malik Shah in 1092. In May 1097 the Crusader and Byzantine armies captured the important town of Nicea and in June 1098 Antioch fell (Source 5). Now the Crusaders had Jerusalem in their sights.

Source 5

Crusaders on the First Crusade attack Antioch. ❓ *What weapons are being used by the attackers and the defenders?*

The fall of Jerusalem

The Crusader armies laid siege to Jerusalem. Battering rams broke into the walls and gates whilst siege towers were used to scale the walls.

The defenders attempted to use bales of straw to soak up the impact of the battering rams but these were easily set on fire. They also threw oil and sulphur down onto the attackers.

The Holy City fell to the Crusaders on 15 July 1099. The story of what happened next was told in *Deeds of the Franks*, written by a Crusader who was in Jerusalem.

> As soon as one of our knights, Lethold, climbed the wall of the city the defenders ran away. Our men chased them, killing as many as they could until they were up to their ankles in blood. When our men captured the Temple they killed whoever they wished. Soon our soldiers took the whole city and seized gold, silver and houses full of treasure.
>
> Those Muslims who had survived were forced to collect the bodies. The dead Muslims were piled up high outside the city and their bodies burned.

Source ❻

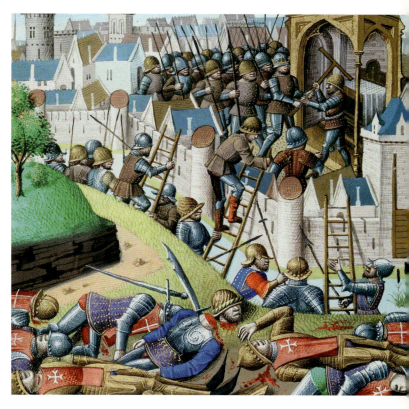

The attack on Jerusalem. ❓ *Compare this with Source 5. Which do you think is a more accurate portrayal?*

Source ❼

A contemporary picture of Saladin. ❓ *What impression does it give of him?*

Perhaps as many as 70,000 Muslims were killed. The holy Muslim site of the Dome on the Rock was wrecked. The victorious Crusaders set up a Kingdom of Jerusalem and elected Godfrey of Bouillon as their first king.

The success of the First Crusade did not end the fighting. The objectives broadened. The Crusaders decided to press on to the capital of the Islamic world at Baghdad. It was a disaster. They were massacred.

However, thousands of Crusaders continued to arrive, particularly from France, and they settled down to live in the region. They built castles to protect their newly conquered lands.

The rise of Saladin

In 1171 a new Muslim leader, Saladin, gained control of Egypt which he then united with Syria. In his next move, Saladin recaptured the southern part of Palestine, which was an important victory. Many Muslims in Egypt went through this region on pilgrimage to the holy cities of Mecca and Medina. Now their passage was assured. Saladin's next mission was to defeat the Crusaders and win back Jerusalem. In 1187 he defeated a Crusader army at the Battle of Hattin and on 2 October he captured Jerusalem. He still allowed Christian pilgrims into the city to visit holy sites but the reaction in the West was one of horror and fury.

THE TEUTONIC KNIGHTS

A number of soldiers from Frederick's army stayed on in the Holy Land to run a hospital at Acre. By 1198 they had turned themselves into the Teutonic Knights. For the next 200 years the Teutonic Knights were a formidable fighting force, conquering parts of eastern Europe.

Did you know?

What happened to the Second Crusade? Well, there were at least fourteen Crusades so we cannot cover them all here. If you want to know more about the ones we have missed, use the internet to look up the Crusades on Wikipedia or a similar site.

Did you know?

Although he was King of England for ten years, Richard I was only in the country for six months. The rest of the time he spent fighting abroad. He only returned to England to raise more money. What is more, Richard's first language was not English but French.

Story 2: The Third Crusade 1189–92

Pope Gregory VIII appealed to the kings of Western Europe to send armies to recapture Jerusalem. The first to respond to his call was Frederick I Barbarossa who set off for the Holy Land in 1189. The Byzantine Emperor had made a secret treaty with Saladin so Frederick could expect no help from him as his army travelled across the Byzantine lands. They crossed as quickly as possible, and captured the Seljuk capital of Iconium on 18 May 1189. Then in June 1190, Frederick was drowned trying to cross a river; his forces split up and were easily defeated when they reached Syria.

In 1188, King Henry II of England and King Philip II of France imposed a tax called a Saladin Tithe on their subjects to pay for a new crusade. They even stopped the war that they were fighting between themselves. The rivalry did not stop. In 1189 Henry II died to be replaced as king by his son Richard I (the Lionheart). In 1190 Richard and Philip set out for the Holy Land. They argued with each other when they met on the way in Sicily. Richard then took a detour and conquered Cyprus.

There is a sense of déjà vu here. The Third Crusade sounds just like a repeat of the First. However, the outcome was different.

Failure to take Jerusalem

The crusading armies eventually reached the Holy Land and BESIEGED the strategically important city of Acre. By July 1191 the city had been captured. However, the rivalries between the Crusader leaders got worse.

- Philip made allies with the French noble, Conrad of Montferrat, who hoped to be made king of Jerusalem.
- Things were complicated further by the arrival of Leopold of Austria who wanted to be accepted as the equal of Richard and Philip.
- Richard would not accept this and took down Leopold's banner which was flying over the conquered Acre.
- Philip became so fed up with Richard that he went back to France in August 1191.

Source check

Saladin had the reputation for being a kind man. Here is one example from a story written by Baha ad-Din Ibn Shaddad.

During a siege of one of the towns, one of the European women came to us asking to see Saladin. She said that her daughter had been taken by Muslims in the night. Tears came to Saladin's eyes and he sent a horseman to the local slave market to look for the girl. He returned soon after with the girl. The girl's mother threw herself to the floor with emotion.

Task
What are the similarities and differences between the First and Third Crusades?

Source 8

The land where Christ was born has fallen into the hands of pagans [people who did not believe in the Christian God]. The bodies of saints have been fed to animals and our churches have been turned into stables. Those of you who join up to free the land of Christ's birth from the pagan will be granted a place in heaven by God.

Pope Celestine III in 1195 encouraging Christians to fight in the Holy Land.

Who is this?

PROPHET
Someone who is given special insight by God so can explain what God wants people to do.

Truce

Richard did not manage to capture Jerusalem. He also acquired a bloodthirsty reputation. In August 1191 he ordered the execution of 3,000 Muslim prisoners because he said that Saladin had not kept to his side of the agreement that ended the siege of Acre. See the practice source exercise on page 180. Richard managed to capture the port of Jaffa, and he and his armies were victorious against Saladin's troops at Arsuf in September. But Saladin's armies were too large and although Richard twice came within sight of Jerusalem he never managed to set foot inside the Holy City. In the end Saladin and Richard agreed a TRUCE. The Crusaders could keep a strip of land which included Acre and unarmed Christian pilgrims could visit Jerusalem. But the city remained in Muslim hands. Richard left the Holy Land for home.

On his way home Richard was captured by Leopold of Austria (who he had offended in Acre). Leopold turned Richard over to the Emperor of the Holy Roman Empire, who demanded a huge ransom for Richard's release. The money was eventually raised and Richard was released.

Source 9

Jerusalem is our Holy City from where the Prophet Muhammed made his miraculous journey. On Judgement Day when we meet God our people will be united there. We do not want to give it up to the Frankish beasts who are only interested in conquering land and riches.

A Muslim writer in the twelfth century.

Story 3: The Children's Crusade 1212

This was not really a crusade but a movement that attracted children and young people from across Europe.

Stephen in France

The movement started with a peasant boy called Stephen who lived in a French village called Cloyes. Stephen's imagination had been stirred by stories of the Crusades. On 25 April 1212, he was further excited by calls made by the priest at his church for the recapture of Jerusalem. Stephen claimed he had a vision of Jesus commanding him to call the children of France to holy war, promising them that they would be successful. According to Stephen, the children would not need to be armed because Jesus had promised to look after them.

Stephen set off on the road to Paris, preaching on the way. Children across France from as young as eight started copying Stephen, claiming that they were prophets and calling all children to war in the name of God. Groups of boys and girls formed and started walking to Paris. The king, Philip Augustus, ordered the children to go home but he was ignored as were the pleas of thousands of parents.

Nicholas in Germany

In a village near Cologne, a ten-year-old boy called Nicholas also started preaching that it was God's will for children to go on crusade. In response, thousands of children answered his call and met in the city of Cologne to start on their way to the Holy Land. The numbers of those involved soon fell because of the lack of food. Hundreds of children died on the roadside. But others pressed on.

Slavery

Some of the German children reached Rome, where the Pope, Innocent III, persuaded the children to go back to Germany. Another German group, after great hardship, walked all the way to Brindisi in southern Italy. There they waited for weeks for the sea to part (as they had been prophesied it would do) so they could walk to Jerusalem on dry land. But the sea did not part, and the children were rounded up and sold into slavery.

The French children met with a similar fate. After a tiring journey south they reached Marseilles. There they were tricked by two Christian slave merchants, Hugh Ferreus and William Porcus. Pretending to be ordinary merchants, they told the children that they would take them to the Holy Land. They packed the children onto seven ships and set sail for the slave markets of Alexandria in Egypt. Two of the ships sank, and the children that survived the journey were brought not to the Holy Land but to the slave markets of North Africa where they were sold to Muslim nobles and merchants.

Source ⑩

In this year occurred an outstanding thing and one much to be marvelled at, for it is unheard of throughout the ages. About the time of Easter and Pentecost, without anyone having preached or called for it and prompted by I know not what spirit, many thousands of boys, ranging in age from six years to full maturity, left the ploughs or carts which they were driving, the flocks which they were pasturing, and anything else which they were doing. This they did despite the wishes of their parents, relatives, and friends who tried to stop them going. Suddenly one ran after another to take the cross.

Thus, by groups of twenty, or fifty, or a hundred, they put up banners and began to journey to Jerusalem. They were asked by many people about who had told them to set out upon this path… especially since only a few years ago many kings, dukes and other powerful people had gone to the Holy Land but had returned with the business unfinished. The present groups, moreover, were still of tender years and were neither strong enough nor powerful enough to do anything.

Everyone, therefore, called them foolish for doing this. The children replied that they were doing God's will and that, whatever God might wish to do with them, they would accept it. They thus made some little progress on their journey. Some were turned back at Metz, others at Piacenza, and others even at Rome. Still others got to Marseilles, but whether they crossed to the Holy Land or what their end was is uncertain. One thing is sure: that of the many thousands who rose up, only very few returned.

Extract from a chronicle, the Chronica Regiae Coloniensis, *written in 1213.*

Task

Read **Source 10** carefully.

1 What reasons did the children give for going to the Holy Land?
2 What is the attitude towards the children of the person who wrote this chronicle?
3 Write your own chronicle about the Children's Crusade using the information on pages 129–30 and Source 10.

The impact of the Crusades

Before the time of the Crusades, Christians and Muslims coexisted fairly peacefully. The Crusades ushered in a new, less tolerant period. Further Crusades were launched against other countries and other religious groups. In Germany and England, for example, the Jews were viciously persecuted. Religious war became a fact of life for hundreds of years. The invasions sparked a call for jihad or holy war that in the end led to the invasion of Europe by the Ottoman Turks in the fourteenth century.

The focus of the struggle between the Christian and Islamic worlds shifted from the Middle East to Europe.

Although the Crusades changed relations between the Christian and Muslim world for the worse, there was greater contact between the two cultures.

- Trade in goods such as sugar, spices and lemons increased.
- European architecture, art and castle building were influenced by the east, such as the use of light and dark stone.
- The west learned mathematical and medical skills. They adopted the Arabic numbers, which made maths easier.
- New weapons of war (such as the trebuchet) were developed and new military tactics emerged.

Pulling it all together

Throughout Section 2 you have been studying different aspects of religion in the Middle Ages. You may have been building up a concept map like this. You are now going to pull all this together to answer one big question:

How do we know that religion was so important to ordinary people in the Middle Ages?

- You could present your findings as an essay, or as a poster, or as PowerPoint presentation.
- You could include ideas from your summary tasks for previous chapters, for example, what going on Crusades shows us about people's religious beliefs and attitudes.
- Use carefully selected examples and evidence from this section that show that religion was a powerful force in people lives.

Aim high

- If you wish you could also add some notes, or an extra paragraph, or an extra slide comparing the power of religion in the Middle Ages with the power of religion in the modern world. Do you think that religion has a less powerful, more powerful or equally powerful influence on events in the 21st-century world?

Summary task

1 Describe the events that led to the First Crusade.
2 Explain why people from Western Europe went on Crusades.

Comment: These are typical of the kind of questions that you may have to answer in Common Entrance exams. If you need help knowing how to answer them see the advice on pages 174–77.

SECTION 3

How did ordinary people live?

If someone visiting the UK from another country said to you, 'I know *all* about your country because I have been to London', you would probably think, 'How stupid – there is more to the UK than London'. And you would be right.

So when you look back in time to the Middle Ages, avoid falling into the same trap. Remember that any period, and any country, is full of rich varieties. Even in the Middle Ages, life in villages was different from life in towns.

Life for the rich was different from life for the poor. Life for men was different from life for women. Life in 1500 was different from life in 1066.

In this unit you are going to look at some of those variations as you study villages and towns (Unit 14), health and medicine (Unit 15), crime and punishment (Unit 16) and the experiences of women (Unit 17).

Your final task will be to prepare a medieval gallery of people you have found out about. Make them as varied as you can. What will they say about their lives?

Task

Can you spot an anachronism?
Another trap to avoid is thinking the past was just like today. Here is a picture of a market in the Middle Ages. There are at least 10 things in the picture that could not possibly have been there in medieval times. These are called 'anachronisms' – things that are in the wrong period of time. Can you spot them all?

1 Work with a partner to list as many as you can.
2 Underline anything in your list that you are completely sure about.
3 Put a circle round anything where you are not so sure.

123

UNIT 14 Villages and towns: how did they change and why?

What is this all about?

Nearly everyone in the Middle Ages lived in the countryside in small villages called manors, which had just a handful of houses each. In 1066 there were only eight towns in the whole of England that had more than 3,000 inhabitants. Through the Middle Ages, this gradually changed. Towns grew, slowly; villages changed, slowly. Find out how and why. At the end of this unit you will write an advertisement for a town or a village to attract people to live there.

Task

These two pictures are illustrations from a Book of Hours, a medieval prayer book. They show people working in a medieval village. Look closely at them.

1 What jobs are the people doing?
2 Which job looks the hardest? Which looks the most pleasant?
3 What dangers are there?
4 What sources of food are there?
5 Which month of the year do you think each picture shows?
6 These pictures are painted in France and show a French countryside. Do you think that means they are useless for finding out about life in England at that time? Explain your reasons.

14.1 How did villages change?

Source ❶

Two illustrations from a Book of Hours (prayer book), made in France in 1412–16. There is a different picture for each month. You can see the entire sequence at http://humanities.uchicago.edu/images/heures/heures.html.

A village = a manor = a farm

It is best to think of a village or a manor as being a large farm or estate, not like a village today. The lord of the manor was granted the land by the king or by another baron. He controlled the land and decided what happened on it. The villagers were his workers or labourers. But it was more complicated than that.

Who's who in the village hierarchy?

- The **lord of the manor** was the most important person in the village, even though he might not have lived there and might have held several manors.
- The **priest** was the next most important person in the village. His land was called glebe land. It belonged to the Church and was usually worked by the peasants for the priest, who was busy doing other things.
- If the lord of the manor owned lots of land, a **bailiff** would work for him, keeping his accounts, making sure rents were properly collected, and generally overseeing the working of his estates.
- Every manor in England was run by a **reeve** on behalf of the lord. A reeve was usually a well-off peasant. He was responsible for seeing that the other peasants turned up on time to work the lord's land, that the right crops were planted at the correct time of year and that the lord's barns were kept in good repair.
- The **hayward** was responsible for the harvest.
- The **constable** made sure that wrong-doers were brought to the manor court, where their case would be judged by the lord, the bailiff and senior peasants.

At the bottom of the HIERARCHY were the peasants who were the labourers. However, there was also a hierarchy among the peasants.

- **Freemen** paid rent to the lord to work some of the lord's land.
- **Villeins**, instead of paying rent, gave the lord a certain number of days' work each week, plus extra work at harvest time. A villein's life was controlled by the lord. For example, in some villages they had to ask the lord's permission to leave the village or to get married.
- **Serfs** were similar to villains but were virtually slaves. They could be sold with land and other goods. However, the lord had to look after them, for example, by taking care of orphaned children.
- **Cottars** were the poorest villagers who could not even farm any of the lord's land. They only had the garden around their cottage to feed them and their families.

Villages also had blacksmiths, carpenters and thatchers, and cowmen, pigmen and shepherds. There would also be a mill run by a miller, where everyone took their grain to be ground, and a bakery run by a baker, where peasants took their bread to be baked.

Task
Draw your own chart to show this village hierarchy.

Source ❷

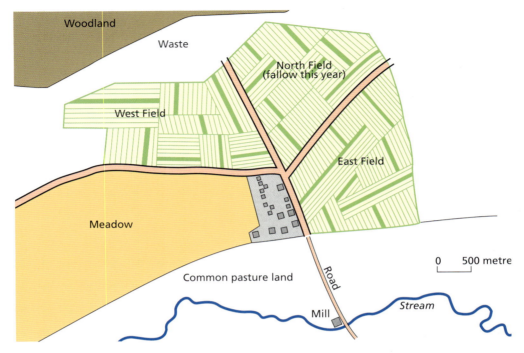

The strip system of medieval farming. One person's strips are shaded green.

How was the land worked?

The three-field system

Peasants would farm strips in each of three fields. Each year, one field would grow wheat, one would grow barley and the other would be left fallow, meaning for that year, nothing would be grown in it. Growing wheat or barley in a field takes a lot of goodness out of the soil. Leaving the field without a crop for the year allows the soil to recover its goodness.

Every year the crops would be rotated (changed around) so that each field had a chance to be fallow.

The lord's fields were called the DEMESNE. These were usually on the best land and the peasants worked for him as part of their feudal service.

Strips and furlongs

- Some of the land was divided into large open fields, which were sub-divided into furlongs.
- Each furlong was divided up into long strips which were cultivated by ploughs pulled by oxen.
- The strips were deliberately long so that the plough teams did not have to be turned round too often.
- Which peasant got which strip depended on the feudal services owed to the lord of the manor. The strips would be scattered around the fields so that all villagers got some good and bad land (see Source 2).

Crops

The most important crops grown on the land in southern England and the Midlands were wheat for bread and barley for bread and brewing. The peasants had to agree which crops would be grown on their strips. They all had to grow the same.

┌ Did you know? ┐

The best form of fertiliser in the Middle Ages was animal manure. When a field was left fallow, animals were put into it to graze. What came out the other end was very good for the soil.

┌ What … ? ┐

FURLONG

A furlong measures about 220 yards (just over 200 metres). Horse races are still measured in furlongs.

┌ What … ? ┐

SUBSISTENCE FARMING

When everything that a village produces is used by the village, with no surplus.

Cottage gardens

Around each cottage was a garden. Peasants could grow what they wanted there and most grew vegetables and herbs. The poorest peasants, called cottars, couldn't afford to pay rent for strips of land and so they only had their cottage gardens from which to feed their families.

Keeping animals

All peasants kept animals for food. They might keep goats, cows, ducks, pigs, hens or geese. Animals that could be eaten and which could produce eggs or milk when they were alive were specially prized. Sheep, for example, produced milk that could be drunk or turned into cheeses, wool that could be spun into yarn and woven into cloth – and they could be eaten, too. Few animals were kept over winter because there was not enough food with which to feed them. The best were kept for breeding the following spring and the rest were killed and their meat salted or cured to keep it edible throughout the long, cold winter months. Everybody who lived in the village was allowed to graze their animals on common land. Each peasant was allowed to graze a certain number of animals according to their feudal rights. All the peasants could use the woodland, too. They gathered firewood there, and let their pigs run loose to root out acorns and other tasty morsels.

Fishing and hunting

The lord controlled hunting rights – who could catch wild animals – but fishing in the river or catching wild boar or birds was an important part of a peasant's food supply.

Did you know?

There were possibly more sheep in England than people. Such was their importance, they were all counted for the Domesday Book in 1086. The Abbey of Ely alone had 13,400 sheep.

Source 3

The plough needed two people, one to goad the oxen, the other to guide the plough. This was a heavy piece of equipment and the oxen were hard to turn. ❓ *How might this type of plough affect the way fields were divided up?*

How did villages change?

Task

The three pictures show an artist's impression of the same village in 1086 (at the time of the Domesday Book), in 1230 and in 1400.

1 Using all that you have so far found out about medieval villages, describe the features numbered 1–10 in the first picture. One has been done for you.

2 Compare each of these numbered features with the same feature in 1230 and in 1400. What has changed? What has not changed?

3 Now write a paragraph to summarise the main changes that you have observed. This does not mean just listing all the changes you have seen. It means picking out the biggest changes and writing in a more general way about the big changes.

The feature we have done for you is number 1.

1 The manor house
Where the lord of the manor lived. He had the largest house – a big hall – and barns to keep his stores over the winter.

1086

1230

1400

139

Why did villages change?

Population change

The population rose then fell over the period. At the time of the Domesday Book in 1086 the population stood at around 2.25 million. By 1230 it had risen to 5.7 million. It then plummeted in the late 1300s to around 3 million.

Woodland clearance

Wood was used to build houses and burnt for cooking and heating. As the population increased, so the demand for wood went up.

Wood was also used in the production of iron. As a result, roughly one third of English woodland had been cleared between 1086 and the middle of the fourteenth century.

Land holding

As the population grew, so some peasants divided up their holdings of land between their children so that they all had land to work. Some lords of the manor made smallholdings out of their original demesne land. These plots of land were rented out to peasants in parcels of an ACRE or so. Eventually, some peasants were able to buy land and owned not only their own strips but also those worked by their neighbours.

Stone buildings

Village houses were made out of whatever local materials were available. In Suffolk, for example, they would be made from wooden frames and wattle and daub in-filling; in north Yorkshire they would be constructed from rough stone. Most houses in most villages, however, were built with a wooden frame and clay walls and floors. Houses were not large and often lasted only for a lifetime.

Later in the Middle Ages, when peasants became freer and relatively richer, people started to build from stone that lasted for many generations. Stone was an expensive building material for people who lived where it was not found naturally.

Improved technology

Better ploughs were developed that were not so heavy and were easier to turn around. This meant that fields did not have to be divided into such long strips.

Did you know?

After the Black Death, a frequent entry in the record held by the reeves was *Defectus per pestilentem* which is Latin for 'vacant due to the plague'.

The Black Death

Nothing changed village life as much as the Black Death (see pages 154–159). This first swept across England in 1348 and further outbreaks followed to the end of the century. It swept through rural villages, killing thousands. Some 1,300 villages were abandoned altogether in the years after 1350. The villages that survived experienced great changes.

- Many fields were permanently left fallow because there were not enough peasants left to work them.
- Lords turned to sheep farming as this needed fewer people to work on the land.
- Parish priests died along with their parishioners. Many villages, in the short term at least, were without a priest. The people could not use the church without a priest.
- The Black Death further changed the land holding. Farmers were able to rent more land and become 'tenant farmers'.
- The price of food went up and tenant farmers got more money for the crops they grew.
- With workers in such short supply the villeins were able to sell their labour to the highest bidder and simply ignore the rule that they could not leave their village without the lord's permission. Now the peasants knew that a lord was desperate to have his land worked and, specifically, to get his harvest in. If the lord would not pay, then many peasants went to find a lord who would. The lords feared that this would cause chaos and, in 1351, persuaded the King to pass the Statute of Labourers. The tension that this statute created was an important cause of the Peasants' Revolt 30 years later (see Unit 5). In the end, however, the measure failed. All villeins had become freemen, who could work where they wanted.

Source check

The Statute of Labourers said that:
- *no peasant could be paid more than the wages paid in 1346*
- *no lord or master should offer higher wages than were paid in 1346*
- *no peasant could leave the village they belonged to without permission from the lord.*

Task

Look back to your paragraph describing the changes in medieval villages between 1086 and 1400. Add a second paragraph explaining **why** things changed so much. Again, don't just list the reasons. Pick the most important ones and explain them.

Put your two paragraphs together and you have an essay on 'How and why did village life in England change in the period 1086–1400?'.

1066

Task
Study the two pictures carefully. Take turns to ask a partner about what has changed, for example, what has happened to the bridge?

14.2 Town life

Just as village life changed from the twelfth to the fifteenth centuries, so the towns of 1500 were very different from those of 1100. Towns changed in size, in number and in what they offered. There were more of them. They grew bigger and more complex. In 1066, 5 per cent of the population lived in towns. By 1300 this had doubled to 10 per cent. Not only had existing towns such as London and York grown in size but also new towns such as Leeds, Liverpool and Hull had emerged.

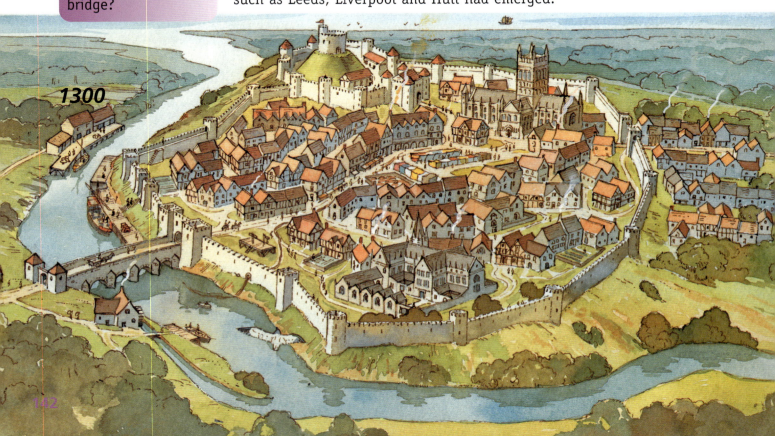

1300

What were the typical features of a town?

A river crossing

Most major towns were built at a crossing point of a river, either a bridge, such as at Cambridge, or a ford such as at Oxford. Because the roads were poor, rivers carried most of the country's trade. Bridges were a meeting place for travellers and where cargo would be unloaded from boats.

Source 4

A medieval shop. ❓ *What do you think it is selling?* ❓ *Do you think this shows a shop in England? Give your reasons.*

A castle

The Normans build strong castles in the middle of existing towns. New towns such as Ludlow were built around the castle. But castles were not only about military might. In many towns the castle became an important part of day-to-day life. For example, a town's law court and prison were often in the castle.

Gates and walls

Many towns had strong walls to protect their citizens. These were to keep intruders out not to keep citizens in. All travellers coming in and out of the town would have to pass through the town gates. These were defended with watchtowers. The watchman would question people to see why they wanted to enter the town. Carts, wagons and goods would be charged a toll at the gate.

Shops and markets

All towns held markets. Many held more than one. You needed the permission of the king to run a market so the right to run a market was both a status symbol and a source of wealth. The buying and selling of goods in the town was governed by detailed rules that were drawn up by the town's officials. Shops or stalls could only be set up in certain districts of the town, depending on what was being bought or sold. The names of streets often came from their shops or trades, for example Baker Street or Mill Lane. Stalls were set out neatly in the market square. Strangers who wanted to set up a new stall had to pay a tax called piccage.

Schools and universities

In villages, very few peasants learned to read. There was no need to. In towns there was more demand for reading. By 1500 many towns contained schools and some had universities: Oxford University was set up in 1167 and Cambridge University in 1209. As the wealth of towns grew, so did the demand for education from the wealthy. Schools and universities were usually provided by monasteries.

Who ran the towns?

In the eleventh and twelfth centuries, in major towns and cities such as London or Canterbury, the most important people were the king's and the Church's officials. The king or the Church was the lord. The citizens of the town had to pay taxes to their lord and ask him for permission for a range of things, from collecting tolls to holding a market.

Charters

As towns grew, so the wealthier townspeople wanted to run their own affairs. They could do this by asking the monarch to grant a Charter. In return for the Charter the monarch would be paid a sum of money every year. Those kings who were short of cash such as Richard I, or John, granted Charters to lots of towns. This meant that those who owned land in the town could become wealthier by charging rents and tolls. They were also free to introduce their own laws, for example, fines for selling bad meat in the market.

Burgesses

Important townspeople were known as burgesses. They would elect the officials of the town including the mayor and the aldermen. Under the town Charter, the burgesses would be granted certain rights and privileges (see Source 5). In return they had certain duties such as guarding the town.

Source

Know that I have granted to my burgesses of Bristol that they should be free of toll and every custom due throughout the whole of my land of England, Normandy and Wales, wherever they or their goods shall come. Wherefore I will and firmly command that they should have liberties and quittances and free customs fully and honourably as my free and faithful men.

Charter of Henry II in favour of Bristol (1155).

Source check

FREEMEN

One of the attractions of the town was freedom. In 1157, the Nottingham Charter stated very clearly that: *If anyone from elsewhere lives for a year and a day in the borough of Nottingham, in time of peace, and without dispute, then no one afterwards except the King shall have rights over him.*
He became a freeman.

Guilds

Guilds were organisations formed by craftspeople or merchants. These organisations made sure that the craft or trade was run properly, that those who needed help or support could get it and that standards were kept high.

This is an example from Bristol Weavers Guild in 1346:

1. No cloth to be made unless it is six bondes in width. If anyone produces narrower cloth, let him be fined 40 pence.
2. If the threads of the cloth are too far apart; the cloth and the instrument on which it was made should be burned.
3. If any of the weavers works at night, let him be fined 5 shillings to the Mayor and 40 pence to the Alderman if he is found doing it a second time.

Within a guild, master craftsmen would train young people known as apprentices in their trade. An apprenticeship would last a long time, often for years.

Source ❻

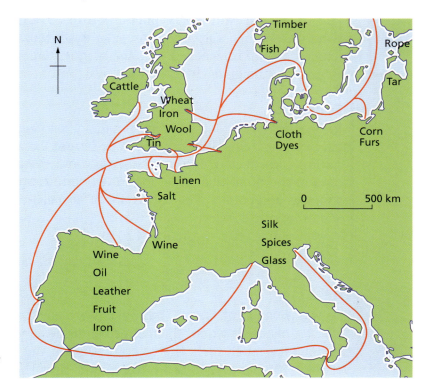

A map of medieval trade routes.

Trade

The most important reason medieval towns grew was the increase in trade. From the end of the eleventh century, trade with the rest of Europe increased dramatically. The single most important raw material produced in England was wool. Most English wool was exported to cities in the area of Flanders (now in Belgium), such as Bruges and Ghent. England was also a supplier of wheat to much of northern Europe. It exported iron from Gloucestershire and tin from Cornwall to the continent. In return, England imported goods such as leather from Cordoba, which would be sold at markets and fairs in towns but also at big annual fairs such as Boston and Stamford in Lincolnshire.

The perils of town life

Town life was dangerous. Despite all of the riches that came from improved trade, towns were threatened by poor hygiene, fire and violence.

Hygiene

Towns stank. Animals were kept in the towns just as they were in the villages. Waste from houses and businesses, including butchers' shops, was thrown into the street or dumped in the river. The river often served as both the town's main sewer and the drinking water supply, as well as providing water for people to wash themselves, their pots and pans and their clothes.

Up to ten per cent of the population in 1316 died from diseases carried in the water, such as typhoid fever or dysentery. Other great killers included smallpox, measles and the plague, which could spread quickly in the cramped housing of the towns.

Source ❼

For that so much dung and filth of garbage and entrails be thrown away and put in ditches, rivers and other waters, so that the air there is grown greatly corrupt and infected, and many diseases do daily happen … any people in London and other cities who do throw or put such annoyances as dung, garbages and entrails [internal organs of animals] in ditches, rivers, waters, and other places, which means that they have to be avoided, and carried away, will have to pay a fine of £20.

An extract from a law passed for London, 1388.

Fire

Fire was a constant threat. Buildings were constructed very close together and were made of wood. Open fires would be used to heat buildings and it did not take much for a fire to start. Once it did it would spread rapidly. Between 1066 and 1230 there were eight fires that destroyed large parts of London. As a result, people were always on their guard and townspeople were all aware of their responsibilities. At curfew all fires had to be covered and raked. If there was a fire the chime of the church bells would ring backwards as a warning sign. All houses had barrels of water outside them just in case. Every house also had to keep hooked poles, which could be used to pull the thatched roofs off houses as a means of preventing the fire spreading.

Violence

Violence was part of everyday town life. Sometimes the violence in medieval towns and cities spiralled out of control, such as the riots of the Peasants' Revolt (see Unit 5) or the massacre of the Jews in 1190 (see page 131).

What is this?

CURFEW
A time at which everyone has to be inside their house. It was signalled in medieval times by the ringing of a church bell. The word curfew comes from the French *couvre feu* meaning 'cover fire', which is just what people did at that time.

The Jews

Occasionally, violence broke out against the largest ethnic minority living in England in the Middle Ages: the Jews. There were around 5,000 Jews in England in 1200, virtually all of them in towns such as London, York and Lincoln. The Jews usually lived together in what was known as a ghetto. In London the Jewish part of the city was called Old Jewry. Although they were allowed to practise their own religion, they were treated differently.

Because they were not Christians, the only job that Jews were permitted to do was lend money. This meant that, while they were useful, they were hated and despised by people who were dependent on their loans. It was too easy for a debtor (someone who owed money) to invent a grievance, start a pogrom, have the Jews turned out and his debts revoked. In 1201, King John issued a charter confirming Jews' rights, but tolerance was not cheap. Jews were to be free from tolls and customs and were placed under royal protection. This meant, however, that they could be taxed whenever the King thought fit. By the late thirteenth century, the French and Italians had started lending money in England and people regarded the Jews as less useful. In 1272, hundreds of Jews were hanged in London and the rest thrown out of the city. Three years later, Edward I ordered that every Jew should wear a yellow armband so that he or she could be identified as a Jew. In 1290 every Jew was expelled from England.

Summary task

It is 1400. You have to compare the advantages and disadvantages of living in a town or a village.

1 Use a table to record as much detail as you can about each category.

	A village	**A town**
Work		
Freedom		
Wealth		
Dangers		

2 Once you have completed your table, work with a partner. One of you has to draw up an advertisement encouraging people to live in a village. Mention all the good things about it. The other person has to do an advert for a town.

3 Compare your adverts with others in the class and decide whether towns or villages win overall.

UNIT 15 Health and medicine: how did medieval people cope with disease?

What is this all about?

By today's standards the people of the Middle Ages had a very tough life. Average life expectancy was around 40 years for men and even less for women. Many babies and mothers died in childbirth. Deadly diseases were ever present and could rampage through villages or towns. People did their best to prevent these diseases spreading but they did not know what caused them, so it was often a losing battle. Even the weather could be a killer. In years when too much rain, or too little, ruined the harvest, tens of thousands could die of famine and malnutrition, much as they still do today in some countries around the world.

So keeping healthy was a challenge. This unit is all about how they responded to that challenge:

- In part 1 you will find out how people at this time treated the sick – and how effective these kinds of treatment were.
- In part 2 you will investigate one particular case study – the Black Death – a devastating epidemic of plague that killed millions of people in England. What does the spread of the Black Death and the people's response to it tell you about health and medicine in the Middle Ages?

Task
Make your own copy of this simple diagram then add to it as you work through the next five pages.

15.1 How were sick people treated?

Plant	Used to treat
Angelica	Coughs and colds
Broom	Bladder infections
Comfrey	Cuts and bruises
Dock	Skin rashes
Hyssop	Stomach complaints
Foxglove	Heart complaints
Marigold	Bee stings
Motherwort	Heavy monthly periods
Nettles	Nose bleeds
Parsley	Kidney problems
Thyme	Whooping cough

Many medieval medical problems were similar to those today. People caught measles and chicken pox, mumps and scarlet fever, influenza and pneumonia. They broke their legs and smashed their skulls; they got appendicitis and blockages in their bowels.

Herbal remedies

Most people, when they fell ill, were given herbal remedies. For ordinary, everyday problems like stomach ache and boils, the women in a family knew what to do. They knew which herbs to gather to make into a poultice to paste on the infected place, and which to make into a medicine that could be drunk. Some women who became particularly skilled would also treat poor people outside their immediate family. The table (left) lists some of the plants and herbs they used. In towns, APOTHECARIES sold herbs and drugs

This treatment for a stye (a painful swelling on a person's eye) comes from an Anglo-Saxon book that was still being used in medieval times.

Take onion and garlic in equal amounts and pound well together; take wine and bull's gall, equal amounts of both, and mix with the onion and garlic. Put the mixture in a brass container and leave it to stand for nine nights. Then strain it well through a cloth. At night-time, use a feather to put some of the mixture onto the stye.

Source ❶

This drawing from the thirteenth century shows King Edward the Confessor (who died in 1066) touching people with the skin disease scrofula. The Kkng's touch was supposed to make them better. This practice continued until the seventeenth century. It was called 'Touching for the king's evil'.

Source ❷

Write these words on the jaw of the patient. 'In the name of the Father, Son and Holy Ghost, Amen' the pain will stop at once, as I have often seen.

A fourteenth-century charm for curing toothache, used by John of Gaddesden, who was a leading doctor of the time.

that people could buy to make themselves or their families better – maybe! Even doctors, treating rich people, used herbs, and these might include more exotic ones from abroad. This was especially so after the 1200s, when public PHARMACIES in Italy began to export herbs and medicines.

Doctors came to believe that sugar was an effective medicine and by the 1400s it was imported in large quantities. Monks kept the best herb gardens. This was because monasteries were centres of care for the sick.

Healers copied treatments that their parents or ancestors had used. They also tried out new ideas to see what worked. By trial and error they arrived at some herbal remedies that worked. We now know that some natural ingredients of herbal remedies have the same properties as modern drugs. For example, many medieval remedies used PLANTAIN as an ingredient. Modern scientific analysis has shown that plantain has antibiotic properties so could combat an infection.

Supernatural treatments

Even today, many people rely on superstition and magic to explain what they do not understand. It is not surprising, therefore, that medieval people often looked to the supernatural for an explanation of why diseases happened and to find a cure.

The Christian Church taught that God was in control of the world. So it followed that God must also control who got ill and when, and who survived. So when someone got ill they would pray and ask God's help. Some believed that becoming ill was God's punishment for past sins so they might also confess their sins, try harder to please God or even punish themselves for their sins to try to get better. They would also seek the help of God's representatives on Earth. A priest might be called on to pray by the bedside of an ill person. For certain diseases the king (who people believed was chosen by God) would be asked to touch the sufferers (see Source 1).

Medieval people also believed in astrology: that the stars and planets had an influence on the world. If the planets and stars were in a 'favourable conjunction' good things would happen. If they were not then the disaster could follow. So surgeons would consult a chart like Source 3 (called a Zodiac man) to determine when was a favourable time to perform an operation. Astrologers would even study the state of the stars and planets at the time of a child's birth to determine whether it would be a dangerous birth and what would be the child's prospects in life.

Source 3

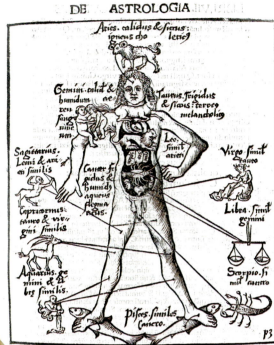

A Zodiac man.

Source 4

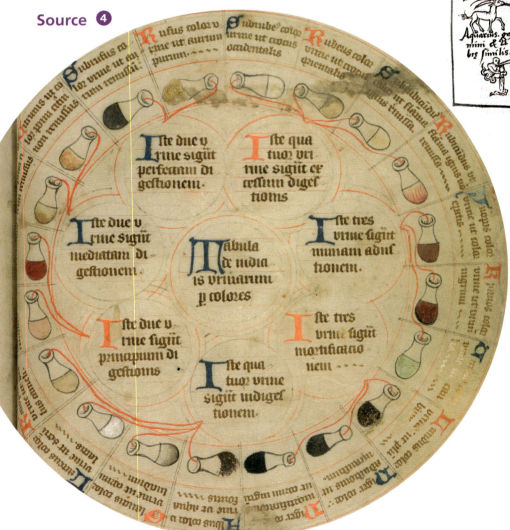

A medieval urine chart. ? *Can you work out which sample is* **a)** *most healthy;* **b)** *least healthy?*

Urine analysis

Most doctors used a urine chart to help diagnose illness. In Source 4, the writing around the chart describes the colour of the urine and whether it is cloudy or clear; the little drawings of urine bottles show the colour of the urine, and the writing in the middle groups the urine samples together according to what they tell the doctor about the patient's condition. Wealthy people might send their urine off for diagnosis every week.

Did you know?

The Theory of the Four humours may sound wrong to you but in the history of medicine it is important because Hippocrates was basing his ideas on scientific methods of observation and recording.

Bleeding

A doctor would open a vein, usually in the patient's arm, and drain some blood into a vessel called a bleeding cup. This may sound a strange treatment. The thinking behind it was the Theory of the Four Humours. Hippocrates, a Greek doctor in the fifth century BC, had suggested that illness arose when the four humours in a body (blood, phlegm, yellow bile and black bile) were not in balance with one another. So, to take blood out of a person would restore the balance of the four humours in his or her body. In fact, bleeding was highly dangerous. It could cause anaemia (not enough red blood cells) and septicaemia (blood poisoning). But it continued in use for 2000 years!

Surgery

Pain

Anaesthetics were not discovered until the nineteenth century. Operations had to be quick so as not to cause too much pain and shock to a person's system. However, even so, it was essential that a person wasn't fully conscious if an operation was to stand any chance of success. The most common method was to get a person drunk before operating on them. This recipe, used by surgeons in the Middle Ages, was a little more sophisticated but had the same effect.

> To make a drink that men call dwale to make a man sleep while men carve him: Take three spoonfuls of the gall of a boar, three spoonfuls of hemlock juice, three spoonfuls of wild nept, three spoonfuls of lettuce, three spoonfuls of poppy, three spoonfuls of henbane and three spoonfuls of vinegar and mix them all together and boil them a little. Put three spoonfuls of the mixture into half a gallon of good wine and mix it well together. Let him that shall be carved sit against a good fire and make him drink until he falls asleep. Then it is safe to carve him.

This mixture would certainly have had the desired effect and might even have put the patient to sleep forever!

Infection and bleeding

Because of the problem of pain surgeons could only do short and quick operations such as amputations. Once the limb was cut off the next challenge for a surgeon was to stop the bleeding – they used a range of methods, including boiling oil to close up the severed veins and arteries. But the biggest problem of all was to follow – infection. Nowadays after an operation a patient is given antibiotics to fight infection and the wounds are covered with antiseptic dressings and ointments. In the Middle Ages they did not know about microbes and bacteria or how to prevent infection so they had to dress the wound and hope for the best. The patients with the strongest immune system and the cleanest wounds would survive. Many would die of blood poisoning and other infections.

Source ⑤

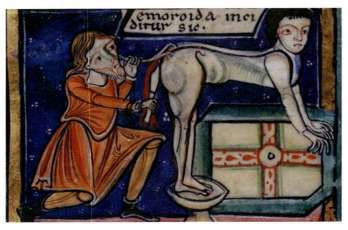

A medieval operation.

John of Ardennes

Some surgeons worked carefully and used their skills of observation, and their knowledge of what had worked for other surgeons, to get things right. The best surgeons learned skills and techniques on the battlefield and passed these on to younger surgeons who were apprenticed to them. John of Ardennes was one of the most famous surgeons in medieval England. He started out as an army surgeon during the wars between England and France and, when the wars were over, returned to London to work there. Source 5 shows an operation on haemorrhoids – one of John's specialities.

Childbirth

Having a baby was a dangerous business and many mothers and babies died in childbirth. Babies died because they were stressed by a long labour, starved of oxygen or because they were born feet or bottom first instead of head first. Mothers could bleed to death or die from an infection caught during or after the birth. Men usually kept out of the way and the dangerous and messy business of childbirth was left to the women.

Hospitals

The word 'hospital' comes from 'hospitality' – and means a place to stay. It did not originally mean somewhere to be treated. Of the 1,200 hospitals in England and Wales in the Middle Ages, only 100 treated or cared for the sick. Nearly all the hospitals were set up or run by the Christian Church and based in monasteries. After 1066 the Church began to open hospitals away from monasteries, although they were still run by monks and nuns.

Most of the hospitals for the sick were opened in the 1100s and 1200s. In London, St Bartholomew's was founded in 1123, St Thomas's in 1170 and St Mary Spital in 1197. Some were very large – St Leonard's in York had over 200 beds – while others could only take half a dozen sick people.

There were some specialist hospitals. In thirteenth-century London there were at least four leper hospitals and six hospitals for the 'sick poor'. Richard Whittington, Lord Mayor of London, paid for an eight-bed extension to St Thomas's hospital for unmarried pregnant women. In Stamford a hospital cared for the blind, deaf and mute and the hospital of St Mary of Bethlehem looked after those who were mentally disturbed.

> **Source check**
>
> It was one of St Benedict's Rules that looking after the sick was a Christian duty:
>
> *Care for the sick stands for all. You must help them, as would Christ, whom you really help in helping them. Also you must bear patiently with them as in this way you will gain greater merit with God. Let it be the chief concern of the Abbot that the sick shall not be neglected at any point.*

> **Source check**
>
> Some hospitals made it very clear whom they would, and would not, admit. The rules of the hospital of St John in Bridgwater stated in 1219 that:
>
> *No lepers, lunatics, or persons having the falling sickness or other CONTAGIOUS disease, and no pregnant women, or sucking infants, and no intolerable persons, even though they be poor and infirm, are to be admitted in the house; and if any such be admitted by mistake, they are to be expelled as soon as possible.*

Source 6

Source 7

Source 8

Source 9

Task

1 Here are four pictures of treatments from the Middle Ages. They all come from medieval manuscripts. Using the information from the past five pages work out what is going on in each picture and write a caption for each one. (For answers, see page 190.)

2 Put these four treatments into order on this scale. A scientific treatment is a treatment based on experiment and careful observation of patients. A non-scientific treatment is based on supernatural beliefs. Write some sentences to explain your order.

Least scientific ⟵——⟶ Most scientific

3 Choose one treatment and write a short advert for the services of this medical specialist.

15.2 Case study: the Black Death, 1346–53

Now you know about the sort of treatments that were available to medieval people. How do you think these services would cope if a VIRULENT disease swept the country, striking without warning, killing within days and carrying off rich and poor alike?

The Black Death swept across most of Europe and Asia in the years 1346–53. It seemed that nothing could escape: millions of people died as well as animals and birds. Whole communities were destroyed. An Arab historian, who lived through it, wrote:

> A devastating plague struck East and West. Whole populations vanished. The entire world changed.

What was the Black Death?

We now know that the Black Death was a combination of three diseases – all caused by the same bacillus (bacterium) – but with different symptoms and spread in different ways.

- **Bubonic plague** was caused by a bacillus that lived in the bloodstream of black rats. When the fleas that lived on the black rat bit the rat and sucked its blood, the bacillus was transferred to the fleas. Then, when the fleas from the black rat bit animals and people, the bacillus was transferred to them. Bubonic plague attacked the body's lymph nodes and caused them to swell (the swellings were known as buboes).
- **Pneumonic plague** involved the same bacillus but affected the lungs. It was spread directly from person to person in their saliva, by coughing or sneezing.
- Either of these two types of plague could in turn lead to **septicaemic plague**, where blood poisoning set in and death occurred before other symptoms could appear.

However, these true causes of such diseases were not discovered until the nineteenth century, and so for medieval people all this was unknown. All they knew was that they were faced with a deadly disease that spread relentlessly, hit without warning and wiped out families and whole communities.

Why did the Black Death spread so quickly?

The Black Death followed the trade routes of merchants, traders and travellers over land and sea. The Black Death was recorded in the eastern Mediterranean in mid-1347 and by the summer of 1348 hit England. It seems to have travelled throughout southern England in the summer as bubonic plague. It hit London in September 1348. Plague fleas die in winter and this would usually stop the spread of plague. But there was no respite in the winters of 1346–49 and this was probably because the bubonic plague changed into the pneumonic version, which could spread

What … ?

PLAGUE
An infectious or contagious disease that spreads rapidly over a large area and has a huge death toll.

from person to person without the help of any fleas. It spread to East Anglia in the New Year, and by the spring of 1349 was devastating Wales and the Midlands. The summer of 1349 saw the plague in the north of England and Ireland.

A monk, William of Malmesbury recorded:

> In 1348, at about the feast of the Translation of St Thomas the Martyr [7 July] the cruel pestilence, hateful to all future ages, arrived from countries across the sea on the south coast of England at the port called Melcombe in Dorset. Travelling all over the south country it wretchedly killed innumerable people in Dorset, Devon and Somerset. Next it came to Bristol, where very few were left alive, and then travelled northwards, leaving not a city, a town, a village or even, except rarely, a house, without killing most or all of the people there so that over England as a whole, a fifth of the men, women and children were carried to burial.

At Ashwell, in Hertfordshire, these words were scratched on the wall of the parish church:

> 1349 the pestilence. 1350, pitiless, wild, violent, the dregs of the people live to tell the tale.

When the Black Death reached Ireland, John of Clyn, an Irish friar, fearing they all would die, recorded what had happened. He recorded how the Black Death came to Ireland and about the thousands who died agonising deaths. He ended:

> Man and wife with their children travelled the same road, the road of death. To stop these notable events from perishing with time and fading from memory, I have set them down in writing whilst waiting among the dead for the coming of death. And to stop the writing perishing with the writer, I leave this parchment for the work to be continued in case in future any human survivor should remain.

Here the writing stops. It is followed by a note in different handwriting:

> Here, it seems, the author died.

The population of England in 1348, before the Black Death hit, was around 3.5 million people. In the outbreak of 1348–50 the Black Death killed 30–45 per cent of them. But it didn't kill evenly. In some villages 80 or even 90 per cent of the population died; in Kilkenny, where John of Clyn lived and worked, everyone died. Other villages got off lightly, with just a handful of people succumbing. Children and young people were particularly badly affected. By the 1370s, the population of England had been halved.

Source 10

'Death' strangling a victim of the Black Death.

What were the symptoms?

The symptoms of the Black Death were terrible and painful and made more dreadful by the mental distress of knowing you were very likely to die.

- A person with bubonic plague would first feel desperately cold and tired.
- Then boils, called buboes, erupted first in their groin and armpits and then all over their body.
- The buboes filled with pus and turned black. If they burst, they stank.
- At the same time the victim would be running a high fever, with migraine-like headaches.

The illness lasted five to ten days and although death was probable, people could and did recover.

A Welsh poet, Ieuan Gethin described at the time what it was like to find a buboe in the armpit. He called it a 'shilling', which is a large coin.

We see death coming into our midst like a black smoke, a plague which cuts off the young, and has no mercy for the fair of face. Woe is me of the shilling in the armpit; it is seething, terrible, wherever it may come, a white lump that gives pain and causes a loud cry, a burden carried under the arms. It is of the form of an apple, like the head of an onion, a small boil that spares no one. Great is its seething, like a burning cinder.

Pneumonic plague attacked a person's lungs, which filled with fluid causing them to have chest pains. They had difficulty in breathing and coughed up blood and pus. The disease was fast-working: people usually died within two to three days.

Explanations: What did people at the time believe caused the Black Death?

There wasn't just one explanation for the plague, but many. Here are some of theories people had about it at the time.

Source ⑪
Between Cathay and Persia there rained a vast rain of fire falling in flakes like snow and burning up mountains and plains and other lands. And then arose vast masses of smoke; and whosoever saw this, died within the space of half a day.

An Italian chronicler.

Source ⑫
The general cause [of the Black Death] was the close position of the three great planets, Saturn, Jupiter and Mars. This had taken place in 1345 on 24th March in the 14th degree of Aquarius. Such a coming together of planets is always a sign of wonderful, terrible or violent things to come.

Guy de Chauliac, a famous doctor of the 1300s.

Task

1 From the information in Sources 11–18, draw up a full list of what or who people in the Middle Ages thought caused the Black Death.
2 Which of these explanations is closest to the truth?

Source ⑬

Terrible is God toward the sons of men. He often allows plagues, miserable famines, conflicts, wars and other forms of suffering to arise, and uses them to terrify and torment men and so drive out their sins.

The Prior of the Abbey of Christchurch, Canterbury, wrote to the Bishop of London on 28 September 1348. This is part of his letter.

Did you know?

The theory in Source 15 arose from prejudice against the Jews (anti-Semitism) but was fuelled by the fact that fewer Jews than other people caught the plague. In fact, this was because of the Jews' strict obedience to the rules of cleanliness laid down in the Book of Leviticus.

Did you know?

Other explanations included over-eating, having sexual relations with an older woman and children being disobedient.

Source ⑭

Sometimes [the Black Death] comes from a privy [lavatory] next to a chamber that corrupts the air in substance and quality. Sometimes it comes from dead meat or the corruption of standing waters in ditches.

A Swedish bishop, writing in the 1400s and basing his views on a book written in the 1360s.

Source ⑮

Some say that it [the Black Death] was brought about by the corruption of the air; others that the Jews planned to wipe out all the Christians with poison and had poisoned wells and springs everywhere. And many Jews confessed as much under torture. Men say that bags full of poison were found in many wells and springs.

A German friar writing in 1348.

Source ⑯

Any person that touched the clothes of the sick, or anything that had been used by them, seemed thereby to catch the disease. The rags of a poor man who died of the disease were thrown into the street. Two pigs came hither and took the rags between their teeth and tossed them to and fro – whereupon almost immediately, they gave a few turns and fell down dead.

In 1349, the author Giovanni Boccaccio wrote about the Black Death in a story called The Decameron.

Source ⑰

This epidemic kills almost instantly. As soon as the airy spirit leaving the eyes of a sick man has struck the eye of a healthy bystander looking at him, the poisonous nature passes from one eye to the other.

A French doctor writing in 1349.

Source ⑱

The plague was carried by infected people who, by sight, or touch, or breathing on others, killed everyone. It was incurable. It could not be avoided.

An Italian historian, who lived in Padua during the Black Death, describes what happened.

Task

1 For each of the explanations in your list from page 156, identify
   a) a preventative measure
   b) a treatment
   that you might expect a person to use if they believed this explanation.
2 Which of these measures or treatments do you think would be most effective? You can find out what they actually did on pages 158–59.

Remedies: how did people try to prevent the plague, and treat and cure victims?

The things people did to try to stop the Black Death spreading and to treat people when they caught it, depended very much on what they believed caused the disease in the first place.

A Some cities and towns tried to quarantine themselves by making rules about who could come in and out of the city gates; others refused to allow strangers to come in. This badly affected trade.

B Many people thought that if they could keep the air moving, the plague wouldn't have time to settle. They rang the church bells to circulate the air.

C The clothes of victims were burned. This was in itself dangerous work because many believed that contact with victims' clothes would spread the Black Death. Those doing the burning dressed in protective clothing with long-nosed masks over their faces and elbow-length gloves. They must have looked terrifying!

D Times at which funerals could be held were restricted so that infected bodies, and those who mourned them, were not on the streets at busy times. Some towns and cities limited the number of mourners who could attend a funeral.

F Laws were passed to keep the streets clean. Butchers, for example, were ordered to remove intestines and wash away blood.

E God-fearing people prayed, and the Church organised special prayers and processions, pleading with God to take the Black Death away from them.

Did you know?

Men, women and children followed flagellants around, mopping up their blood with cloths. People believed that this blood had miraculous powers and would protect them from a plague death.

G Men, women and children who were hit by the Black Death were treated with the usual range of 'cures' available to healers and doctors – if these people could be persuaded to enter a house where there was a plague victim. So plague victims were, for example, bled and given herbal medicines. Some tried putting softened bread mixed with herbs on the buboes to draw out the infection. Others thought a dried toad would be more effective.

H Some took this even further. Men called flagellants, up to 600 in a single group, travelled the country. They stripped to the waist (and sometimes stripped naked) and whipped themselves in public. Their whips had knots in them and sharp nails stuck through them and the men bled a lot.

I John of Burgundy wrote one of the first books about the plague. He gave this advice to people on what they should do:

First you should avoid too much eating and drinking and also avoid baths which open the pores, for the pores are doorways through which poisonous air can enter the body. In cold or rainy weather, you should light fires in your room, and in foggy or windy weather you should inhale perfumes every morning before leaving home. If, however, the plague occurs during hot weather, you must eat cold things rather than hot and also drink more than you eat. Make little use of hot substances such as pepper, garlic and onions.

J Many, terrified and desperate, simply ran away. An Italian historian, who lived in Padua during the Black Death, described what happened:

Wives fled their husbands, fathers their sons, brothers fled each other. Even the house or clothes of the victim could kill. One death in the house was followed by the death of all the rest, right down to the dogs. Doctors admitted that they had no cure for it. Indeed, the best of them died of it.

Summary task

How did the Black Death change Britain?
Here are some notes about the impact of the Black Death.

BLACK DEATH
Effect on villages
* Helped dismantle the Feudal System
* Changed farming
* Changed land ownership

Helped change medicine
* Short term – increased people's sense of powerlessness – nothing they could do
* Longer term – more positive
  – challenged religious explanations – plague hit good and wicked equally – a 'just God'?
  – challenged rational explanations – e.g. Theory of the Four Humours did not help
  – so looked for other explanations e.g. dirt, disease
  – helped progress in scientific understanding

Use these notes to write two paragraphs on the topic 'How did the Black Death change Britain?'. Make sure you back up each point with some evidence.

What is this all about?

If you were transported back in time from now to the Middle Ages what do you think is the biggest change you would notice? What do you think would be the greatest similarity?

In this unit you are going to investigate an aspect of medieval life – crime and punishment – that in some ways is very similar to how it is today but in other ways can be very different. See which you think are the greater – the similarities or the differences.

Task

The person in Source 1 has been caught red-handed. Let's give him the benefit of the doubt and say it is a first offence.

1 How do you think this person would be punished today?
2 How do you think this person would have been punished in the Middle Ages?

Record your ideas and, once you have finished studying this unit, look back and see if you want to change them.

Source ❶

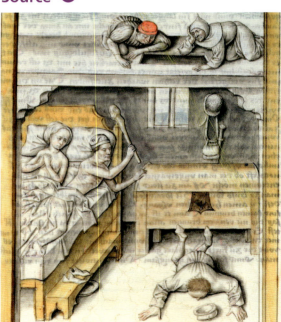

An illustration from a medieval manuscript. ❓ *What crime do you think has been committed?*

What crimes did people commit?

The most common crime committed in the Middle Ages was theft. Records of crime in eight counties between 1300 and 1348 show that theft accounted for 74 per cent of all crimes. But far more serious crimes were regularly committed. In the same period, nearly a fifth of all criminals were tried for murder. Indeed, it seems that outbursts of violence were common in medieval society.

In London in 1244 a rather painful but clearly not uncommon incident was recorded:

> Roger struck Maud, Gilbert's wife, with a hammer between the shoulders and Moses struck her in the face with the hilt of his sword, breaking many of her teeth. She lingered until the feast of Mary Magdalen, and then died.

In London, riots and fights between gangs of apprentices were common. But violent gang crime also happened outside the capital. In some areas, gangs of criminals roamed the countryside attacking and plundering homes. The royal records tell of a gang in Leicestershire in the 1320s, led by Eustace de Folvill, that terrorised honest people. In one instance the gang attacked the home of:

> Joan, late the wife of Ralph Basset of Drayton, and carried away her goods and held the manor by armed force.

Who ... ?

APPRENTICES
Young boys who spent years learning a trade such as a silversmith or cooper (someone who makes barrels).

The apprentices of London were well known troublemakers. The court records of 1244 tell of an incident when watchmen had arrested a group of apprentice boys who had filled a barrel with large stones and then rolled it down Gracechurch Street towards the River Thames, terrorising those in its way.

And what do you make of this crime? In 1310 a Justice of the Peace in Colchester heard the case of Henry Fylbrigge, William Paccard, Thomas Causton and the servant of Thomas Whitmersh. They were accused of gambling:

> … until the early morning, then stripping off their clothes they go home naked, to the scandal of the people.

How were criminals caught in the Middle Ages?

Catching and bringing to court those who had broken the law was no easier in medieval times than it is today. However, in medieval times the responsibility for making sure that criminals were brought to justice lay with all the members of a community, whether it was a village or a town.

Hue and cry

If a crime was detected, then it was the responsibility of all who had witnessed it to raise the 'hue and cry'. They had to make a lot of noise to attract the attention of other people so that the wrongdoer was caught.

Constables

Some towns and even some villages had constables or watchmen who had the power to arrest wrongdoers.

In London, the watchmen were instructed to arrest anyone who was wearing a 'visor or false face' (a mask). In the Middle Ages, as now, masked people were thought to be potential criminals. If the watchmen suspected anyone of wrongdoing, they had the right to go to that person's house, take out the windows and remove the doors.

Curfew

As many crimes were committed after dark, most towns had a curfew at sundown. Those caught breaking the curfew could end up in court. One such person was Henry Derex, who was brought before a court in Colchester in 1310 accused of:

> Being found with a long knife after the ringing of the last bell [which is] against the custom of the town.

What ... ?

CURFEW
When nobody is allowed out of their house after a certain time. The signal for the start of a curfew was often a ringing of a bell.

What was that?

COMMON LAW
The term is used to mean that the law was applied in the same way across England. The king best known for making sure that there was a Common Law was Henry II.

Sanctuary

A criminal who managed to take refuge in a church when on the run could claim sanctuary under the protection of the Church. If the criminal then confessed to the crime he or she would be allowed to 'abjure the realm' (leave the country) instead of being punished. All property left behind automatically belonged to the king. In Oxfordshire in 1241 it was recorded that:

> Alice of Kingham stole a tunic at Newton Purcel and fled to the church there. She admitted the theft and abjured the realm. She had no chattels [belongings].

In another case in London in 1244, it was reported that:

> Henry de Buk killed a certain Irishman, a tiler, with a knife in Fleet Bridge Street, and fled to the church of St Mary Southwark. He acknowledged the deed, and abjured the realm.

Source 2

This fifteenth-century illustration shows the court of King Henry's bench which was based in Westminster. It was set up by Henry II and became one of the most important royal courts. ❓ Can you find: the judges, the jury, the accused waiting for their cases to be heard?

Trials

Most court cases were heard at a local court.

In **villages** in the countryside these courts were known as manor courts. They were presided over by the local lord or his representative known as the steward or bailiff. Often these courts dealt with local disputes over day-to-day issues such as people ploughing someone else's land. Most of the villagers would attend the court and witnesses would often be called on to give evidence.

In **towns**, the mayor would sit in judgement at the mayor's court. Disturbances of the peace and petty crimes were either dealt with in the local courts, or were passed to the shire or county court that was presided over by the local Justice of the Peace.

Royal courts

Royal courts tried people under Common Law for crimes ranging from poaching game in royal forests to murder.

Eyre courts

Many cases ended up in a royal court known as the eyre court. The monarch appointed travelling judges. These men visited all the counties of England on a regular basis, and heard cases that were thought to be too difficult for the local courts to sort out, usually property disputes and questions of land ownership. For example:

Case study: Joan Arsic loses her land

More often than not, the courts were called upon to make judgements on the ownership of land and belongings. The law about who owned what was quite complicated. That is why most monarchs tried very hard to uphold the idea of Common Law. The case below from 1241 is a good example of the kind of things that the royal courts had to deal with. In this case, the judge wanted to make sure that the king got his feudal rights.

- If someone held land directly from the king he or she was called a 'tenant in chief'.
- If an unmarried woman became a tenant in chief she was known as being 'in the king's gift'. This meant that it was up to the king who she married.
- If she got married without asking for the king's permission, as here, she lost her right to the land.

The jury say that Joan Arsic, daughter of Robert Arsic, holds £7-worth of land in Somerton of the king in chief, and she is in the king's gift. Evidence is given that Joan has married Stephen Simeon without the king's permission. So the sheriff is ordered to take all the land she holds off the king in chief and place it into the king's hand.

Judges were not always as honest as they should be. Indeed, in 1178 Henry II reduced the number of eyre court judges from eighteen to five because of the complaints about them.

Most cases at the eyre court lasted less than half an hour.

- Firstly, the evidence against the accused would be put to the court.
- The accused then had the right to defend him or herself.

- Sometimes witnesses would be called to give evidence on behalf of the prosecution or the accused.
- The judge would listen to each side, perhaps asking a few questions.
- The cases would be heard in front of juries of twelve local men.
- The judge did not always ask the jury for their verdict but when he did, they did not leave the courtroom but would talk about it amongst themselves and then announce their decision. The juries would often make up their minds based on what they knew about the character of the accused.

However, there is evidence that, on other occasions, the jury did have to listen to the evidence as well as make a decision based on the personalities of the people involved.

Source ❸

Emma, wife of Walter of Elsfield, claims that, on the Thursday after Epiphany [6 January] 1238, Roger Mock came to her in her house and hit her with a pair of tongs in the eye so that she lost her right eye. Roger comes [to court] and denies everything, and it is shown that Emma did not mention this until now, and this event happened 3 years ago. The judge lets an enquiry be made by jury. The jurors say that Roger is not guilty, so he is ACQUITTED, but they say that Walter of Elsfield, Emma's husband, hit her so that she lost her eye, so he is sent to GAOL.

Another case from 1241.

Task

Study Source 3. How is the role of the jury different from the role of a jury today? You may need to do some research. Try www.cjsonline.gov.uk/juror and click on 'the trial'.

Church courts

Who ...?

ACCOMPLICE
Someone who helps another person to commit a crime.

CLERK
An official in a cathedral, church or chapel.

Alongside these courts there was a separate system of Church courts. Ever since the reign of William I, cases involving members of the priesthood or religious orders could only be tried in a Church court. Such was the case of Richard Mansel who, in 1241, was charged with being an accomplice to murder. He was brought in front of the eyre court but once the judge found out that he was a clerk, he handed him over to the Church court of the Bishop of Lincoln. It was well known that Church courts were often more lenient, which means that they gave out less harsh punishments. Therefore, some accused would try to claim that they were in some way a member of the Church and should be tried in the Church court, not the King's court.

Trial by ordeal

In the early Middle Ages, if a jury was unable to come to a verdict, they could ask that the accused stand trial by ordeal. Many of the ordeals took place in a church. The accused was put in a potentially dangerous position as his or her fate had to be decided by God. There was a range of ordeals that the accused might be put through including:

Ordeal by hot water The accused had to pick a stone out of a cauldron of boiling water. If their burns healed in a few days they were believed to be innocent. If a burn got infected or blistered the judges would rule that person guilty.

Ordeal by cold water The accused man or woman was tied up in a crouching position and thrown into water. If he or she sank, the verdict was innocent. If the accused floated, it was thought that the water had rejected him or her, and the verdict was guilty.

Ordeal by iron The accused had to carry a red-hot iron bar for a certain distance. The distance and the weight of the bar differed according to the seriousness of the crime. If the burnt hand healed in a few days, the person was regarded as innocent. If the blisters got infected, the person was guilty.

In 1215 Pope Innocent III banned trial by ordeal.

Trial by battle

This was a way to find out who was right and who was wrong in a dispute between two nobles. The Normans liked this method. The two people in dispute, or people chosen as representatives, would fight each other. The victor was assumed to be in the right because it was thought that he had won because he had God's protection. This practice had more or less died out by the later Middle Ages.

Source **4**

Trial by battle at the Hampshire eyre court in 1249. It shows two men fighting and, in the background, what happened to the loser.

Punishments

The severity of the punishments handed down by the courts depended on the nature of the offence. Those convicted of a first offence of stealing apples might have got away with paying a fine. Most cases in the manor courts ended in a fine.

Humiliation

Certain kinds of crime were thought to deserve a public humiliation. This served as a DETERRENT to others.

In London in 1244, a certain baker called John Mundy was placed in a pillory for selling 'false bread' (which was bread of poor quality); the same punishment was handed out to Agnes Deynte because she sold 'false mangled butter' (poor quality butter). Those placed in the pillory or stocks were humiliated in front of their families, friends and neighbours. They also had to put up with the abuse of passers-by. In some cases rotten food would be thrown at them. The more unfortunate criminal might be pelted with sticks and stones.

What was this?

PILLORY
Also known as stocks, these were wooden frames into which the feet and/or hands of criminals were locked.

Those convicted of sexual offences often had their heads shaved and were paraded through town before being placed in the pillory. The parade to the pillory was part of the humiliation. The London court records tell of a priest in the thirteenth century who was caught in bed with a woman. He was paraded through the streets with his trousers down, his priest's robes carried before him. Often those paraded through the streets would be accompanied by a minstrel who would make up songs about the criminal's wrongdoings to the amusement of the watching crowds. When the criminal arrived at the pillory, the show usually continued. Those accused of cheating people by selling them poor standard goods might have these goods burned in front of (or even underneath) them.

There were hardly any prisons in the Middle Ages. They were used simply to hold someone before their trial. They were not used as punishment.

Execution

Murder was almost always punished by hanging, unless the accused was a woman and could prove that she was pregnant. Every town and city had an execution site. In London it was at Tyburn. The first person to be executed at Tyburn was a man named William Longbeard who died in 1196. Those condemned to death would be led through the streets to their death. There are records in the fourteenth century of a man riding through the streets on the back of a horse dressed 'in a striped coat and white shoes' being accompanied by the hangman with the hanging rope in his hands for all to see. Some would escape justice by fleeing. They were then branded as outlaws, as in this case of a woman who had been accused of murder:

> Rose, widow of Robert King, and Maud her sister killed Robert and fled. So they were called to trial and outlawed. They had no belongings. No one else is suspected.

The most common way to avoid execution was to claim 'benefit of clergy' because Church courts would never condemn anyone to death. To prove you were a churchman, you had to read out loud a verse from the Bible. Many criminals memorised the verse so that they could claim benefit of clergy. The verse was Psalm 51, verse 1: 'Oh loving and kind God, have mercy. Have pity upon my transgressions.' It was called the neck verse because it saved many criminals from the hangman's noose.

The ultimate punishment

The most serious charge anyone could face was that of treason, which was a crime against the king. Those accused of treason usually had led rebellions against the monarch and they were tried in the monarch's court. When the leaders of the Peasants' Revolt were put on trial in 1381 they were condemned to death by the young king, Richard II, and the mayor of London. Rebels and traitors were tortured and executed in public to act as a deterrent to others.

To combine execution with humiliation, many traitors were hanged, drawn and quartered. This involved the hanging of the condemned person and splitting his body open whilst he was still alive. The head of the traitor was then boiled and placed on a pole on London Bridge. The rest of the body was then hacked into four quarters and sent to different parts of the country. This was the fate of the Scottish rebel, William Wallace, who was found guilty of treason in 1305 (see pages 46–48).

Summary task

Now it is over to you to write a newspaper report on a medieval trial. In this unit there have been brief descriptions of court cases and punishments and acquittals of real people. You can either choose one of these real cases or invent another case of your own. If you invent one, you must make sure it follows the patterns of crime, policing, trial and punishment described in this unit. Make your report as close to medieval reality as possible. Your report will need the following:

- A crime
- The capture of the criminal
- A court case, perhaps in an eyre court
- The verdict of the jury and the sentence.

If guilty:
- The parade to the punishment
- The punishment.

What is this all about?

A woman in medieval England was generally regarded as belonging to a man. She was one of his possessions. So men could, more or less, do what they liked with women but they were also responsible for them. Men were expected to control 'their' women folk. For example, fathers and husbands spoke for their wives and daughters in court and were responsible for their punishment afterwards. The Church taught that women should obey their husbands.

Men also wrote the medieval chronicles, and most of the time the affairs of women were ignored. Women were simply background, their stories seldom recorded or described; indeed hardly even mentioned. A bit of a shame for half of the population!

In this final unit we redress this balance as we focus on a few particular women. The evidence about them is very different. For some we know not much more than a mention in a court record. For a precious few we have their letters.

For your final task you will write a letter to a publisher suggesting which of these five women most deserves to have a whole book written about her.

Task

Look at the pictures on this spread.
1 a) Which of the pictures show men? What jobs are they doing?
   b) Which of the pictures show women? What jobs are they doing?
2 Choose one of the pictures of women and put yourself in her place. Describe to a man why the job you're doing is important, for you, your family and the village.

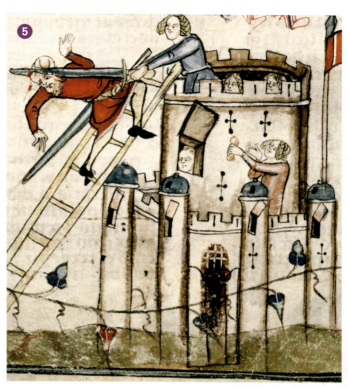

A peasant woman: Alice de Attwood

In Unit 14 you found out what life was like for peasants in English villages. Women worked in the fields, sowing seeds, weeding, harvesting and threshing the grain; they fed animals, milked cows and collected eggs. They brewed beer. They spun wool and FLAX and wove cloth. At home, they cooked, washed, scrubbed, and looked after babies and young children. Very few medieval women lived beyond the age of 30. Childbirth was a particularly dangerous time.

In 1370, William Langland wrote a story called *Piers Plowman*. This is part of what he said about peasant women:

> The poorest folk are the widows with children. The landlords keep putting their rent up. The money they make by spinning has to be spent on rent, or on milk and oatmeal for the hungry children. The women are often miserable with hunger and cold. They get up before dawn to card and comb the wool, to wash and scrub and mend, and wind yarn.

One fascinating source of information about the lives of ordinary women in the Middle Ages is the court records. For example, this extract is taken from the Court Rolls of the village of Halesowen between 1270 and 1307. This is **all** we know about this particular woman, Alice de Attwood.

> Ralf de Attwood has five daughters. The third, Alice, has married without the lord's permission. For this, Ralf is fined 2s. If this happens again, his goods are to be confiscated.

A mystic: Margery Kempe

One of the ways that ordinary women could find some degree of independence was through the Church. In Unit 11 you investigated the motives and opportunities of those who became nuns. Here is someone who became a holy woman who worked independently of any nunnery.

A married woman, Margery Kempe had a breakdown after the birth of her first child and then went on to have thirteen more children. She set up and ran two business enterprises, both of which collapsed. She then began to evaluate her life. It seemed to her that all she had wanted was profit and pleasure. Now she changed direction. She gave up sex, went on pilgrimages to Rome and the Holy Land and became a visionary, a holy woman. She gave away her money and visited the sick. She had fits of loud weeping at intense moments. These impressed some but irritated others, especially priests who had their sermons interrupted by her loud sobbing. However, Julian of Norwich supported and encouraged her. The Archbishop of Canterbury allowed her to take communion every Sunday (once a year was usual for ordinary people) and she was admitted to the Guild of the Holy Trinity, a powerful religious club. In 1438 she finished her book *The Book of Margery Kempe*, extracts of which were printed. Margery Kempe shows what a determined fifteenth-century woman could do – provided she was born rich.

A merchant: Dame Claramunda

On pages 144–145 you read about the restrictions that different trades put on who could practise their trade and how. Trade guilds were particularly keen to control the entry of women into business. Only a few women were able to become merchants or traders, and here's one of them.

In the thirteenth century, Dame Claramunda was a well-known and successful Southampton wine merchant. We know she was successful because in 1258 she won an important contract to supply King Henry III with wine from France. We know, too, that she had been widowed twice and that she had been given permission to trade in Southampton as a *femme sole*. Dame Claramunda had combined two successful businesses and made them even more profitable. Widows in towns were often given permission to carry on with their dead husband's businesses, and this is one way in which town women managed to lead independent lives.

We know from town plans and from Southampton's taxation records that Dame Claramunda lived in one of the large merchants' houses on the quay. We know, too, that she owned property elsewhere in the town that she let out to tenants. Dame Claramunda had no children to whom she could leave her business. When she died, therefore, she left her wooden chest full of jewels and silver jugs and plates, together with her houses, to various churches and monasteries in and around Southampton. Many rich people left money to the Church in the hope it would speed their journey to heaven.

What ... ?

FEMME SOLE
A legally independent woman, married or single, who had the right to trade on her own account.

A landowner: Margaret Paston

Women in rich families usually lived longer than peasants because they were better fed, usually lived in warm, dry houses and had decent clothes to wear. However, even though they had time for leisure activities like dancing and music, they were expected to supervise the management of their household – and little else. Here is one of the best-known land-owning women from the Middle Ages.

Margaret Paston was a great letter writer, and it is because of her letters that we know a great deal about everyday life in England in the fifteenth century. We also know a great deal about Margaret Paston herself, because of what she unwittingly reveals. She was certainly not a SUBSERVIENT wife!

Margaret started life in the Norfolk village of Mauntby, where her father was a wealthy landowner. On his death she inherited his lands and, in 1440, entered an arranged marriage with a neighbouring landowner, John Paston. This meant that John had to administer a very large estate indeed. Or did he? He was a lawyer and spent a lot of time away from Norfolk.

Margaret Paston to John Paston 22 March 1451

As for herring, I have bought a horseload for 4s 6d. I can get none eels yet. I sent to Joan Petche to have an answer for the windows. She sent word that she had spoken to Thomas Ingham and he said he would speak to you himself and come to an agreement.

Margaret Paston to John Paston 20 April 1453

Thomas Howes has got four great beams for the private rooms and the malthouse and the brewery, three of which he has bought. As to the rest of the work, I think I must wait until you come home because I cannot get either joists or boards yet. I have measured the private room where you want your chests and accounting board, and there is no room beside the bed, even if it was moved to the door, to have space to move and sit down as well.

Margaret Paston to John Paston, April 1465

Many of the properties at Mauntby have great need to be repaired. The tenants are so poor that they cannot afford to do the work. If it pleases you, I would like the peasants to have rushes with which to repair their houses. Also there is windfall wood at the manor that is of no use and might help them make repairs.

Task

1 What different things enabled Dame Claramunda and Margaret Paston to behave as independent women?
2 How independent of her husband do you think Margaret Paston really was? Explain your answer.

A queen: Eleanor of Aquitaine

The whole of Section 1 of this book was about the actions of kings. Nearly all of these kings had queens. Here we focus on one of those queens, Eleanor of Aquitaine. You read a little about Eleanor on pages 35–36. She was a lot more than just the wife of King Henry II or the mother of King John!

Eleanor was determined, arrogant, forceful and free-thinking. She started out in life as the very wealthy daughter and heiress of Duke William X of Aquitaine. Her lands and wealth made her very marriageable and when she was just fifteen, she was married off to King Louis VII of France. Once she had become Queen of France, Eleanor turned her attention to the old-fashioned, fusty French court. She encouraged poets and TROUBADOURS (many of whom were half in love with her), dancing and good manners, turning the French court into something of a trend-setter in medieval Europe.

Sitting at home and encouraging courtly love wasn't enough for Eleanor. When Europe was gearing itself up for the Second Crusade, she was determined to join in. Appearing before the startled Abbé Bernard of Clairvaux, dressed as an Amazon (a mythical female warrior), Eleanor offered him thousands of her fighting men. Delighted to accept her troops, the Church must have been considerably less delighted when it became clear that Eleanor intended to go on the Crusade herself, planning to 'tend the wounded' along with about 300 of her ladies.

But money talked, then as now. Eleanor, her ladies and their servants, along with countless wagon-loads of supplies, set off for the Holy Land. Reaching Antioch, where her uncle, Raymond, was in charge, Eleanor agreed with him that the best plan would be for the Crusaders to make the recapture of Odessa their first objective. But King Louis disagreed. He was fixed on reaching Jerusalem and demanded that Eleanor fulfil her marriage vows and follow him there. Furious, she announced to the world that their marriage was not all that it should be – and in any case they should not have married at all because of some distant family connection. Louis asserted himself as her husband and insisted she rode with him to Jerusalem. She did. The expedition failed and Louis and Eleanor returned to France in separate ships.

Maybe Eleanor did try to be a dutiful wife. Back in France, she produced two daughters for him. But all was not well and when she was 29, the marriage was annulled (declared invalid). Eleanor left her two daughters to be brought up in the French court and the vast estates of Aquitaine came back under her control.

Not one to linger, within a year Eleanor threw herself into a new marriage to Henry Plantagenet, Duke of Anjou, eleven years her junior. They were well-matched in wealth and in temperament; this marriage was to be a stormy one. In 1154 Henry became King of England as Henry II.

What ... ?

COURTLY LOVE

A very formal type of behaviour at a royal court involving poems, songs, music, singing and dancing where men and women acted out the 'proper' ways of approaching each other.

Did you know?

When plans began for the Third Crusade, the Pope announced that no women whatsoever, rich or poor, were to be allowed to join in. All the Christian kings of Europe, including Louis of France, agreed. However, plenty of women still went.

Task

1 What do you find most surprising about Eleanor's life?

2 Compare Eleanor's career with that of
  a) Matilda (see Unit 2). She was Eleanor's mother-in-law
  b) Elizabeth Woodville (see page 80), the wife of Edward IV.
In what ways was Eleanor similar to, and in what ways was she different from, these other two queens?

Eleanor was pregnant for much of the next thirteen years, giving birth to five sons (William, Henry, Richard, Geoffrey and John) and three daughters (Mathilda, Eleanor and Joan). Over a number of years, through tough bargaining, clever alliances and some fighting, Eleanor and Henry created a strong and powerful kingdom, stretching from the Pyrenees to the Scottish borders. But Eleanor wasn't satisfied with this. Exasperated by Henry's string of affairs (he wasn't unusual here: most medieval kings had mistresses and illegitimate children), vehemently disagreeing with many of his decisions and weary of having to share the ruling of Aquitaine with him, she joined with two of her sons, Richard and John, in rebelling against Henry. The rebellion was soon put down, and Eleanor was imprisoned by Henry for the next fifteen years.

She was released when Richard succeeded to the throne in 1189, but she wasn't ready for retirement even though, at 67, she was a very old lady by medieval standards. She repeatedly intervened to defend Richard's land when he was away fighting in the Holy Land, and raised vast sums of money with which to pay his ransom when he was captured. Travelling constantly throughout Europe, she managed her army and her estates, supported English subjects and even found the time to search out a bride for Richard.

She died aged 82 at Fontevrault, her favourite religious community, where older aristocratic women went to find spiritual comfort.

Summary task

Which of these women do you think most deserves to have a book written about her? Choose one and write a letter to a publisher suggesting a new book. Explain:
a) why the woman is so interesting
b) what else you would like to find out about her
c) what this woman's life can reveal about the roles and lives of women in the Middle Ages.

Pulling it all together

You have now met a lot of medieval people and discovered many things about their lives. Prepare a medieval gallery of the five that interest you the most. Start with a picture of each, either draw them or find them on the internet. Then write a speech or interview that explains what each person does for a living or what they have achieved in their lifetime.

Answering questions on a Common Entrance Paper

The Common Entrance History examination is set by the Independent Schools Examinations Board (ISEB) but it is marked at the senior school to which you have applied. ISEB sends a marking scheme to all schools to guide them as they mark the papers, although each school will have its own rules too. So, while these four pages can't tell you everything or guarantee you success, they can help you know what your marker should be looking for in your answers.

The history paper has two parts: Part A is an evidence question; Part B is an essay question. They test different kinds of history skills and require different kinds of answers.

You can answer questions from Medieval Realms, the Making of the UK or Britain 1750–1900; as this is a book on Medieval Realms, all the examples below are drawn from medieval topics.

TOP TIPS – First things first
Before you start writing in an exam:

- Read the instructions on the front page.
- Check the time that you have available to answer the questions. You only have sixty minutes for the whole exam. Sixty minutes is a short time!
- Work out how you are going to spend that time. Match the time you spend to the marks available. Evidence questions are worth 20 marks. Essay questions are worth 30 marks. ISEB advise that you spend 5 minutes reading through the paper, 20 minutes on the evidence question and 35 minutes on the essay question.
- It is good idea to allow time to read through your answers at the end. You won't have time to revise the whole thing but it is worth reading through to check for obvious errors.
- Finally, whoever is marking your paper will want all your work to be neat (easy to read) and clear, with a good use of English. It is always worth working hard at that.

Part A Evidence questions

For the evidence question there will be only one topic. You will be told in advance which topic you will be examined on. There will always be **three sources**, and there will always be **four questions** on these sources. There are examples from each of the set topics for Medieval Realms on the pages 178–183. Your exam will feature one of these.

TOP TIP – Evidence questions

- Read through **all** the sources before you start to answer the questions.

Questions 1 and 2: Comprehension of sources
The first two questions test if you comprehend (understand) the sources.

The first question will be on Source A. The second, on Source B, will be a little more demanding. But all you need to do is look closely or read carefully, just as you would for an English exam.

TOP TIPS – Comprehension questions

- Write in complete sentences.
- If a question has two marks, one statement is enough.
- If it has three marks, you need to mention at least two points.
- If it is a written source, include a phrase from the source in your answer.
- If it is a picture, describe the relevant detail from the image.

Question 3: Cross-referencing and comparing sources

This question asks you to compare the sources and explain how far they support each other.

You are expected to compare the sources in the following ways:

- **content** – the information in them
- **tone** – the style and the kind of language a writer uses
- **implication** – what you can infer from the source about the topic or about people at that time.

TOP TIPS – Comparing sources

Although the question may start something like this: 'Look at Source C. With which source does it most agree…', our advice is to set out your answer as below, i.e. start by comparing Sources A and B, then bring in Source C.

- It is likely that you will have time to write only one paragraph. In your paragraph you should try to:

1 Write a short sentence of introduction.
2 Explain the extent to which the first two sources agree and then back up your points with information from the sources. It is better to do it this way, i.e. mention both sources rather than dealing with the sources in turn. This makes your answer more analytical.
3 Show how the first two sources **disagree** and explain why. Again, back up your points with information and quotations from the sources.
4 Write a clear concluding sentence that **brings in Source C**. Point out what Source C says or shows and compare it with the other two sources.

- NB You can only get top marks if you compare **all three** sources.
- Don't stray into provenance or usefulness in answering this question – keep all that for question 4.

Question 4: Evaluating sources

Evaluating means weighing the value of a source to a historian. To evaluate sources you need to consider:

- the **provenance** of the source (who wrote/made it, when and why)
- how those circumstances might affect the **usefulness** of a source.

This can be hard, but here are some tips.

TOP TIPS – Evaluation questions

- Use these Who, When, Where, What and Why questions to think about the provenance.

  - **Who** produced the source?
  - **When** and **where** did they produce it? What is the author's/artist's situation at the time of writing/painting and how would this affect his/her reliability? For example, is the person in a position to know what is going on?
  - **What** genre is it? Some sources naturally set out to tell the truth, others set out to distort it. For example, a cartoon, by its very nature, sets out to distort the truth.
  - **Why** was the source written/painted and who was it for? Is the author/artist trying to inform or persuade someone? Is he/she trying to make things look good or bad? What does the source tell us, and does it match up to what you already know?

- Remember that the source caption is there to give you important information about the provenance. Always read it carefully as well as reading the source.
- Remember that every source is useful to someone at some time but you have to decide how far it is useful in answering the particular question.
- Make sure you consider the provenance and usefulness of **each** of the sources. You can only get top marks if you consider the provenance and usefulness of all three sources.
- Use your background knowledge to help you evaluate the source (see panel overleaf).

Using your background knowledge

You will probably not have seen the sources used for the evidence question before but you should have studied the topic. So remember this background knowledge. It is very important. Use it for two reasons:

● It should help you judge the usefulness of a source. For example, your background knowledge might make you doubt whether a source was accurate and so help you judge its reliability.

● It should impress the marker. One thing that examiners often say about Common Entrance answers is that candidates don't have much background knowledge, or if they have they don't use it to inform their answers. So if you can do it well you will really impress the marker.

Practice

Now use this advice to have a go at the practice questions on pages 179–184. There is one question on each of the nominated topics for Common Entrance Medieval Realms.

Part B Essay questions

Essay questions have a lot of marks: 30. So it is worth spending time getting better at this. There have been practice opportunities as you have worked through this book for example pages 49 and 131.

TOP TIPS

Whatever the topic of the essay question' remember:

● Choose your question carefully. You only have to answer one and there will be lots of choice. Make sure it is on a topic where you are confident of your knowledge.
● Answer the question directly. One way of doing this is to make sure that you use key words from the question in your answer.
● Plan your answer.
● Structure your answer with paragraphs.
● Always make sure that your answer has an introduction and a conclusion.

There are usually two parts to each essay question:

● **describe** – which tests your knowledge
● **explain** – which asks you to analyse.

Usually the question will be 'generic', for example:

For a battle you have studied,
a) describe the main events …
b) explain why …

or

For a monarch you have studied,
a) describe …
b) explain …

So you will have a lot of choice, meaning you can pick the topic best for you.

The 'describe' question

This question will be worth 20 out of the 30 essay marks so aim to spend two thirds of the time on it. You should have time to write:

● a sentence introduction
● a few paragraphs
● a sentence conclusion.

The marker wants you to show your knowledge and in particular your ability to:

- **select** relevant features or information to describe. He/she does not want a long list of everything you know about this topic. Focus on a few key features that are important or relevant. If you want the highest marks make sure you select more than two features. To describe only two features might lead to lower marks.
- **use** relevant detail to back up the points that you make. That is, give examples or evidence.
- **connect** – make sure that all the paragraphs link to the main point and to each other. Use linking phrases and sentences to make your description hang together and which show understanding of the importance of what you are writing.

This may seem a bit difficult but the secret is to plan before you start writing the essay. Every minute of planning will help you.

TOP TIPS – Describe questions
- Think of it like telling the story.
- Jot down all the elements that could be included. This is where your revision will be all important. You can't describe something you have not learned about.
- If there are more than three elements on your list, decide which three you are going to focus on. You can write a paragraph on each one.
- Decide what order to describe them. If you are describing events, it is usually best to do it in chronological order (the order they happened in), otherwise you could work thematically (group them together according to common features).
- Note one or two points to make in each paragraph.
- Now you have a plan – off you go!

The 'explain' question
This question will be worth 10 out of the 30 essay marks so aim to spend one third of your essay time answering it.

You will probably have enough time to write only one or two paragraphs. It should build on what you have already written for the describe question. In the describe section you covered the knowledge, now it is time to do something more analytical. In these questions your examiner is looking for:

- **analysis** – your ability to analyse, to consider important factors and evaluate them, not simply list or describe them.
- **argument** – your ability to create and develop an argument that addresses the point of the question
- **evidence** – your ability to back up your argument with evidence that supports it.

TOP TIPS – Explain questions
- Think of this like analysing the story after you have told it.
- You won't be including lots of new information or knowledge. Instead you will be doing a lot of thinking about the information that you have already included in the 'describe' part of the question.
- Plan: if the question is asking you to 'explain why…' something happened jot down at least three factors that affected it then choose one that you are going to argue is most important. Your first paragraph can then argue why that is so important. The second paragraph can argue why others are less important or how they are linked to your main factor.
- If the question is asking you to 'explain whether someone was a success or a failure', you need to jot down reasons why that might be the case, for both options, then decide which you are going to argue. The first paragraph can argue why some people might think this person was a success. Your second paragraph can explain why you think they were a failure (or the other way round!).
- Now you have a plan – off you go!

Practice

Here are four examples of essay questions from past papers for you to have a go at. Remember, for each one, part (a) is worth 20 marks and part (b) is worth 10 marks.

WAR AND REBELLION

From this period choose one battle in which the King or Queen of England was challenged for his or her throne, such as Hastings, Lincoln, Towton, Bosworth or another you have studied.

a) Describe the main events of the battle.

b) Explain the reasons why the challenger fought against the ruler.

GOVERNMENT AND PARLIAMENT

Choose one king who argued with the Church during this period, such as William II, Henry II, John or another you have studied.

a) Describe the main events of the argument.

b) Explain whether you think the Church or the king was right in the argument.

RELIGION

a) Describe the main buildings and their roles in either a nunnery or monastery.

b) Explain why nunneries and monasteries were important in Medieval England.

SOCIAL HISTORY

a) Describe how people tried to avoid and to cure the Black Death.

b) Explain how the Black Death affected Britain in the long term.

Practice source exercises

KING JOHN

The sources all provide evidence about King John.

1 Look at **Source A**. According to this source what was one of John's good points? (2)
2 Look at **Source B**. What impression does it give of King John? (3)
3 Look at **Source C**. With which source, A or B, does it most agree? (7)
4 Look at all the sources. Which one do you trust the most as evidence about what King John was really like? (8)

SOURCE A: from a chronicle written by an anonymous monk at Barnwell Priory in 1212. It describes events in 1212.

Then the king began to have more consideration for his people. He set in motion a deed of great memory. For when the forest officials harassed many in all parts of England with new demands for money, the king seeing the misery of the people forced the officials to swear that they would only exact the amount which they collected in the days of his father.

He restrained those who had imposed new taxes and had molested citizens, travellers and merchants, and abolished the new taxes so that he would be said to be merciful and concerned to keep the terms of the peace.

SOURCE B: from *Chronica Majora* by Matthew Paris. Paris was a monk at St Albans Abbey and wrote his account about 20 years after John had died. The abbot of St Albans was a friend of the barons in John's reign. John was not in favour with most churchmen because of his row with the Pope. Paris based most of his account on the chronicle of Roger of Wendover, another monk at St Albans. Wendover was also critical of John and some of his account was simply made up.

John was a tyrant not a king, a destroyer instead of a governor, crushing his own people and favouring foreigners, a lion to his subjects but a lamb to foreigners and rebels. He had lost the duchy of Normandy and many other territories through laziness, and was actually keen to lose his kingdom of England or to ruin it. He was an insatiable extorter of money and he invaded and destroyed his subjects' property. He detested his wife and had given orders that her lovers were to be seized and throttled on her bed. He himself was envious of many of his barons, and seduced their more attractive daughters and sisters. As for Christianity he was unfaithful.

SOURCE C: a medieval drawing of King John.

RICHARD THE LIONHEART

The sources all provide evidence about the surrender of Acre to Richard during the Third Crusade, and the massacre of Muslim prisoners that followed.

1 Look at **Source A**. How has King Richard acted towards the Muslims? (2)
2 Look at **Source B**. According to this source why did Richard carry out the massacre? (3)
3 Look at **Source C**. With which source, A or B, does it most agree? (7)
4 Look at all the sources. Which one do you think is the most useful as evidence about the massacre? (8)

SOURCE A: from Baha ad-Din's biography of Saladin. Baha ad-Din was a senior official in Saladin's household.

The defenders were at their last gasp. They therefore made an agreement handing over the city with all its munitions and equipment, in addition to 200,000 dinar, 500 ordinary (Frankish) prisoners and 100 important ones chosen by the Franks, and also the True Cross. In return they were to be allowed to leave the city freely.

When Richard saw that Saladin delayed in carrying out the terms of the treaty he broke his word to the Muslim prisoners with whom he had made an agreement and from whom he had received the city's surrender in exchange for their lives. If Saladin handed over the agreed sum, he was to allow them to go free with their wives and children, but if the money was refused him he was to take them into slavery as his prisoners. Now, however, he broke his word and revealed the secret thought he was hiding and put it into effect even after he had received the money and the prisoners. He and all the Frankish army marched to the central plain. They they brought up the Muslim prisoners, more than 3,000 men in chains. They fell on them as one man and slaughtered them in cold blood.

SOURCE B: from a history book published in 1988.

It was agreed that Acre be surrendered to the Christians with its contents and ships; 1,500 Christian prisoners should be released by the Muslims; the Muslims were to make money payments and the True Cross was to be restored to the Christians. Richard was anxious to continue the Crusade. His army was burdened by a large number of Muslim prisoners. On 20 August, when there was some delay in the transfer of the money that the Muslims had agreed to pay, Richard had 2700 Muslims, including women and children, brought outside the city walls and killed in cold blood, in full view of Saladin's army. Chroniclers claimed he had been trying to avenge the massacre of the Templars and Hospitallers. Others have said he was trying to shock the Muslims into returning the True Cross, and still others suggested that Saladin had been delaying paying the money and that Richard wanted to teach him a lesson.

SOURCE C: an engraving of the massacre of Muslim prisoners. This was created in in the nineteenth century as an illustration for a French book on the Crusades.

EDWARD I

The sources all provide evidence about King Edward I.

1 Look at **Source A**. What can you learn from this picture about Edward I? (2)
2 Look at **Source B**. What qualities does it claim that Edward had? (3)
3 Look at **Source C**. With which source, A or B, does it most agree about the character and achievements of Edward? (7)
4 Look at all the sources. Which one do you think is the most useful evidence about Edward? (8)

SOURCE A: a nineteenth-century drawing of Edward.

SOURCE B: written by Sir Richard Baker in his *A Chronicle of the Kings of England* published in 1643, a time of great difficulty for English monarchy. The book was dedicated to Charles, Prince of Wales (the future Charles II).

He had in him the two wisdoms, not often found together: an ability of judgement in himself, and a readiness to hear the judgement of others. He was not easily provoked into passion, but once in passion, not easily appeased, as was seen by his dealing with the Scots; towards whom he showed at first patience, and at last severity. If he be criticised for his many taxations, he may be justified by his good use of them; for never prince laid out his money to more honour of himself, or good of his kingdom.

SOURCE C: from a website about Edward I.

Edward never got a chance to fight that last campaign. The covetous king did die, leaving a mess for his son to deal with as best he could. The mess he left behind is what impresses me most about Edward I. The power he inherited was very great, unprecedented in centuries. His personal talents were exceptional. His situation seemed to offer great opportunities for extending his rulership even further. But despite the conquest of Wales, Edward, so popular in his youth, lost the devotion of the political class long before he died. They resented his demands and feared his techniques of rule, which verged on the arbitrary. He bequeathed to his son great debts, an endless guerilla war on the northern frontier, and a restive baronage.

THE BLACK DEATH

The sources all provide evidence about the causes of the Black Death in the fourteenth century.

1 Look at **Source A**. Name one detail in the picture that tells you these are religious people. (2)
2 Look at **Source B**. Why has the mayor ordered the cleaning to take place? (3)
3 Look at **Source C**. With which source, A or B, does it most agree about the causes of the Black Death? (7)
4 Look at all the sources. Which one do you think is the most useful evidence about what fourteenth-century people believed caused the Black Death? (8)

SOURCE A: a painting from the fourteenth century. It shows flagellants whipping themselves to prevent the Black Death.

SOURCE B: from a letter from King Edward III of England to the Lord Mayor of London, 1349.

To the Lord Mayor of London

An order: to cause the human waste and other filth lying in the streets and lanes in the city and its suburbs to be removed with all speed. Also to cause the city and suburbs to be kept clean, as it used to be in the time of the previous mayors. This is so that no greater cause of death may arise from such smells. The King has learned that the city and suburbs are so full with the filth from out of the houses by day and night that the air is infected and the city poisoned. This is a danger to men, especially by the contagious sickness which increases daily.

SOURCE C: from a letter written by leading doctors at Paris University to the King of France in 1348. The King had asked them to explain what was causing the Black Death.

The distant cause
The first cause of the plague is the position of the heavens. In 1345, at one hour after noon on 20 March, there was a major conjunction of three planets in Aquarius. This caused a deadly corruption of the air.

The near cause
The present plague has happened because evil smells have been mixed with the air and spread by frequent winds. This corrupted air when breathed in penetrates to the heart and destroys the life force.

Hippocrates agreed that if the four seasons do not follow each other in the proper way, then the plague will follow. The whole year has been warm and wet and the air is corrupt.

THE FIRST CRUSADE

The sources all give evidence about the First Crusade

1 Look at **Source A**. What reasons does it give for the launching of the First Crusade? (2)
2 Look at **Source B**. According to Anna Comnena, what was one of the real reasons why Peter preached in favour of a Crusade? (3)
3 Look at **Source C**. With which source, A or B, does it most agree about the role played by Peter the Hermit in the First Crusade? (7)
4 Look at all of the sources. Which one do you think is the more useful evidence of the causes of the popularity in Europe of the First Crusade? (8)

SOURCE A: from a history book written in 1991.

In 1085 the Seljuk Turks seized Jerusalem and attacked the Byzantine Empire. The Byzantines were Christians. They appealed to the Pope for help. At a meeting in France in the year 1095 Pope Urban II urged the knights and princes of Europe to fight a crusade. Pope Urban's speech was so effective that kings and knights at once made plans to sail to the Holy Land. They wore a cross on the front of their armour as they went.

SOURCE B: from *Alexiad* by Anna Comnena. Anna was the daughter of the Byzantine Emperor Alexus I. She started the writing *Alexiad* in 1138. Throughout the work she shows her dislike for the Crusaders.

A Frank [Frenchman] called Peter had gone on a pilgrimage to Jerusalem but had been forced by the Turks and Saracens to turn back to France without reaching his destination. Peter was angry at having failed to get to Jerusalem and he was determined to succeed next time around. However, Peter realised that it would be difficult to reach Jerusalem on his own and that he would need company. So he came up with a cunning plan. He preached across Europe that God had told him to raise an army to relieve Jerusalem. His plan really succeeded. For after inspiring the souls of all he assembled a large army that filled every highroad. And those Frankish soldiers were accompanied by an unarmed crowd more numerous than the sand or the stars, carrying palms and crosses on their shoulders; women and children, too, came away from their countries.

SOURCE C: a picture of Peter the Hermit leading the Crusaders. The picture was drawn in France in the beginning of the fourteenth century.

WOMEN IN MEDIEVAL SOCIETY

The sources all provide evidence about the role of women in the Middle Ages.

1 Look at **Source A**. What can you learn from this source about the work women did in medieval times? (2)
2 Read **Source B**. What does this source tell you about the relationship between Margaret Paston and her husband John? (3)
3 Read **Source C**. With which source (A or B) does it most agree about the role of women in medieval society? (7)
4 Look at all the sources. Which one do you think gives us the most useful evidence about the role of women in medieval society? (8)

SOURCE A: the *Luttrell Psalter* is a medieval manuscript commissioned by a wealthy Lincolnshire landowner, Sir Geoffrey Luttrell, sometime between 1320 and 1340. Written in the Psalter are the 150 psalms that make up the Book of Psalms in the Old Testament. What makes the *Luttrell Psalter* special is that it is illustrated with hundreds of tiny pictures showing scenes from everyday life on the Luttrell estates. This is one of the pictures:

SOURCE B: from two letters written by Margaret Paston to her husband, John, in 1483. The Pastons owned a large amount of land in Norfolk. John was a lawyer and was often away from home, working in London.

Right worshipful husband, I commend myself to you, begging that you will not be angry with me, even though my stupidity caused you to be so.

I am sending the roll of parchment: it was found in your travelling chest. As for herring, I have bought a horseload for 4s 6d. I can get none eels yet. I sent to Joan Petche to have an answer for the windows. She sent word that she had spoken to Thomas Ingham and he said he would speak to you himself, and come to an agreement. As for all the other errands you have asked me to do, they shall be done as soon as possible.

SOURCE C: from a history book published in 2004.

In an age when living conditions and health were at the mercy of the weather, and when survival often depended on physical strength, life for women was not rosy. According to the Bible, God had created Adam first and Eve from Adam; therefore women were inferior to men. Their role was domestic; they had children, brought them up, ran the house, cooked for their husbands. Most women's horizons were limited to the house, children and animals. In law, women are rarely mentioned, as a woman was the property of either her father or her husband.

Make your own revision quiz

There are many ways to revise. You may already have worked out which is best for you. Do you prefer to make notes; read a book; draw concept maps; set your notes to music; or something else completely?

Some people like quizzes, but the person who learns most from a quiz is usually the person who does the research to set the questions, not the person who answers! So, your final task in this book is to make your own revision quiz based on what you have learned. Here are some types of questions you could devise. You will be able to think of others.

When you have written your quiz, swap with a partner and see who can get most answers right, or split the class into teams and do some of the quizzes together.

Multiple choice

Question
Roughly how many people in England were killed by the Black Death?
a) 15,000
b) 150,000
c) 1.5 million

Answer
1.5 million

Question
Becket and Henry II quarrelled over:
a) Taxes
b) War with France
c) Church courts
d) Ugly cathedrals

Answer
Church courts. Becket wanted priests to be tried in the Church courts not in the King's courts.

Pairs

Question
Match each event with a correct date

1066	The Battle of Bosworth
1215	The Battle of Agincourt
1348	The Norman Conquest
1383	The Black Death
1415	Magna Carta
1485	The Peasants' Revolt

Answer
- 1066 The Norman Conquest
- 1215 Magna Carta
- 1348 The Black Death
- 1383 The Peasants' Revolt
- 1415 The Battle of Agincourt
- 1485 The Battle of Bosworth

True or false?

Question

A villein was a medieval criminal. True or False?

Answer

False. A villein was someone who owed feudal duties to a Lord.

You could use the Did you know? or What...? boxes throughout the book to set your multiple choice or time challenge questions.

Time challenge

Choose one mini-topic from this book and set five questions on it. The answerer has to answer as many questions as they can in 30 seconds. Here is an example set on the chart on page 3 which shows all the kings of the Middle Ages.

Questions

1 Who was the first Angevin king?
2 Which king reigned for the longest time?
3 Which king had to deal with the Peasants' Revolt?
4 Which king's cousin took over while he was in prison?
5 How many kings were murdered or possibly murdered?

Answers

1 Henry II
2 Henry III
3 Richard II
4 Stephen
5 One murdered (Henry VI); four possibly murdered (William II, Edward II, Richard II, Edward V)

Blockbusters

Questions

1 Which A is a person who prepares and sells drugs and other medicinal cures?
2 Which BOH is where William I defeated Harold?
3 Which C means troops who fight on horseback?
4 Which D is the oldest son of the King of France?
5 Which L is Richard I's nickname?
6 Which M is a king or queen?
7 Which MC is a document signed by King John giving more power to the nobles?
8 Which O is someone who has broken the law but has not been caught?
9 Which P is a person who makes a journey to a holy place?
10 Which U is someone who takes power illegally?

Answers

1 Apothecary
2 Battle Of Hastings
3 Cavalry
4 Dauphin
5 Lionheart
6 Monarch
7 Magna Carta
8 Outlaw
9 Pilgrim
10 Usurper

GLOSSARY

ABDICATE Give up the throne

ACQUIT To release without charge, to clear an accusation

ACRE A measure of land equivalent to approximately 4,047 square metres

ALDERMAN A senior officer of a town council, next in importance to the mayor

ALLIES People with whom you have a friendly relationship

AMBASSADOR A person chosen to represent their government/kingdom diplomatically

APOTHECARY A person who prepares and sells drugs and other medicinal cures

ASUNDER Separate or split into separate parts

BESIEGE To lay siege to somewhere, to surround it

BURGESS An important person in a town

CAVALRY Troops who fight on horseback

CONCENTRIC Of circles, sharing the same centre

CONTAGIOUS Describes a disease that can be passed on by touch

CORRUPT Dishonest

CRUSADE A military expedition, often religious in nature

DAUPHIN The eldest son of the King of France

DEMESNE Anglo-French word for 'domain'

DETERRENT Something to discourage an attack, a means of stopping something bad happening

ESTEEM High regard

FEUDAL Relating to the social system whereby poorer people held land belonging to a richer person in exchange for allegiance and service

FLAX Plant from which linen is made

GAOL Jail, a prison

HARRYING The act of raiding or attacking

HIDE A measure of land area

HIERARCHY A society with clear social ranks

HOMAGE Honour and allegiance shown to a lord/king

KINSMAN A person related by blood or marriage, a relation.

LOLLARDS The name 'Lollard' comes from the middle Dutch word 'lollaerd' which means 'mumbler'

MARTYR A person who dies for their cause

MEN-AT-ARMS Servants who are also bodyguards

MONARCH A king or queen who rules a country

NOBLES People of high rank in society

OATH A formal promise, often sacred in nature

OUTLAW Someone who has broken the law but is still free (has not been caught and punished)

OVERLORD A powerful feudal ruler

PENANCE Self-punishment for doing something wrong

PHARMACY The place where an apothecary works

PHYSICIAN Doctor

PILGRIM A person who makes a journey to a holy place

PLANTAIN A type of plant

PROTECTOR Someone who rules for a monarch when he/she is too young to rule by him/herself

SECULAR In medieval times, it meant not attached to an abbey. Now means non-religious

SEDITION Activity or speech encouraging people to rebel

STONEMASON Someone who carries or carves stones

SUBSERVIENT Subordinate or submissive

SUCCESSIION The process by which the Crown passes from one person to the next

TITHES A system whereby a tenth of what everyone produced was given to the Church

TROUBADOURS Travelling players

TRUCE An agreement to stop hostilities or fighting temporarily

USURPER Someone who takes power illegally

VIRULENT Of exceptional severity

INDEX

ACKNOWLEDGEMENTS

Photo credits

Cover By permission of the British Library (MS Royal 16 G. VI f.360); **p.2** *t* © Michael Holford, *c* By permission of the British Library (MS Yates Thompson 11 f.6v), *b* By permission of the British Library (MS Add. 42130 f.171); **p.4** By permission of the British Library (MS Royal 2 A. XXII f.219v); **p.5** By permission of the British Library (MS Royal 14 C. VII f.8v); **p.7** akg-images/Erich Lessing; **p.8** Musée de la Tapisserie, Bayeux, France/With special authorisation of the City of Bayeux/The Bridgeman Art Library; **p.12** *l & r* akg-images/Erich Lessing; **p.16** *t* akg-images/Erich Lessing, *b* © Michael Holford; **p.18** © James Bartholomew/Collections; **p.24** Private Collection/The Bridgeman Art Library; **p.26** © Michael Freeman/Corbis; **p.29** By permission of the British Library (MS Royal 20 A. II f.6v); **p.31** *l* By permission of the British Library (MS Cotton Nero D. VII f.7), *r* National Portrait Gallery, London (NPG 4980-3); **p.33** *t* TopFoto/British Library/HIP, *b* © R. Sheridan/Ancient Art & Architecture Collection; **p.37** TopFoto/British Library/HIP; **p.39** *l* Courtesy Roy Bunn, *tr* Houses of Parliament, Westminster, London/The Bridgeman Art Library, *br* TopFoto/Balean; **p.40** By permission of the British Library (MS Royal 14 C. VII f.9); **p.43** *t* By permission of the British Library (MS Royal 14 C. VII f.9), *b* By permission of the British Library (MS Cotton Claudius D. VI f.9v); **p.44** Courtesy the Dean and Chapter of York; **p.48** *t* TopFoto/Seale, *b* The Royal Collection © 2006 Her Majesty Queen Elizabeth II; **p.50** *t* Reconstruction painting by Mike Codd, Chichester District Museum Collection. © Chichester District Council, *b* © Michael Jenner/Collections; **p.51** © Simmons Aerofilms Ltd.; **p.52** akg-images; **p.53** Cadw. Crown Copyright. (Painting by Ivan Lapper); **p.56** *t* National Portrait Gallery, London (NPG D19149), *b* TopFoto/Woodmansterne; **p.57** TopFoto/HIP/The British Library; **p.58** © Michael Holford; **p.62** By permission of the British Library (MS Royal 18 E. I f.172); **p.64** By permission of the British Library (MS Royal 18 E. I f.165v); **p.69** Renaissance Films/BBC/Curzon Films/The Kobal Collection; **p.71** akg-images/Jérôme de Cunha; **p.72** TopFoto/Woodmansterne; **p.73** By permission of the British Library (MS Royal 20 E. VI f.9v); **p.76** Society of Antiquaries, London/The Bridgeman Art Library; **p.78** TopFoto/Woodmansterne; **p.82** Sonia Halliday Photographs; **p.84** TopFoto; **p.94** akg-images/Bildarchiv Monheim; **p.96** TopFoto/Woodmansterne; **p.99** By permission of the British Library (MS Harley 5102 f.32); **p.105** *l* By permission of the British Library (MS Cotton Domitian A. XVII f.122v), *r* By permission of the British Library (MS Cotton Domitian A. XVII f.177v); **p.108** *l* By permission of the British Library (MS Yates Thompson 11 f.6v), *tr* By permission of the British Library (MS Cotton Cleopatra C. XI f.27v), *cr* The Bodleian Library, University of Oxford (MS Bodley 264 f.79r), *br* The Bodleian Library, University of Oxford (MS Bodley 264 f.22r); **p.111** © English Heritage (drawing by Alan Sorrell); **p.114** *l* Trinity College, Cambridge/The Bridgeman Art Library, *r* Musée de l'Assistance Publique, Hopitaux de Paris, France/Archives Charmet/The Bridgeman Art Library; **p.115** By permission of the British Library (MS Sloane 2435 f.44v); **p.116** The Travel Library/Rex Features; **p.118** Sonia Halliday Photographs; **p.120** akg-images/British Library; **p.121** *t* Victoria & Albert Museum, London/The Bridgeman Art Library, *bl* akg-images/British Library, *br* Sonia Halliday Photographs; **p.123** akg-images; **p.125** By permission of the British Library (MS Royal 2 A. XXII f.220); **p.126** Bibliothèque Municipale de Lyon, France/The Bridgeman Art Library; **p.127** *t* akg-images/Erich Lessing, *b* British Library, London/The Bridgeman Art Library; **p.134** *l* Victoria & Albert Museum, London/The Bridgeman Art Library, *r* Musée Condé, Chantilly, France/Giraudon/The Bridgeman Art Library; **p.137** By permission of the British Library (MS Add. 42130 f.170); **p.143** Österreichische Nationalbibliothek, Vienna/Alinari/The Bridgeman Art Library; **p.149** By permission of the Syndics of Cambridge University Library (MS Ee.3.59 f.21v); **p.150** *t* Wellcome Library, London, *b* The Bodleian Library, University of Oxford (MS Ashmole 391, Part V, f.10r); **p.152** By permission of the British Library (MS Sloane 1975 f.93); **p.153** *tl* By permission of the British Library (MS Add. 42130 f.61), *tc* Wellcome Library, London, *tr* By permission of the British Library (MS Sloane 1975 f.93), *b* By permission of the British Library (MS Royal 6 E. VI f.301); **p.155** Werner Forman Archive/National Museum, Prague; **p.162** Inner Temple, London/The Bridgeman Art Library; **p.160** Musée Condé, Chantilly, France/Lauros/Giraudon/The Bridgeman Art Library; **p.165** National Archives, Kew (KB-26/2231249); **p.168** *t* By permission of the British Library (MS Add. 42130 f.171), *bl* By permission of the British Library (MS Add. 42130 f.172v), *br* By permission of the British Library (MS Add. 42130 f.158); **p.169** *tl* By permission of the British Library (MS Add. 42130 f.166v), *bl* akg-images/British Library, *bc* By permission of the British Library (MS Add. 42130 f.193), *r* By permission of the British Library (MS Royal 10 E. IV f.18v); **p.179** Topfoto/British Library/HIP; **p.180** Private Collection, Ken Welsh/The Bridgeman Art Library; **p.181** Mary Evans Picture Library; **p.182** Getty Images; **p.183** By permission of the British Library (MS Egerton 1500 f.45v); **p.184** By permission of the British Library (MS Add. 42130 f.193).

Written sources

p.92 *G* Paul Kendall *Richard III* Allen and Unwin, 1955, *H* Philip Lindsay, article in *Argosy* 1972; **p.178** questions from History paper 2005, ISEB; **p.180** *A* Francesco Gabrieli *Arab Historians of the Crusades* Routledge and Kegan Paul, 1984, *B* Karen Armstrong *Holy War: The Crusades and Their Impact on Today's World* Macmillan, 1988; **p.181** The Online Reference Book for Medieval Studies; **p.183** Philip Sauvain *Old World* Stanley Thornes, 1991; **p.184** Toby Purser *Medieval England 1042–1228* Heinemann Educational Publishers, 2004.

Every effort has been made to trace all copyright holders but, if any have been inadvertently overlooked, the Publishers will be pleased to make the necessary arrangements at the first opportunity.

Answers to tasks

p.108

Source 2 – nuns attending mass with priests; Source 3 – a novice monk having a tonsure cut; Source 4 – a friar preaching in the open air; Source 5 – drunken nuns being taken home in a cart.

p.153

Source 6 – a doctor bleeding a patient; Source 7 – men consult the stars (astrology) while women attend to the practicalities of childbirth; Source 8 – a surgeon performing an eye operation; Source 9 – monks suffering from the plague are blessed by a priest.